# LEYTON ORIENT
# GREATS

# LEYTON ORIENT
# GREATS

by Matt Simpson

DB
PUBLISHING

First published in Great Britain in 2008 by The Breedon Books Publishing Company Limited
Breedon House, 3 The Parker Centre, Derby, DE21 4SZ.

This paperback edition published in Great Britain in 2013 by DB Publishing, an imprint of
JMD Media Ltd

ISBN: 9781-78091-370-4

Printed and bound in the UK by Copytech (UK) Ltd Peterborough

# CONTENTS

# DEDICATION

To my gorgeous wife, Nicki – it can't be easy being married to an Orient fan. To my dad, Alan, for the countless Saturday afternoons. And to my mum, Wendy, for standing in the freezing cold to watch 0–0 draws at Brisbane Road on at least two occasions over the years!

# ACKNOWLEDGEMENTS

Firstly, a huge amount of gratitude goes to the players featured in this book, who all gave up their time to share their stories. It was an honour to meet all of you. None of this would have happened, however, without the huge amount of assistance given to me by David Dodd at the Leyton Orient Supporters' Club and Leo Tyrie, Leyton Orient's press officer. Apologies for all the annoying emails.

Thanks also to the following people for contributing their recollections: Roy Anderson, Dennis Barefield, Frank Clark, George Gatward, Mike Gold, Alan Harvey, Stephen Jenkins, Jean Johnston, Mickey Kasler, Cyrille Regis, Dick Richards, Alan Simpson, Mark Waters, Laurie Woolcott and Gabriel Zakuani.

Thanks to Steve Caron and Michelle Grainger at Breedon Books for all their help and for letting me do this in the first place.

With regard to the photographs, a big thank you to Simon O'Connor and Tim Reder for donating their images, to my brother David Simpson for his Photoshop wizardry and to Martin Ellis for his generosity. Photographs copyright: Leyton Orient Football Club, Simon O'Connor, Tim Reder and West Bromwich Albion Football Club.

There are a number of books to which I'm indebted: *The Goal Gourmet: The Peter Kitchen Story* by Neilson N. Kaufman; *Leyton Orient: A Season in the Sun* by Kevin Palmer; *Leyton Orient: The Complete Record* by Neilson N. Kaufman and Alan E. Ravenhill; *The Men Who Made Leyton Orient Football Club* by Neilson N. Kaufman; *Never Walk Alone* by Gavin Peacock and Alan Comfort with Alan MacDonald; *Oooh – The Autobiography of Terry Howard* by Terry Howard and Trevor Davies; *Samba in the Smethwick End* by Dave Bowler and Jas Bains; *Tommy Johnston: The Happy Wanderer* by Neilson N. Kaufman; and *The Untold Story of the O's Best Ever Team* by Tony McDonald.

Thanks should also go to my wife Nicki for putting up with the fact that I spent a good part of a year writing this book instead of taking her on romantic holidays; and to my grandfather Ernest Warwick who, as the family's first – and proper – author, is an inspiration to me.

# FOREWORD

## By Leyton Orient chairman Barry Hearn

I am delighted to welcome you to *Leyton Orient Greats*, a journey through the careers of the finest players to have pulled on an Orient shirt.

There are numerous fascinating stories behind the footballing success of these Orient legends, and I'm particularly pleased to be writing this foreword at a time when we are enjoying our best Football League season in well over a decade. Our current playing squad is undoubtedly the finest we have assembled during my time as chairman at Brisbane Road, and credit for our success in the past five years must go to Martin Ling, who has improved our League position year-on-year in every season he has been at the helm. He has attracted players of the calibre we need to keep this club moving forward, and we stand a realistic chance of pushing on to Championship level football in the near future. If that were to happen, then surely we would have a whole host of names fit to stand alongside those featured in these pages and many more stories to tell.

That's for the future, but for now we can reflect on the tales of those who have helped make Leyton Orient as special as it is, and I hope you enjoy reading this book as much as I have.

Up the Os!

Barry Hearn
25 March 2008

# INTRODUCTION

The words 'Orient' and 'great' rarely appear in the same sentence – except perhaps in ones such as 'There were great holes in the Orient defence', or 'He was a great waste of Orient's money'. Since the club's inception in 1881 it has spent just one ill-fated season in the top tier of English football and won no significant trophies. Indeed, the only silverware you will find at Brisbane Road is the posh cutlery the chairman brings out for special occasions.

But for Orient's devoted fans the many years of despair makes the occasional triumphs all the more satisfying, all the more worthwhile. We feel like we have damn well earned them. Similarly, on the rare occasions that a truly great player graces the Brisbane Road turf, it is somehow more special, more meaningful, than perhaps it would be to followers of teams for whom success is more commonplace. Orient heroes are cherished forever by the fans and, so it transpires, the feeling is mutual. All the greats featured in this book speak passionately about how much Orient means to them, and its unique qualities as a warm, friendly and welcoming club.

What, then, makes an Orient great? And, furthermore, how does one whittle the list down to the 12 players that feature in this book? Firstly, it should be said that the dozen that appear are not necessarily the best 12 players ever to pull on an Orient shirt. After all, England internationals such as Peter Taylor, Stan Bowles, Ray Wilkins and Peter Shilton all turned out for the club in the twilight of their careers, though admittedly the latter was, by then, 47 years of age and his weight not far off that in stones. The greats in this book, however, spent some of their best playing years at the club.

The list is not one decided by pure talent alone, otherwise players such as Vic Groves, John Chiedoze or Amara Simba might well have been included. (Many of the 12 that do feature in these pages would certainly fulfil that criterion, though.) Over and above talent, the greats in this book all bring with them a sense that Orient was their club, be it through their loyalty, their commitment, their passion, their influence, their achievements or because, as in Alan Comfort's case, they almost missed their own wedding because of it.

Some of the players featured would surely be on every Orient fan's list. At a club where, throughout its history, lethal strikers have been as rare as a transfer-window spending spree, two names demanded inclusion: Tommy Johnston, the club's all-time leading scorer, and Peter Kitchen, the moustachioed bandit who plundered 29 goals in the famous 1977–78 season. Others featured are perhaps more contentious and, as is so often the case with lists such as these, it is the names left off that fuel debate, rather than those that made the final cut.

Both Stan Charlton and Sid Bishop appear thanks to their endeavours in the team that won promotion to Division One in 1962, but there are many others from that side who could also lay claim to Orient greatness, such as David Dunmore, Terry McDonald, Malcolm Lucas, Cyril Lea and Malcolm Graham. Similarly, Tommy Taylor, Dennis Rofe, Peter Allen, Laurie Cunningham and Tony Grealish represent the Orient sides of the late 1960s and 1970s in this book, though arguably Terry Mancini, John Jackson, Phil Hoadley, Glenn Roeder and Bobby Fisher are all just as worthy of recognition.

Alan Comfort and Steve Castle feature from the 1980s, but then again perhaps Terry Howard, Shaun Brooks or Lee Harvey could also have been included. And while Matt Lockwood surely stands out as the greatest player of recent times, Carl Griffiths remains a favourite of many for the fact that, unlike many of the club's strikers over the years, he had an uncanny knack of actually scoring goals.

Other names might glare as omissions: Owen Williams, John Townrow, Ted Crawford, Stan Aldous, Ray Goddard, Ian Bowyer, Bill Roffey...everyone has their own favourites. Even Mark 'Sooper' Hooper might make some fans' lists, if only for his winning goal in the 1988–89 Play-off Final and the brief 'embarrassing uncle at a wedding' jig with which he celebrated it.

A special mention should also go to another name that does not feature in these pages: Richard McFadden, who from 1911 to 1915 scored 68 goals for the club before he was killed in action in World War One – a true Orient great whose story is recorded in Stephen Jenkins' book *They Took The Lead*.

I hope that most supporters would at least agree that the 12 players who do form this book all gave that little bit extra to the club and helped to make those often difficult afternoons at Brisbane Road a genuine pleasure.

Matt Simpson
31 March 2008

# Chapter 1
# THE GENTLEMAN MIDFIELDER
## Peter Allen 1965–78

Although many things changed at Leyton Orient between 1965 and 1978 – six different managers, two chairmen, one relegation, one promotion, numerous narrow escapes, a couple of near misses, one or two very close shaves with bankruptcy and a pitch that alternated between swamp and rock quarry – there was one thing that remained constant. Well, two actually: Peter Allen and his impeccable manners.

The polite, well-spoken midfielder was a continuous presence at Brisbane Road for 13 seasons who, before his eventual transfer to Millwall, clocked up a total of 490 games in an Orient shirt. He holds the club's all-time appearances record and – in these days when anyone who can control a ball in less than five touches starts dreaming of a move to the Premier League – could well do so forever.

Teammates referred to Peter as 'Posh Pete', and while he is hardly aristocratic or privileged (his father was a stock manager at Woolworths and then a milkman), he's certainly cut from a different cloth to your typical footballer. His conversation is peppered with expressions like 'my goodness' and 'old chap'. He refers to a training ground altercation as a 'contretemps' rather than a 'ding-dong' or a 'tear-up'. And he's incredibly placid; softly-spoken, with a mild Sussex accent, courteous and kind. He's a gentleman, and you would presume that he would not have lasted a second amid the testosterone-pumped bravado of the football dressing room, let alone on the receiving end of a bone-shattering lower-League challenge out on the pitch. You'd be wrong.

An all-round midfielder, Peter combined incisive distribution with a shuddering tackle. He was an intelligent, articulate player – as you'd expect from a grammar school boy with seven O levels and three A levels – but also one not afraid to mix it up a bit when the situation required. 'Sometimes my job was to kick people,' he says. 'People used to

Peter before Orient's home game against Reading on 11 October 1969. Orient lost 1–0.

say to me that they wouldn't recognise me on the pitch from when I was off it. I was aggressive. I really liked to tackle, and in my day it was much more physical. Dick Graham and George Petchey used to say "What's the point in tackling if you don't hurt somebody?"'

In the dressing room, meanwhile, he commanded enough respect to captain the side for four seasons. 'I wasn't afraid to bawl people out,' he says. 'I once went head-to-head with Mickey Bullock. About three or four times in succession he played the ball back to me with a little chip on it rather than just sidefooting it which, on our pitch, wasn't on at all. It really got under my skin and I told him as much.'

In Peter's vernacular, 'getting under his skin' is about as bad as it gets and, he reveals, he was similarly irked by Jimmy Bloomfield – twice his manager – with whom he had a troubled relationship. That aside, his memories of Orient are nothing but fond ones, and he talks with great affection about his many years at Brisbane Road. These days he is a solicitor with his own partnership in Hove, where he lives with his wife, Jill. The couple have been together since the age of 15 after meeting at a bowling alley.

Peter was born in that same Sussex town on 1 November 1946 to dad Bert and mum Frances. He had two older brothers, David and John. Peter recalls that, unsurprisingly, most of his early memories are of sport. 'Generally I was better than average at most of them,' he says. 'I was a decent long distance runner, but most of the time I was playing football.'

Peter showed early promise and by the age of 10 was playing for the district team, Brighton Boys. 'We had a good side,' he says. 'We beat someone 11–0. I used to play centre-forward then, and I got a hat-trick in the first five minutes.' By the time he was 14 – and attending Hove Grammar School for Boys – Peter was playing a year above himself for the Brighton Boys team that reached the semi-finals of a national knockout tournament. His performances earned him a call-up to the South of England Schoolboys, where he caught the attention of scouts from a number of top clubs: Chelsea, West Ham and, most significantly, Tottenham. He played one season for the Spurs youth team and did well enough to be offered an apprenticeship at the club. This was in 1962, when Spurs had just won the double under Bill Nicholson and boasted the likes of Danny Blanchflower and Jimmy Greaves in their side. Peter was being offered the chance to turn many a young boy's dream into reality – and he turned them down. 'My headmaster told my parents that it would be better if I stayed on at school until I was 18 and got my A levels,' he explains. 'They agreed with him and convinced me that football would be there for me when I was 18, but when football had finished with me it would be harder for me if I only had O levels rather than A levels. It wasn't that they didn't want me to play football – they just wanted me to have an education to fall back upon.'

Spurs, however, were presumably used to getting what they wanted, and pulled out the stops to try and snare Peter. 'They were desperately trying to get me to sign,' he says. 'They said, "What can we do? Would you like some boots?" So I said that that would be nice, and they took me to the boot room. They asked me if I wanted one of the players' old pairs. But I said no, I wanted a new pair. So they got me a new pair. But to think now I could have had Danny Blanchflower's boots hanging up.'

Tottenham's courting was to no avail – Peter decided to stay on at school. To any football fan, it seems a crazy decision. 'I don't think I realised how good an opportunity it was,' says Peter. 'I was 15 and I thought, well, if that's what Mum and Dad think is best then that's what I should do.' But Peter says that he doesn't regret the choice he made. 'You can't look back and say "what if?" You do what you do and live with the consequences. I suppose sometimes I do wonder what might have been had I signed, and I think I would have been a decent player in a Spurs side. But when you look at the team they had – so many stars – I think that's all I would have been, just a good team player.'

So it was back to studying for Peter as he embarked on three A levels: Geography, English and History. He continued to play football and made the Sussex Grammar Schools side, where he was converted from a centre-forward to a midfielder. It was while playing for Sussex Grammar Schools at the age of 18 that Peter caught the eye of Orient manager Dave Sexton who, at the time, lived in Brighton. He invited Peter up to Brisbane Road to train and play a couple of reserve games. Next thing Peter knew, he had a visitor. 'I was just coming up to doing my A Levels and I was out with Jill,' he says. 'When we got home there was a message at both of our houses that a chap who looked like a film star had been looking for me.' The good-looking fellow was Dave Sexton – 'He was always very dapper and suntanned,' laughs Peter – and he'd come proffering a contract with Leyton Orient. It wasn't Peter's only choice at the time, as he'd also been offered places at Birmingham University to study social history and the London School of Economics to study economics. This time the decision was easy. 'I'd chosen education once and now it was time for football,' he says. 'My parents were fine about it – they accepted that I'd done the education bit. So when Dave asked me to sign it was a "Yes, please!"'

Peter signed professional terms with Orient in July 1965, commanding a wage of £25 a week, and made his debut in September of the same year in a home League Cup tie against Coventry City, playing alongside the likes of Dennis Sorrell, David Webb and David Methick. The team lost 3–0, giving Peter a taste of what much of his time at Orient would be like. 'I thought that I'd played alright,' he says, 'but outside the ground a long-standing Orient supporter came up to me. He didn't realise who I was, and started saying that Peter Allen was crap. He said that Orient could have signed the ex-Spurs forward Bobby Smith, but instead they'd ended up with Peter Allen. He was slagging me off terribly, and I didn't have the heart or nerve to tell him who I was, so I just said "Yes, you're right." It wasn't good for my confidence.'

In actual fact, Peter says he didn't suffer from self-doubt, and even at 18 he felt he could hold his own as a professional and made 22 starts and two substitute appearances for the club in that first season. 'I always thought that if I worked hard I'd be a decent player,' he says. 'I've been lucky in that I've never doubted my ability.'

Unfortunately, the Orient team at the time did not appear to be imbued with similar levels of self-belief, as the 1965–66 season in Division Two was an unmitigated disaster. The great promotion-winning side of Stan Charlton, Sid Bishop, Malcolm Lucas, Cyril Lea and Dave Dunmore had been disbanded and a younger – or rather, cheaper – side was struggling. By December, with Orient bottom of the table, Dave Sexton paid the price. 'I don't think anyone realised what a good coach Dave was at the time,' says Peter. 'He brought a lot of new ideas, continental ideas, but we were doing badly so I guess he had to go.'

With no manager and the club facing relegation, Orient did what they always did: allowed Les Gore to take over. But loyal Les could not stop the rot and the club ended the season at the foot of the table and relegated to Division Three. Midway through the summer of 1966, Orient brought in former Crystal Palace boss Dick Graham as the new manager, and he wasted no time in letting the players know who was in charge. 'He invited us all in to meet him in the middle of the summer break,' says Peter. 'We all thought that was a bit of a bore, but when we arrived it was worse – he made us do a really hard training session. It was typical of Dick. He was a real disciplinarian. If he didn't think you were giving your best he could be very fierce. But you knew where you stood with him.'

Peter recalls one time in particular when he felt the sharp end of Dick's tongue. 'We'd lost 2–0 at home to Walsall at the end of the first season Dick was in charge, and I'd been run ragged,' he says. 'Dick spent so long tearing strips off us after the game that it was going to be impossible for me to get back to Hove. But Dick realised this and said I could stay the night with him, and he made me a nice cup of cocoa. He was quite a character.'

On the pitch, Dick had some innovative schemes to unsettle the opposition, including changing the team strip at random between orange, blue and red and refusing to name his own side until five minutes before kick-off. His methods met with limited success, and Orient finished the season in mid-table mediocrity. To be fair, he faced some serious financial constraints, and 1966 was one of the (many) years Orient nearly went bust. Thankfully, due largely to the efforts of chairman Arthur Page and director Harry Zussman, the club survived and Peter – though troubled by a recurring groin injury for much of the season – found himself a regular in the side, making 36 appearances and winning plaudits for his mature performances.

The following season Orient continued to struggle on the pitch and flirted dangerously with relegation. In February 1968 Dick Graham resigned, frustrated by the lack of funds, and the ex-Arsenal and Birmingham City midfielder Jimmy Bloomfield was brought in as a player-manager. This immediately spelt trouble for Peter. 'There was a bit of friction between Jimmy and me because we played in the same position, so I was the first person to be dropped,' he explains. 'And I don't think Jimmy rated me as a player.'

Peter, for his part, is pretty lukewarm about Bloomfield's ability as a manager. 'He didn't give us a way of playing,' he says. 'He'd just tell us to do the right thing – if it's on to whack it, whack it; if it's on to play it, play it. And fitness wasn't his priority. He thought that enthusiasm would take us through the games. But I thought that we could have done more to get us through the last 20 minutes.' Though initially dropped from the team, Peter did force his way back into the side for the remainder of that season, and Orient avoided relegation, although he says he remained convinced that Bloomfield did not believe in him. Off the pitch, things were happier, and Peter married Jill on 25 May 1968.

Peter did play the majority of the 1968–69 season – one in which only a 4–0 thumping of Shrewsbury on the final day of the season ensured that Orient did not drop down to Division Four – and his performances remained consistently good, if apparently unappreciated by his manager.

Bloomfield decided to concentrate solely on his managerial duties for the 1969–70 season, and Peter's consistency ensured that he was untouchable in the centre of midfield – he played every single game. It was the year that Orient won the Third Division Championship, and Peter puts the success down to the experience of some of Bloomfield's signings. 'We had players like Ray Goddard, Mickey Bullock, Mark Lazarus and Peter Brabrook,' he says. 'I think that's what Jimmy was good at – getting the best out of the older players. We had a good balance. And we had a bit of luck.'

Orient in 1967–68. Back row, left to right: Michael Jones, Ray Goddard, Ronald Willis, Bert Howe. Middle row: Eddie Werge, Brian Wood, Tony Ackerman, John Snedden, Peter Allen. Front row: Malcolm Slater, Barry Fry, Brian Whitehouse, Cliff Holton, Tommy Anderson, Terry Price.

Peter heads the ball away from Fabio Capello in a friendly against Roma at Brisbane Road in May 1970. He insists he is not scoring an own-goal.

Peter certainly did when he scored the winning goal against Luton on Boxing Day. He says 'I was going in for a 50–50 ball with a Luton lad just outside their box. He got there a fraction of a second before me, but he hit the ball against the inside of my foot and it flew into the top corner of their net.' The title was confirmed with a 1–0 win against Shrewsbury, though the celebrations left Peter feeling a little green. He says 'We had a meal at a hotel, and when we'd finished eating, Harry Zussman started handing cigars around. I wasn't a smoker, but I thought they smelled nice so I had one. But it didn't taste as good as it smelled, and I felt really ill. So I don't remember the game, I remember the cigar.'

In May, to commemorate the promotion, Orient played a game against the Italian side Roma at Brisbane Road, in which Peter pitted his wits against, among others, a young Fabio Capello.

Peter lived in Hove throughout his time at Orient and would travel to east London by train. He enjoyed a drink or two but was not really a gambler. After training he would go to a café with some of the other players and put the world to rights. But, he says, the days just seemed to drift by. 'I wasted my time, really. I had promised myself that I was going to keep my education going and do a degree while I was playing, but I was enjoying myself too much. It just didn't happen.'

Peter's teammates attest that their slightly posh and rather clever midfielder had nothing but respect from the dressing room. 'He did get a bit of light-hearted stick from the likes of Terry Mancini and Mark Lazarus,' concedes Dennis Rofe, who played alongside Peter from 1968 to 1972. 'But everyone respected Peter because of what he could do on the pitch. He was a credit to the game and to himself and never gave anything less than everything he had on the football pitch. The words "model professional" are overused, but they apply to Peter. And he was a gentleman. If I ever wanted a letter written I'd get him to do it – he knew far more big words than me.'

Tony Grealish, who played with Peter from 1974 to 1979 adds 'He was very quietly spoken, and you'd never see him in a violent temper. He'd get angry, but a look was a bad as a punch on the nose from him. But he was a great encourager and a lovely guy.'

In the 1970–71 season Orient, though avoiding relegation, struggled in Division Two, suffering from a chronic lack of goals – just 29 in the League in total. Peter's performances attracted the attention of First Division Everton, who made a bid for him. Orient, however, wouldn't sell. Peter

Peter in the promotion season of 1969–70.

didn't dwell on it too much. 'I was always very happy at Orient,' he says. 'There was no reason I wanted to get away.'

For Peter, it is as simple as that, really. He was content at Orient, and claims he never had a burning drive to play at a higher level. 'Perhaps I wasn't ambitious enough,' he reflects. 'But then I think about what I've got now in my life, and it's great. I've got a nice home, wonderful kids, a lovely wife. Why would I want to change anything? If I'd gone up north I might not have what I have now.' He does concede that he feels he could have played at a higher level if a move had come about. 'I think I had my better games against better sides – like in our Cup runs – so I always thought I could have done it. It was flattering to know that Everton wanted me, and there would often be things in the papers or on the grapevine about other clubs being interested. It's nice to think that I could have held my own at that sort of level. If I'd had an agent on my shoulder chipping away saying 'I can get you this, I can get you that', it might have been different. But in those days the club held your registration, so if they didn't want to sell you, then you stayed. I could have stopped trying or become a troublemaker if I wanted to leave, but I never felt I had any reason to do that.'

In June 1971 Jimmy Bloomfield left to take over as manager of Leicester, something that Peter was rather pleased about. 'There was no love lost between Jimmy and me so I wasn't sad to see him go,' he says. 'He was dismissive of me. We had no relationship – he wouldn't talk to me and I wouldn't talk to him.'

Confusingly, Peter later heard word that Bloomfield had tried to take him to Leicester. Peter isn't quite sure how to take this. 'Maybe he did think I was a better player than I thought he did,' he muses. 'Perhaps he thought that the way to get the best out of me was to handle me the way he did.'

Either way, Peter was happy to meet the new manager, George Petchey. 'When George first joined he had everyone in individually to introduce himself and to tell us what he'd be expecting from us. I thought that at least he was laying his cards on the table from the off. He was honest. But he was also the first manager I played for who really said how he wanted us to play. He put a lot of thought into the game, and he got together a good group of players. He was the best manager I played for.'

In Petchey's first season he could do nothing to improve Orient's League form – they finished 17th, the same as the previous year – though he did oversee one of the club's most famous FA Cup runs. A 3–0 victory over Wrexham in the third round had set up a fourth-round tie with Jimmy Bloomfield's First Division Leicester side. And though no one could ever accuse Peter of being malicious, he does confess – under duress – that the 2–0 win was particularly satisfying, especially as he himself had scored. 'It's sad, but it was pleasing,' he admits. 'I had to do an interview after the game with Brian Glanville and George had a quiet word in my ear beforehand and told me "Don't say anything about Jim." George was quite cute like that.'

The programme from Orient's famous 3–2 victory over Chelsea in the FA Cup in 1972, a game Peter says was the highlight of his career.

The fifth round brought a home tie against a Chelsea side containing the likes of Peter Osgood, Alan Hudson, John Dempsey and Peter Bonetti. The famous names showed their class in the opening exchanges, and with 20 minutes gone Chelsea were 2–0 up. 'I felt we were chasing shadows and I thought we were in for a hard afternoon,' says Peter.

A Phil Hoadley goal before half-time gave Orient hope, and then Mickey Bullock made it 2–2 from Peter's long ball into the area. 'It was probably a hit and hope,' Peter laughs. 'It was just a case of getting the ball up there because we were ankle deep in mud. In fact, the state of the pitch was a constant feature of my time at Orient. Some of our team talks were about which bits to avoid – the big quagmire in the centre circle, for example. When it was wet it was just mud, and when it was dry it was rock hard.'

Thankfully it didn't seem to trouble Barrie Fairbrother, who scored in the final minute to record a famous victory for Orient – one that Peter rates as his greatest in his entire time at the club. 'I don't think at the time we realised what a great achievement it was. That was the Chelsea team that won the Cup-winners' Cup – a terrific side.'

The quarter-final brought Arsenal to Brisbane Road, though the luck was not with Orient that day and they lost 1–0. 'Barry Dyson hit the crossbar, I hit the post, and I think we were having the better of the game, but it wasn't meant to be,' says Peter. 'We all thought their goal was a foul on Ray Goddard. But we all thoroughly enjoyed it. We had acquitted ourselves well – that was our consolation. We lost with a bit of glory.'

Following the departure of Terry Mancini, Peter was made captain for the season of 1972–73. 'It was an honour, and I enjoyed it,' he says. 'I think George thought that on the pitch I was the one who could ensure we were playing the way he wanted us to play, to do the simple, straightforward thing.'

Peter led mostly through example, and his commanding performances in midfield continued to impress. The team struggled, though, and managed only a 15th-place finish in the division.

When it came to renewing Peter's contract for the next season – in those days most contracts ran year-on-year – he found himself locked in disagreement with the club for the first time. 'I thought I was being seriously underpaid,' he reveals. 'I'd had a good year and there were senior players who'd come in and were getting more money just because they were older. I thought that it was my last chance to get what I'm worth so I dug my heels in. I said that unless I got paid what I was worth I would leave.'

Initially the club refused to give Peter any more money but, thankfully, compromise was reached. 'In the end George talked me into staying,' he says. 'He said "have a crack at it this year and if we have a good one I'll look after you." In the end I signed for £80 a week, which wasn't a lot of money. But George also suggested that I could write for the *Walthamstow Guardian*, as they wanted a player to do a column every week. I got paid for that and I really enjoyed it.'

The beginning of the 1973–74 season saw the introduction of the new three-up, three-down system and, in what is apparently a much-cherished annual ritual in the world of football punditry, the experts predicted that Orient would be one of the teams to be relegated. Amusingly, by Christmas the east Londoners found themselves near

Peter is presented with the *Evening Standard* Player of the Month award in 1973.

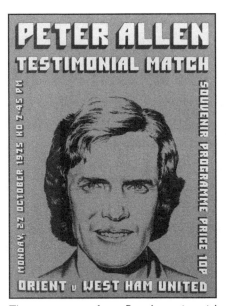

## PETER ALLEN
## TESTIMONIAL MATCH

MONDAY, 22 OCTOBER 1975. KO 7.45 PM

SOUVENIR PROGRAMME PRICE 10P

ORIENT v WEST HAM UNITED

The programme from Peter's testimonial against West Ham on 27 October 1975.

the top rather than the bottom of the division. Peter, however, suffered a bad injury in a New Year's Day game against Bristol City, damaging the ligaments in his ankle. He was out for five weeks and had to play the rest of the season with heavy strapping and pain-killing injections. His was one of a handful of injuries in the team, and they lost momentum, winning only two of their last 15 games. The final match of the season was against Aston Villa in front of nearly 30,000 fans at Brisbane Road, and Orient needed a win to secure promotion to the top flight. It wasn't to be: the game ended in a 1–1 draw. 'We thought we could do it,' Peter says. 'We were so close. It was the chance to play in Division One and I thought we'd be lucky to get that chance again. I had a little weep after the game. I'd played half the season with painkillers, and I thought what a waste it had been.'

Expectations were high that the following season of 1974–75 would be the one where Orient finally did secure promotion, but in reality things were a little more difficult on the pitch. 'The expectations were unrealistic,' says Peter. 'We were a team of old war horses that had taken a bit of a battering, and we weren't quite as sharp as we used to be. I know that my left ankle was never the same after my injury. I was never as mobile again.'

Orient finished in 12th place, scoring just 28 League goals – a record low. Peter then spent virtually the entire 1975–76 season sidelined by an injury to his right knee, though he managed to make a handful of appearances in March. One of them, against Sunderland, made Peter Orient's all-time record appearance holder, beating Arthur Wood's 373 games. 'It was a proud moment, but I wasn't consciously chasing records,' he says. 'At the time I didn't realise what an achievement it was. Now I think the record is unlikely to be broken because players move around so much more.'

That season Peter was also awarded a testimonial, a match against West Ham in front of over 6,000 fans. 'I felt a bit of a fraud because I wasn't playing,' says Peter. 'But I have good memories of all the people that helped me. I was very lucky.'

Peter also began to think about his future outside of football. 'I realised that I wasn't the player that I used to be,' he says. 'With my left ankle then my right knee, I thought that I didn't have many years left in me. I started to do a bit of work for one of the supporters, who was an accountant, but it made me realise that I was never going to be an accountant. So I was thinking about what else I could do. Then Jill's father, who had a furniture shop and removals business, asked me if I wanted to work for him with a view to taking over the company in the future. I thought I'd give it a crack and asked Orient if I could go part-time. I needed to see what life was like outside of football.'

Though initially reluctant, Petchey agreed that Peter could train on Tuesdays and Thursdays but would work in the business on Mondays, Wednesdays and Fridays. Peter concedes that his part-time status affected his standing at the club. He was replaced by Phil Hoadley as team captain, though retained the title of club captain. He also found himself out of the side on occasion. 'There were times when I thought I should have played when I didn't,' he says. 'I wasn't particularly happy about the whole situation, but I knew it had to be done. It was good to try it – I realised that working for Jill's dad wasn't the right thing to do for the future anyway. But being part-time I missed the day-to-day life of a footballer and having a laugh with the lads.'

In contrast to the earlier part of Peter's Orient career – when, he says, players would tend to drift home after matches – there was plenty of socialising going on. 'There were three groups: the ones who always went in early, the ones who always stayed out to the bitter end, and the ones in between. I was in the middle group – being responsible and looking out for everyone! But we'd get into trouble sometimes. On a pre-season tour to Antwerp we'd all been drinking and had been thrown out of numerous strip clubs. It was two or three in the morning and three of the lads – who shall remain nameless – went off to get some food. Minutes later they came running back being chased by some transvestites, each one with their hitched-up dress in one hand and a brick in the other. Then the police turned up with Sten guns – that sobered us all up.'

Perhaps with moments like this in mind, Petchey began to invite the players' wives along to social events and pre-season tours. 'He thought it would help control us,' Peter laughs. 'We weren't as much trouble when the wives were knocking us into shape.'

Back on the pitch, Orient struggled terribly in the 1976–77 season and needed to avoid defeat against Hull City on the last day to avoid relegation to Division Three. They managed to hold on to a 1–1 draw to avoid the drop – 'We would have kicked our own grandmothers,' says Peter, although it is difficult to imagine him kicking any grandmother, let alone his own.

The poor season meant George Petchey was a marked man and, after losing the first two League games of the following season, he was given the boot in August 1977. 'You could see it coming,' says Peter. 'Brian Winston and George fell out of love with each other a bit. Brian couldn't understand why if you had one good season you couldn't do it again the next. But football doesn't work like that.'

Unfortunately for Peter, Orient's new manager was in fact an old manager: Jimmy Bloomfield. 'I wasn't best pleased,' says Peter with diplomatic understatement. 'It was never going to be easy for Jimmy and me to hit it off.'

Peter realised that, finally, the time was right to leave Orient. 'I sat down with Jimmy and told him that I knew I wasn't his type of player, that my right knee was gone, my left ankle was gone and that he should let me go. But he refused. He said "Where am I going to get another player like you?"' The response seems somewhat at odds with Peter's perception of the manager's opinion, but he remains adamant that Bloomfield did not rate him, saying 'He might not have been able to find another player like me, but he didn't think I was particularly good.'

A few months later, during an away game at Sheffield United on Boxing Day, things came to a head. 'I was a bit aggrieved with him already that day because the players travelled up to Sheffield on Christmas Day but he hadn't joined us,' says Peter. 'At half-time we were losing 1–0, but I thought we'd been doing OK – Sheffield were a good side. But when I got into the dressing room he said "You're off". I just took my shirt off, threw it on the floor and told him what I thought about that. And he told me that I'd never play for the club again.'

Peter was immediately relegated to the reserves and – just to rub his nose in it a bit more – was made to get changed in the referee's room, away from the other players, and train on his own. It was a pretty humiliating thing to do to the club's record appearance holder, but Peter did not take it as such. 'I knew I hadn't done anything wrong so the problem was with Jimmy,' he says. 'It made him look like he was the one in the wrong. It showed him up. The other players treated it as a joke. They were on my side.'

By late February, a number of injuries meant that Bloomfield had little choice but to allow Peter back into the team, and he played his last three games for the club. One of them was Orient's famous 2–1 victory over Chelsea in the FA Cup. 'When we beat Chelsea in 1972 we'd had our fair share of luck – they'd been the better side, but we'd battled through and won. This time round I thought we played really well and deserved to win.'

It was a last hurrah for Peter, and within a couple of weeks he was on his way. 'Brian Winston had a quiet word with me and asked me if I thought Jimmy and I would ever be able to hit it off. I said no. I didn't want to play for him. I wanted to leave.' Winston and Bloomfield insisted on putting a £10,000 price tag on Peter's head, something the player was at a loss to understand. 'I said to Jimmy "I've been at this club so long, I didn't cost you anything, I've played all these games, why do you really want a fee for me?"'

Fourth Division Wimbledon under Dario Gradi were keen to snap up Peter, but baulked at the asking price. However, Second Division Millwall, where George Petchey was now manager, were prepared to pay the £10,000 and after 13 years and 490 appearances, Peter finally said goodbye to Brisbane Road. 'It was all so easy,' he recalls. 'I went in one morning and the coach Terry Long told me that Millwall wanted to speak to me. One of their scouts took me over to The Den in the car and we agreed terms there and then. The next day I went back to Orient to collect my boots. Peter Angell was the only one there. I took my boots and left. That was it. I thought someone might have said "thanks for all you've done".

Though he knew it was the right time to go, Peter was still sad to leave. 'I'd fallen out of love with playing for the manager, but not out of love with the club,' he says. 'I'd been there a long time and had a lot of friends, so it was a wrench to leave.'

Peter made 13 appearances for Millwall at the end of that 1977–78 season, but early into the next campaign, in a game against Brighton, he suffered the injury that would end his career. 'I was running out of joints,' he quips. 'This time it was my left knee. I was standing on my left leg and played the ball with my right and the Brighton lad hit my knee and it went all different ways.' Peter had ligament damage, and though he had two operations and tried to regain his fitness, it was to no avail – his knee was shot. At 32, his career was over. 'It was a big blow,' he says. 'Suddenly I'm thinking: wife, two kids, mortgage. How was I going to pay the bills?'

Petchey offered Peter a coaching job at Millwall, but Peter turned it down. 'I would have been taking the youth team, the reserve team and the amateurs,' he explains. 'It would have been all day every day in London, so I didn't think it was the most sensible option.' Instead Peter decided to go back to college to study to become a solicitor. He graduated in 1984, and set up his own partnership in 1988, where he works to this day.

Peter and Jill have one grandchild, Charlie, born in 2006 to their daughter Sam. Their son Tim has represented Great Britain as a triathlete. Though in his 60s, Peter still has enough of the old magic to regularly play five-a-side football with some friends – 'no tackling though,' he says – and claims the thing he misses most about the game is the dressing room banter. But he's happy. 'Things have worked out well for me,' he says. 'I had a good time at Orient, and I've got a good practice here in Hove. I don't have any regrets. I don't think there's anything that I can say I would have done differently if I had the chance. Perhaps the only thing is that I would have taken better care of my body. When you're a youngster you think you're indestructible. If I was injured it was "run it off, take a tablet, strap it up, have an injection" But overall I was very lucky.'

Peter manages to get to Brisbane Road two or three times a season and, showing impeccable taste, has never been tempted to swap allegiance to the nearby Brighton and Hove Albion. 'What amazes me is that I left in 1978 and even now when I go back to Orient people remember me warmly,' he says. 'I'm proud to say that I played for Orient for most of my career. And I'm proud to say that I'm an Orient fan.'

# Chapter 2
# THE FAMILY MAN
## Sid Bishop 1953–65

Sid in the late 1950s.

If ever one needed evidence of how much football has changed, then it would be worth glancing at the career of Sidney Harold Bishop. Despite being courted by Manchester United and other big clubs, and being the subject of repeated calls for inclusion in the England squad, the inspirational centre-half chose to spend his entire professional football life at Leyton Orient. Were a player of Sid's calibre to come through the ranks at Brisbane Road today he would be off like a shot, racing towards Premier League glory in a Ferrari Maranello with only the slightest of glances in his rear-view mirror to check that his diamond earring was correctly adjusted.

For Sid, life was much simpler. His priority was the happiness of his family, and they found it in east London. 'We were set up perfectly there, and I wouldn't have wanted to see it all go up in smoke,' he says. It meant that Orient supporters had the pleasure of seeing one of the finest centre-halves of the time turning out at Brisbane Road for over 12 years. 'Sid is by far the best defender we've ever had,' says fan Mickey Kasler. 'He never put a foot wrong, he was sheer class. He wasn't tall but he could beat most people in the air. He had a fantastic tackle but he wasn't crude. And he had tremendous pace. If the ball was played down the middle and the forward had a three-yard start on Sid, you wouldn't worry. He'd catch them up and get a sliding tackle in every time.'

In all, Sid made 323 first-team appearances for Orient, and formed part of a formidable half-back line with Malcolm Lucas and Cyril Lea that helped take the club into Division One in 1962. These days he lives alone in Harlow, Essex. Tragically, in February 2003, his beloved wife of 50 years, Vera, died after a hospital blunder during a routine operation. His son Warren, who works as an air-conditioning engineer, and daughter Denise, a former hairdresser, live nearby and between them have given Sid four grandchildren, two boys and two girls.

Sid is quite a character, and spending time with him is an entertaining experience – his enthusiasm, warmth and humour make him great company. He smokes like a trooper – he has done since he was 20 years old – and is not shy of an opinion. Get him going on the state of football today (in summary: not good) and you are in for a long afternoon. And he is quick to point out that he is still slightly upset by the fact that nearly 50 years ago Orient chairman Harry Zussman refused to sell him the club house that he and Vera were renting. But that aside, he has nothing but good memories of his time at Brisbane Road. 'I couldn't see how it could be any better,' he says.

Sid owes his very existence on this earth to football. His father, Harold, was involved in the day-to-day running of amateur club Tooting Town. His mother, Lou, volunteered at nearby Mitcham Wanderers. When the two clubs merged in 1932 to form Athenian League outfit Tooting & Mitcham United, the couple's eyes met over a muddy field. The rest, as they say, is history. Sid arrived two years later, born on 8 April 1934 in Tooting. Harold worked as a foreman for Crittles, a heating and ventilation company, while Lou volunteered at a local hospital. Sid has an elder sister, Betty, and a younger brother, Clive. His earliest memories, then, are of football shirts strewn around the house – Lou was the official team kit-washer – and regular trips to Sandy Lane, Tooting & Mitcham's old home ground. It seems Sid had a destiny. 'At times I scratch my head and think "was my life set out like this?"' he says, while literally scratching his head.

Unsurprisingly, Sid took to sport – and pretty much all of them. 'I just loved being involved in anything active,' he says. 'I was hardly ever in the classroom. I was reasonable at table tennis. I used to do gymnastics on a Friday with the Boys' Brigade. I won a ball-throwing contest in the playground. I tried ice-skating. I played cricket. I have an old school mate who still rings me up and says "I remember you at cricket – I'd go home, have my tea, come back and you'd still be batting."'

It was football at which he really excelled, captaining his school team at Defoe Secondary Modern and representing South London Schoolboys. It was for the representative side that he first came up against future Fulham legends Johnny Haynes and Trevor 'Tosh' Chamberlain, both of whom featured in the North London Schoolboys team. Even at that young age Sid claims that he was never anything but a defender. 'To get your name in the paper you had to be a forward, but I never craved that,' he says. 'I felt that I could talk to the lads as defender. And I enjoyed winning games, keeping clean sheets.'

At 15, after impressing in a trial, Sid began turning out for Chase of Chertsey Football Club, at the time Arsenal's nursery side. A year later he travelled with the Chase of Chertsey team to a youth tournament in Sanremo, Italy, where they eventually lost 1–0 to Barcelona in the Final. He returned to England to find that Chase of Chertsey had been taken over by Leyton Orient, which no doubt sent many of the youths involved scuttling for the safety of careers in plumbing and carpentry. Not Sid, though – upon leaving school he was one of the handful of players invited to join the ground staff at Brisbane Road. He says he was made to feel at home at Orient. He was also made to work hard. 'I spent the morning cleaning the ground, sweeping the terraces, goodness knows what. In the afternoons we'd do some training – mainly ball control and head tennis.'

Sid continued to skipper Chase of Chertsey and began to turn out for Orient in the midweek league. In January 1952 he was offered a professional contract at £4 a week. 'It spins a young person's head around,' he says of his first few months as a salaried footballer. 'It's a wonderful feeling. You sat there in the dressing room with your ears open and did what you were told.' One player in particular stands out in Sid's memory. 'Tommy Brown!' he exclaims. 'He ruled the roost at Orient; a real character. In the mornings he'd come in, look at himself in the mirror, slap his face and say "How do I look lads?" He'd been out all night.'

Sid began to turn out for the reserves, but his pathway to the first team was blocked by two obstacles. One was the fact that just a few months after signing his contract he was due to do his National Service. The second was Stan Aldous. The former Bromley player had made the centre-half position his own at Orient since signing in 1950 and he wasn't going to be dislodged easily. 'I idolised Stan,' says Sid. 'He was a big, strong centre-half. Hard as nails, he was. Down on the ground he was lacking a bit, but he was very good in the air. His timing was perfect.'

Just after he turned 18, Sid began his two-year stint in the army, stationed in Aldershot, Hampshire. He was given the job of physical training instructor and played for his regiment's football team alongside Ben Cook, then of Arsenal but later to sign for Orient. He also had an accommodating, sport-loving sergeant major, who saw to it that Sid didn't have any duties on Saturdays so that he could continue to play in Orient reserve fixtures. He'd play midweek too on occasion. Sid recalls 'Sometimes I'd be put on a five-mile walk – or a run, jog and walk – at 10 in the morning, then I'd have to play for Orient in the afternoon. But I managed it. That really helped with my stamina.'

Fitness was to play a big part in Sid's career – the 20 cigarettes a day notwithstanding – and it was something that he prided himself on. 'It was always important to me, ever since I was at school,' he says. 'At Orient I would do a bit of extra training on my own to sharpen the edges. The physical training there was a joke. Later on Eddie Baily used to take it and he was hopeless. I just used to laugh.'

It was while he was on leave from the army that Sid met his wife-to-be, Vera, at Wimbledon Palais. As he was nearing the end of his National Service, on 27 February 1954, he finally made his debut in the Orient first team, playing centre-half in place of the injured Stan Aldous in a 1–1 draw with Swindon at Brisbane Road. He went on to make a further seven appearances that season. Sid says that by then he was confident that he had the ability to play at that level, but that it wasn't easy for a teenager. 'I took a few bad knocks. One player said to me "You'd better watch yourself, son. You haven't been in the game long."'

With his National Service completed, Sid could devote all his time to football. Unfortunately, in the 1954–55 season that meant reserve football, and he did not make one single appearance for the first team. 'I was disappointed, but I knew in my mind that I still had things to learn,' says Sid. 'By then I was whacking a good ball, especially a dead ball, but I was struggling with my timing for jumping. I was only 5ft 10½in, so I had to get it right. But I worked on it, and in the end I had a good jump.'

That season, under the stewardship of Alec Stock, Orient came within a whisker of promotion, finishing second in Division Three South in the days when only one team was promoted. In the next season, 1955–56, the team went one better and topped the table – and this time they did need to call on the services of Sid. He played a total of 16 games, mostly covering at right-back in place of Jimmy Lee. It was Sid who twice hooked the ball off the line in the 1–1 draw with Brighton in April that effectively sealed promotion to Division Two. Sid describes the season as a battle, and in a game against Shrewsbury at Gay Meadow in December he found himself under attack. 'I'd gone in hard on the winger and ended up with my back against the terrace wall. Then suddenly, WHACK! An old lady hit me over the head with an umbrella.' She wasn't the only one unimpressed with Sid that day. 'I'd given away a few fouls, which wasn't like me,' he says. 'As I came off the pitch at half-time I walked past Alec Stock, and he said "You dirty bastard". That's what he called me! It was one of his favourite

Sid, third from the right, is wearing the new Adidas boots that prompted manager Alec Stock to call him a 'flash bastard' in the 1955–56 season.

swear words. And it was in earshot of a few of Shrewsbury's players and officials. I felt horrible. I thought, whose side is he on?'

This was symptomatic of Sid's relationship – or lack of one – with his manager. 'You didn't see Stocky standing around having a laugh with the players,' says Sid. 'And he wasn't afraid of giving a bollocking. He was a good motivator, but he didn't do much coaching – that was at a minimum. And he seldom praised people. He never once said to me "well played, terrific".'

Sid's Championship-winning medal of 1956, which he says was thrown to him by manager Alec Stock.

Sid recalls a time he invoked the ire of Stock during that 1955–56 season. 'One afternoon Vic Groves and I went down to a sports shop on Fleet Street to buy a new pair of Adidas boots with the white stripes down the side. They were £4, which was the top price for boots in those days. We must have been two of the first players to wear them – they were like carpet slippers. The next day we went out to train with them on and Alec Stock said to us "You flash bastards". I said "Oi! We paid for these ourselves".'

Most galling for Sid was the way in which he received his medal for being part of the promotion-winning side of 1955–56. 'I'm not sure why, but I wasn't presented with the medal after the last game,' he says. 'But a couple of days later I was in the tunnel going towards the dressing room and I bumped into Alec Stock. He said "Here you are" and this black box came floating in the air towards me. The medal flipped out and hit the bleedin' concrete! There wasn't a smile on his face.'

During that summer Sid proposed to Vera and they set a date for an October wedding. Alec Stock was not impressed. 'He said "For Christ's sake do it bloody right, young 'un – get married before then,"' Sid explains. 'So we brought the wedding forward to the week before the first League game of the season, when we used to have the 'possibles versus probables' match at the club between the first team and the reserve team. The goalkeeper Pat Welton was my best man, but Alec said that he'd have to play the first half of the game. So I went to the ground with the two hired morning suits, and when Pat came off at half-time we put them on. But at that time there was building work going on at the ground, so we had to climb over bleedin' scaffold poles in our suits to get out.'

The wedding itself went off smoothly, though Sid didn't have much time to enjoy a honeymoon. 'I asked Mr Stock how long I got off and he told me I had to be back by Wednesday,' says Sid. 'So we had two nights at the Savoy Hotel in London then one night in the Grand Hotel in Brighton and then I was back in training.'

Disappointingly for Sid, his performances in the promotion-winning season were still not deemed good enough to warrant a permanent place in Orient's starting XI, with Stan Aldous continuing as centre-half and Jack Gregory and Stan Willemse taking the full-back slots. Sid made just four appearances in that 1956–57 season. 'It was frustrating but you took it on the chin,' he says.

'I did think that I deserved to be playing by then but I said this is part and parcel of the routine, this is what professional football is about – you have to fight for your place. And if you're keen enough you know you're going to make it in the end. And I was thinking to myself, Stan Aldous has to retire one day.'

It was actually the next season, after five years as a pro, that Sid finally made the centre-half spot his. 'Stan Aldous was struggling in the end,' he says. 'He couldn't keep the pace up.'

They were big boots to fill, as Aldous was much-loved by the Orient fans. But Sid did not feel any added pressure. 'I was turning out performances in the reserves off the back of my hand,' he says. 'A lot of the fans thought the world of me for that. And once I got in the side I knew that if I put in 100 per cent every week and was consistent, I'd always be one of the first names on the team sheet.'

Sid quickly proved that he had the temperament and the skills to play regularly in Division Two and he helped Orient to a respectable 12th-place finish. He also showed that, although young, he was not to be messed with. 'If I had someone giving me a dig I'd just have a word in their ear. I'd say to them "Oi, I've given you a quiet game so far. You better start looking for me now." And it used to affect them. There was one game where one guy kept nibbling me from behind and fouling me.

Sid in action in the late 1950s.

I thought, right, I'll sort him out. So I said to the referee "Can I hit him in a minute?" And he replied "Well don't let me see you." So that player got three-penneth – when I could get near him, that is. Because he knew I was after him.'

He also showed his versatility when, during a Challenge Cup game against Arsenal in December, he filled in for goalkeeper Pat Welton, who was injured after six minutes. The *Walthamstow Guardian* reported that Sid gave 'an eye-opener of a display. He took everything any experienced League keeper might have been expected to stop – and was often better than most with his work in the air'.

Sid chuckles at the memory of his one and only game in between the sticks. 'I thought it was terrific,' he says. 'I was clapped off the field. I was quite proud of that. Les Gore said to me "We've found your position after all!"'

Asked if he thinks he could have made it as a goalkeeper, Sid replies emphatically 'Yes, I really think I could.' That said, it was as a centre-half that he was really impressing, which must have made it a little galling that at the beginning of the 1958–59 season Alec Stock brought in Welsh amateur international Trefor Owen and stuck him straight in the first team in Sid's place. 'He was always getting other centre-halves in, top amateurs and so forth,' says Sid. 'I thought, what's this bloke trying to do to me? Am I not good enough? People used to stop me in the street and say "What's he got him for?" The boys in the reserves would say "What the hell are you doing here, Sid?" It was ridiculous. I can count the number of times I had a bad game on one hand.'

Does he think that Alec Stock never quite trusted him? 'I don't know,' he replies. 'But I think I must have registered in his head as a good player because he'd always pick me for the key games. I felt let down when he dropped me for Trefor but I just swallowed it, did my training and hoped my name was on the team sheet for the next week.'

Sid did force his way back into the side by mid-October and stayed there. Orient were struggling in the League that season and only managed a 17th-place finish. It marked the end of Alec Stock's rein at the club, and he resigned in February 1959. The coach Les Gore took over as manager. 'Nothing too much changed, though there were a few less bollockings about the place,' says Sid. 'Les was a nice guy and things just rolled along.'

By now Sid and Vera were living in a club-owned house in Woodford – the same property previously occupied by Tommy Johnston and his wife Jean. He socialised with the likes of Frank George, Stan Charlton, Dave Dunmore, Ronnie Foster and Terry McDonald – all players who liked the occasional drink. Sid was partial to a pint of bitter but, ever mindful of his fitness, would always be in bed by 9pm from Wednesday onwards. He points to a good atmosphere at the club. 'We had a terrific social side,' he says. 'There was good, happy banter. If anyone wanted an argument they could sod off outside – there was no point in upsetting the dressing room.'

Sid's pastime of choice outside of football was snooker and he would spend many an afternoon at Jelks Snooker Hall on Leyton High Road. In the summers Sid would top up his salary by getting a part-time job. 'I was being paid £12 a week in the winter and £10 in the summer,' he explains. 'So if I got a job for six or seven quid I'd be much better off. I used to do work on the stadium, or digging holes – anything really. A few of us did a bit of grass cutting at the City of London Cemetery.'

The 1959–60 season saw Orient's fortunes improve slightly and the team managed a 10th-place finish. Sid remembers in particular his battles with Middlesbrough's Brian Clough. 'He was

Sid at home in Woodford Green with his wife Vera and their five poodles in 1961.

never any trouble to me,' he says. 'You couldn't take away the fact he got 40 goals a season, but the way I played him stopped him scoring. I didn't kick him all over the place either. You had to be on the ball with him, and not let him turn. If you let him come at you he'd hardly get to you – Cloughie would shoot from anywhere.'

Unfortunately Orient couldn't build upon their good work, and the following season of 1960–61 saw them slogging it out in a relegation dogfight. 'We had to dig in at the back, by Christ we did,' says Sid. Aside from holding the defence together, Sid also contributed to the cause with his first three goals for the club (he was hardly prolific – he only scored four in his whole time at Orient). One of them – against Bristol Rovers in February – was a full-blooded drive from near on 40 yards that surprised the opposition keeper and slipped through his legs. 'I'm not too sure what happened,' Sid laughs. 'But I could clout a ball.'

It was a goal from a more likely source that secured Orient's status as a Division Two club – Tommy Johnston's winner against Norwich in the penultimate match of the season. They had avoided relegation, and Sid has an insight into what may have given the players the extra resolve that was needed. 'The chairman Harry Zussman promised us a holiday in Jersey if we stayed up – so we did,' he says. The chairman was true to his word and the players got their holiday. Zussman even came out to visit and, intoxicated by the sea air – that or the potent Jersey ale – promised the team that if they got

The team that won promotion to Division One in 1962. Back row, left to right: Malcolm Lucas, Stan Charlton, Bill Robertson, Sid Bishop, Eddie Lewis, Cyril Lea. Front row: Norman Deeley, Derek Gibbs, Dave Dunmore, Malcolm Graham, Terry McDonald.

promoted the next season he would take them all to Majorca. The promise of a holiday in a Spanish tourist resort proved to be all the incentive the players needed, for they went on to do exactly that. If Zussman had upped the offer to Tenerife they would probably have won the FA Cup too.

That famous season of 1961–62 began with two arrivals. The first was Sid and Vera's first child, a boy they named Warren. The second was a new boss at Orient, the former Manchester United player and Everton manager Johnny Carey. 'We were glad to have someone like that – a big name – at the helm,' says Sid. 'He had a good reputation as a manager and I think that inspired the players mentally. He wasn't supernatural or anything, but I think he was the right guy to have at the time.'

Sid describes Johnny as a 'pleasant enough bloke' and says 'He always had a bleedin' pipe in his mouth. And he had a quiet sense of humour. One time we'd just finished training and he turned to Les Gore and said "Les, has Sid been out there training with us today?" I didn't have a bead of sweat on me. I said "What are you talking about, Guv? Of course I've been out there." But that was just his sense of humour.'

Sid finds it difficult to pinpoint why Orient performed so heroically in 1961–62 when they had almost been relegated the season before. But he singles out the fifth League match of the season as a significant one, a 5–1 win at Walsall. 'There was nothing special about us, but we steamed away and Walsall went for a burton,' he says. 'It was the hottest day I've ever played football. We came off the pitch at half-time and one or two of the boys were complaining about the heat and saying they were knackered. I said "We're knackered? How do you think they bleedin' feel, they're three goals down?"

And then we went out and knocked in another couple. And to get off to a bang like that. It gave us a boost, and we had the feeling among us that we could win every game. We had a fantastic record up until Christmas.'

Sid also says that the strength of the team was built from the back, and the 1961–62 season was the first in which the half-back line of Sid, Malcolm Lucas and Cyril Lea really came to the fore – none of the three missed a single game of the entire campaign. 'When Malcolm and Cyril first came to the club a couple of years before, the other players were having long looks at one another as if to say "Where have they got these two from?" But they worked hard, they did some afternoon training and they proved to be good players. I'd do all the calling and talking. Sometimes I'd say that I would be preoccupied with a certain striker so they would have to fill up the hole. In the end I didn't have to talk because they knew what to expect. The defence had a good understanding; it moulded.'

It needed to, because in the second half of the season Orient's goals dried up. Sid marks the turning point as the two fourth-round FA Cup ties against Burnley, in which Orient creditably held the First Division high-flyers to a 1–1 draw at Turf Moor before unluckily losing 1–0 at Brisbane Road. 'In the away game I got knocked out cold twice,' Sid recalls. 'They'd come on with the sponge and the smelling salts, and I'd carry on playing.'

In the last 13 games of the season Orient conceded just eight goals. Their bid for promotion came down to the last day of the season, when the team needed to beat Bury at home and hope that Sunderland failed to beat Swansea at Vetch Field. 'It was an interesting day,' says Sid with a smile. 'You couldn't think about what was going on in Swansea, you just had to make sure you did the right thing at Brisbane Road. Then all of a sudden Malcolm Graham decided to go and whack in two goals. Malcolm had a terrific left foot, but if he'd used his right foot as well he'd have got even more goals. I'd give him a bollocking sometimes, saying "Use your right foot – and not just for standing on either!"'

As the final whistle went and the news that Swansea had held Sunderland to a 1–1 draw filtered through, Sid realised that all his hard work had paid off – Orient were promoted to Division One. 'I was just elated,' he says. 'All the various people that volunteered at the club on match days were tearing around like headless chickens. You couldn't get a sensible word out of anybody. Then we were in the bar celebrating afterwards, and it wasn't beer in our pint glasses, it was champagne. The director Leslie Grade got so carried away that he told us he would buy all of us a Jaguar if we got to the FA Cup Final the next year. That was a promise that would never have to be honoured.'

No matter, for the players did get to enjoy the reward of a trip to Majorca they'd been promised by Harry Zussman at the start of the season. 'He had to keep his word,' says Sid, 'because if he didn't he'd have had 11 wives on his back.' Sid says that with all the wives in tow, there was not too much opportunity for mischief in Majorca. The team did manage an outing to a bullfight, though for Sid

Sid leaving the pitch after Orient's 2–0 win over Bury secured them promotion to Division One on 28 April 1962.

it was not the beginning of a Hemingway-esque love affair. 'I didn't think much of it, all that prancing about,' he says dismissively. 'The animal was half-dead by the time they met up with it for the final kill. I thought, sod this, and left.'

Orient's first game of the 1962–63 season in the top flight was a home fixture against Arsenal. Incredibly, Sid was nutmegged by striker Joe Baker. The memory still prickles 46 years later. 'Lucky sod,' Sid scoffs. 'He was a good player, but he didn't give me what I'd call a hard time. I applauded him when he pushed the ball through my legs.'

Sid soon realised that Orient's stay in Division One was going to be a short one. 'The leap in quality was very noticeable,' he says. 'I felt straight away it was going to be too tough. The season before, we'd fought a long, hard promotion battle, and the season before that was a long struggle against relegation. They took a lot out of certain players. We were well and truly knackered.'

He continues 'We'd lost a bit of that edge from the promotion season. It just drifted away. The players had a challenge in front of them: do they want to be better players or don't they? And what do they have to do to achieve it? I don't think enough players took it into their heads to do that. In the end we were flogging a dead horse. We weren't beating the teams we should have been.'

Even though Orient won four matches in September – including a famous victory over Manchester United – Sid still doubted the club could escape relegation. 'I just couldn't see it happening,' he admits.

Sid does have some happier memories of the season, such as his goal in the 2–1 victory over Liverpool in May. He recalls 'I took it up from the back and did a push and run with Malcolm Musgrove. I was just outside the box and the goalkeeper was staring at me. I just walloped it and in it went. We didn't have many moments like that. It was a shame.' He says that his own form remained good throughout the season, and one of his regrets is that he didn't have the chance to play at the highest level again. 'I was on a learning curve. It was my first season in Division One. I've often looked back on it and thought I'd like to have improved even more.'

But Sid's performances were getting him noticed. He remembers a cryptic conversation he had with Johnny Carey on the way home from an away game. 'The train was passing through Manchester and Johnny turned to me and said "Would you like to live up here, Sid?" I replied "No, not really. I'm quite happy at Woodford Green".'

Sid made a connection between this and an earlier chat he'd had with the short-lived Orient player Don Gibson, who was Manchester United manager Matt Busby's son-in-law. 'He told me that Busby had had three looks at me over the past few weeks, and that he'd be looking again at the weekend,' says Sid. 'So linking this up with what Johnny Carey said, I assume there was a bit of interest from Manchester United.'

Sid appears remarkably non-plussed by the fact that he was potentially being courted by a team containing names like Bobby Charlton and George Best. It comes back to the stability he craved for his family. 'I was just settling into a house at Woodford Green so I didn't want to be selfish and say to Vera, look, we're moving. She was in glory land – her mother was just down the road at Hackney Wick, and we had a good life. She worked as a dressmaker, even once the kiddies came along – our second child, Denise, was born in May 1963. So if I'd have gone to Manchester I might have regretted it. I'd pushed so hard to get where I did and set up a good life for the family.'

Sid does admit to occasionally wondering what might have been if he had ended up at the northern club – or one of the others that were rumoured to be interested in him – but says 'There's no use in regretting anything. I might have regretted not going there if I had a bad time at the Orient, but I didn't. People-wise, I was with a good club; a happy club.' There were also calls for him to be included in the England squad. And while Sid was never convinced that the national selectors even knew there was a football club in Leyton, he believes he could have acquitted himself with three lions on his shirt. 'Big Jack Charlton was playing for England and while he was good in the air he needed to sharpen himself up a bit on the floor. Then there was Bobby Moore. He was a great player and good at reading the game, but when it came to hard graft I can't remember seeing a lot of Bobby. I was being looked at and noticed and was getting top marks in the paper every week. I couldn't get any more consistent. I think if I'd done another season in Division One, or if I'd been playing for one of the bigger clubs, I'd have been straight into the international set-up.'

It doesn't appear to trouble Sid too much that he wasn't. 'I was just happy trying to play a good, consistent game,' he says.

After relegation – the team managed just 21 points – Orient began the next season of 1963–64 back in Division Two and, surprisingly, Sid claims there were no big ideas about bouncing straight back to the top flight. 'I don't remember a single conversation about it,' he says emphatically. 'There was no chance. We didn't have enough strength in depth.' The fact that by then Johnny Carey had left to take over at Nottingham Forest and been replaced by ex-Colchester United boss Benny Fenton was also significant. 'To me he was laughable,' Sid scoffs. 'I thought, what can he do to save this club? Early on he came up and put his arm around me, Cyril Lea and Malcolm Lucas and said "The team is going to be built around you three. You're the kingpins." I replied "Well, these two want transfers and I'm retiring."'

It seems strange that Sid was already thinking of hanging up his boots. He was only 29, he was fit and his performances were as good as ever. Even Sid himself struggles to explain it. 'I'm not exactly sure why, but I think I was getting anxious about how I was going to provide for Vera and our two children. I didn't want to be travelling all over the country living out of a bleedin' suitcase. I wanted something stable. I thought I'd done enough at Orient and that I was too old to go to a really big club.'

Though Sid did play the entire 1963–64 season – a pretty unmemorable one in which Orient finished 16th in Division Two – he was committed to leaving. What he wanted before he said his goodbyes, however, was the chance to buy the club-owned house he and Vera had lived in since 1958. With some anger, Sid recalls 'I went to Harry Zussman's office in Shoreditch and said "Look, you can have a couple more years out of me, can you let me buy the house?" But he refused. I was disgusted. After all the time I'd been at the club, and the consistency I'd given them. Surely they could have respected me and helped me out? It wasn't as if I'd clawed money from Orient.' Worse still, in Sid's eyes, was the fact that although he was allowed to go part-time, Orient retained his registration so he was unable to move to another League club. 'It was all about money,' he says. 'They didn't want someone to come in and take me on a free transfer. They wanted a fee for me. But I thought, that's it, I'm digging my heels in now, sod it. I wasn't going to move.'

Sid actually stayed at the club as the 1964–65 season kicked in, and he made four appearances. In January 1965, after the sacking of Benny Fenton, Chelsea coach Dave Sexton took over as manager. Once an Orient player, he was a former teammate of Sid's and looked upon his situation favourably. Sid explains 'Dave said to me "What's all this about you packing up?" I said "I've had enough, Dave. I'm worried about the wife and the two kids now. I love this place but I've got to go." Then he told me

Sid with son Warren during his spell as caretaker manager of Guildford City in 1968.

that I was free to leave. Just like that.' It was a sad ending to an Orient career that spanned over 13 years – and the club's refusal to let Sid buy the house in Woodford Green still rankles with him today.

Sid took a job as player-manager at Southern League outfit Hastings United but dismisses his year there as 'a ridiculous waste of time'. Boardroom politics – or 'jiggery pokery', as Sid puts it – sent him scuttling away to another non-League outfit, Guildford City. He remained there for 18 months, first as a player, then as caretaker manager.

It was Sid's curtain call as a footballer, and in 1968 he left to manage a pub in Leigh Park, Hampshire. A year later he relocated to Harlow, Essex, and ran another pub for 18 months before becoming a storeman at various local factories, a job he retained until he retired at 60. Aside from a couple of charity games, Sid never played football again. 'It wasn't in me,' he says. 'I was working hard. I only used to have a day and a half off. So it was unfair to the family to have a day of football.' He did manage to squeeze in the odd game of cricket, and continued to turn out for a local over–50s side until he was past 60 – despite the cigarettes.

Sid remains in the same house in Harlow which, since the death of Vera, he shares with his dog, Belle. He still gets to Brisbane Road a few times a season and those in earshot will always be well aware of Sid's opinions on the current state of the club, football in general, the country...and so on! Looking back, Sid is rightly proud of his playing career. 'I think I brought a little bit of football at the back,' he says. 'Not just kick and bleedin' rush stuff. People knew I liked to play a proper game.' But over and above that it's Sid's family that most fills him with pride. 'That was always the most important thing to me,' he says. 'And I've got a smashing family. I think that's worth a lot of money, being really happy.'

# Chapter 3

# WHATEVER HAPPENED TO THE FANCY DAN?
## Steve Castle 1984–92, 1996–97 and 2000–02

Steve in 1992.

Steve Castle has no doubt been called many things – mostly by opponents who had just felt the brunt of one of his clattering tackles. Brisbane Road regulars, however, will be surprised to learn that 'Fancy Dan' was a term of abuse once levelled at the midfielder. Steve, after all, was Castle by name, castle by nature; a fortress in the centre of midfield, unafraid to get stuck in against the various lumbering hard nuts that tend to populate the lower divisions of English football. He was more skilled than the lot of them, certainly, but 'Fancy Dan'? Surely not.

Steve insists it's true. At least it used to be. 'I nearly didn't make it as a professional footballer because I was thought of as a bit of a fairy,' he explains. 'I was one of those Fancy Dan players that would only play when I got on the ball.' Orient coach Jimmy Hallybone told the 14-year-old Steve as much when he came for a trial in 1980. Then something clicked. 'Jimmy's words really did have an effect on me,' Steve says. 'I started to play less and less football and really concentrated on the strength and fitness side of things. I probably owe my career to Jimmy, because he instilled in me something that I have to this day.'

So, it was out with the step-overs and drag-backs – pretty much sending-off offences in Division Four anyway – and in with tough tackling, simple but effective distribution and an eye for goal: in other words, the Steve Castle that supporters came to know and love. 'He was one of those players that always gave 100 per cent and a little bit more,' says fan Mark Waters. 'He wasn't afraid to get stuck in. He was always giving the team everything, and it rubbed off on people around him.' Supporter Alan Harvey agrees: 'We haven't had a midfield player as strong as Steve Castle since Steve Castle. He was the ultimate. He was the last Orient player that could really dominate the midfield.'

In eight full seasons, plus another two shorter spells at the club, Steve scored an incredible 67 goals from midfield in just under 300 full appearances. 'He'd always be lurking around the edge of the box when we were attacking, especially at corners and free kicks,' says Mark Waters. 'If the ball was half-cleared he'd always be on hand to put it back in. Most of his goals came that way.'

Brisbane Road observers will note that since Steve Castle's departure, half-cleared balls invariably end up bouncing straight back to the opposition. On the rare occasion that an Orient player does get on the end, those in the back rows of the South or North Stands take cover immediately. Steve is sorely missed. His career took him to Plymouth, Birmingham and Peterborough, but it is Brisbane Road where he played most of his football and where, according to Steve, he was always happiest.

These days Steve does not live too far from his old stomping ground, sharing his Bishop's Stortford house with wife Kate, daughter Charlotte – born on 14 November 2001 – and twin boys Harry and Charlie, who were born on 3 February 2005. Perhaps he has mellowed with age, but Steve's personality seems a little at odds with his on-field persona of old. He is warm, thoughtful; gentle even. He's also genuinely humble – 'I don't want to blow my own trumpet' is a phrase he frequently employs when asked to discuss his footballing achievements. When, as he often does, he refers to his 'youthful exuberance' – and this is someone who once ended up in court for legging it from a pizza restaurant without paying the bill – there is still a glint in his eye, but now Steve's priority is providing for his family. He's carving out a career as a coach, but the taxi that sits on his driveway – Steve drives it at night to make ends meet – is testament to the fact that the life of a retired lower division footballer is a world away from that of a Bentley-driving Premier League star.

A genuine east-ender, Stephen Charles Castle was born in Barkingside in the London borough of Redbridge on 17 May 1966. His dad, Sid, was a printer in Walthamstow; his mum, Betty, worked at the large electronics and communications firm Plessey in Ilford, in between bringing up Steve and his older sister, Lynn. Steve describes himself as a 'mischievous' child, but says that it was easy to punish him: just prevent him doing the thing he loved most. 'I was a Sport Billy. I was brought up on football and cricket. My dad was an amateur player for Leytonstone, Woodford and Crawley so it was always in my blood.'

It was cricket that seemed to be Steve's destiny – a promising bowler, he represented Essex from the ages of 11 to 13. He was not a bad footballer – he was always playing in teams with older kids – but, then again, he doesn't believe he was all that good either. 'I wasn't better than the kids around me. I made the district team as a lad but struggled to make the county side. I wasn't really fit enough and was probably a bit lazy. I did hope that I could become a professional footballer, but it was more a dream than a goal. Realistically, I thought that if there was a queue of kids who'd become professional footballers, I was at the back of it.'

Steve – modest to the core – is probably doing himself a bit of a disservice. He did make the county side in the end and tasted much success playing for the junior side Romford Royals alongside the likes of Tony Cottee and a young John Cornwell, who Steve later played with at Orient. He must have been doing something right, as he was invited to train at Arsenal, Chelsea and West Ham before signing on schoolboy terms for Tottenham at the age of 14. But a year later Steve realised that it was not happening for him at White Hart Lane, and the club let him go. 'I got badly disappointed,' he says. 'It's never a nice thing to be told that you're not wanted.'

Steve could feel his chance of making it slipping away, but he was given a final shot by Orient coach Jimmy Hallybone, a friend of Steve's father. Though initially unenthusiastic, Jimmy managed to purge the flowery excesses from Steve's game and in 1982, at the age of 16, the youngster was offered an apprenticeship with Orient. He left Fairlop School in Hainault with a handful of CSEs and says that he was simply in awe of the whole experience of signing up with a professional football club. 'The biggest thing that struck me was what a privileged position I was in,' says Steve. 'I'd gone beyond the realms of what my dad had achieved as a footballer, and I thought that I had to give it a really good go. I really concentrated and between the ages of 16 and 18 progressed more than I ever did as a kid.'

Steve puts much of his improvement down to the youth-team coach at the time, Dario Gradi. 'His enthusiasm, his coaching techniques...he was fantastic,' he says. 'I don't think I'd have had a professional career without him.' It was hard work too, because these were the days when the senior players treated the apprentices like Roman slaves. 'They'd talk to us like dirt,' Steve smiles. 'I lost count of the times Tommy Cunningham or Bill Roffey would throw their boots back at me because there were knots in the laces.' But while his boot-care left something to be desired, his performances on the pitch ensured that he was awarded a professional contract at the age of 18. He made his first-team debut on 29 September 1984 in a 1–0 win over Bradford City at Brisbane Road, playing left-back. 'Dario was convinced that's what I was going to be,' Steve says. 'But I was still sure that I was a midfielder.' He went on to play 24 times that season at full-back and scored a goal in his second game, away at Preston North End. It was the season that Orient got relegated from Division Three, but Steve was just happy to be getting games. 'I didn't feel totally part of the team,' he explains. 'I was in and out, and I was only 18. The dressing room was an intimidating place, and I didn't feel comfortable. But it seemed like some of the senior lads were a little bit complacent that season. Many of them had been at bigger clubs and perhaps thought that they just had to turn up to get themselves off the bottom of the table. But they got kicked up the backside and got relegated.'

The following season Steve did manage to make the first team in his favoured central midfield position, but again he found himself in and out of the side. He finished the campaign – one in which

Orient finished fifth in Division Four, missing out on the Play-offs – with 26 appearances and five goals. The turning point for Steve was that four of them came in the same game – a 4–1 win against Rochdale in the last match of the season. 'It was just one of those days when everything went right,' he says. 'I actually class it as scoring five goals, because after the second goal I scored another one that got disallowed. Alan Comfort had put the ball over, I jumped but the defender didn't jump with me, and I headed the ball into the net. But the referee gave a foul. I went absolutely crazy because he was denying me a hat-trick. I got booked for dissent.

Steve was Orient's designated penalty-taker for many years.

'When the fourth goal went in I just laughed. Shaun Brooks – who was very reluctant to give me the ball in general – passed to me about 15 yards outside the penalty area and I just hit it. It was swinging and flew into the back of the net. Shaun was laughing too.'

From that point Steve grew in confidence, and from the beginning of the next season had established himself as the mainstay of the Orient midfield. He recalls 'Frank Clark said to me, "If you're fit you're always in my team." I was one of his favourites. And I took it the right way – I didn't get complacent.'

Frank Clark is highly complimentary about his midfield dynamo. 'Steve was strong and powerful,' he says. 'He had a terrific left foot – he could really strike the ball. He was a great athlete, very determined. And he was the perfect foil to play inside Alan Comfort – when Alan went drifting out wide or crossing over to the right wing, Steve was capable of pushing out wider on the left and doing a job there for a while.'

And though Orient failed to win promotion in the 1986–87 season, Steve's form was one of the positives. One of his personal highlights was scoring the penalty that earned the team an impressive 1–1 draw with local rivals West Ham who, at the time, resided four tiers higher than Orient in Division

One. It was an FA Cup third round game in front of nearly 20,000 fans at Brisbane Road, which left Steve feeling somewhat shaky at the thought of taking the spot-kick. 'It was the first penalty I'd ever taken professionally,' he says. 'I'd been nominated to take them about six games earlier, but this was the first penalty we'd had, so when the ref blew his whistle my first thought was, great, who's taking it? Then Tommy Cunningham handed me the ball and I thought, oh s**t, it's me. Tommy asked me if I was OK to take it. I think I might have said "Why?" But thankfully it went in.'

Steve ended the season with six goals in 26 starts and three substitute appearances. The following season of 1987–88 – another in which Orient failed to make it out of Division Four, eventually finishing eighth – Steve was made captain for the first time in an away fixture against Bolton in November. He was just 21 years old. 'Frank took me aside and told me I was captain material,' Steve recalls. 'He said "You're young, but you're ready for it. Do you feel ready for it?" With the confidence of youth I said yes. I also thought, well, you can't easily drop the captain. And I loved the responsibility of it.'

Captain or not, Steve admits that by now he was one of the loud characters in the dressing room. 'Terry Howard and I were probably the catalysts of the nights out,' he says. 'It was the era where you worked hard and played hard, and we had plenty of jaunts up to Epping Country Club. Terry and I were both single guys so we'd spend a lot of time at Walthamstow dogs.'

The 1987–88 season ended for Steve with 10 goals in 48 games. At the start of the 1988–89 season he found himself sidelined by an inflammation of the pelvis until mid-January. Steve's return to the team, as Orient sat 14th in the table, coincided with the arrival of Kevin Campbell, on loan from Arsenal, and Mark Cooper, signed from Gillingham. All three were to have a profound impact on the team's eventual promotion that season. Goals helped – Campbell got nine, Cooper seven and Castle six – but it was Steve's all-round play that was one of the reasons the team went on to lose just twice in their 17-match run-in to the Play-offs. 'That season Steve really came into his own – he became a man,' says teammate Alan Comfort. 'He was amazingly strong and absolutely determined. He wanted to win so much and that always shone through. He was fair, although very aggressive. But he wasn't nasty – he didn't leave his foot to finish people. He'd love to come off at the end of the game having had the most incredible battle with somebody. He was a natural leader and he led by example. You didn't want to let him down.'

Orient overcame Scarborough in the two-legged Play-off semi-final, before coming away with a hard-fought 0–0 draw against Wrexham in the first leg of the Final. This meant that a win at Brisbane Road would be enough to send the team into Division Three. Steve says that he didn't have any doubts that Orient would prevail, but that he was disappointed with his own form. 'I have played poorly in every single Play-off game I've been involved in. It's not that I got nervous, but maybe I was always trying too hard. I tried to do as much as I could, and if people weren't doing their jobs then I'd try to do it for them. So I'd end up not doing anything.'

Steve captained Orient between 1987 and 1990 and is seen here before an away game against Stoke City.

With the scores locked at 1–1 with 13 minutes to go, Steve began to wonder where the winning goal was going to come from. 'I wasn't having the best time in the world and wasn't getting any shots in on goal,' he says. 'But Mark Cooper was the one who was going to be a hero. He came up with a great bit of skill, which he did on a semi-regular basis, to win the game.'

Orient were victorious, and Steve was ecstatic. Fans there on the day will recall his bare-chested, fist-pumping celebrations on top of the players' tunnel, drinking in the adulation like a victorious gladiator – or a member of the Chippendales at least. 'I went really overboard,' he laughs. 'But then again, we deserved to on a day like that. I was singing and dancing in the supporters' club after the game, and then we all went out to a restaurant and loads of fans joined us there. They were fantastic times.'

The following season, with Orient back in Division Three, saw Steve in the last year of his contract. He scored nine times in 32 appearances before a medial knee ligament injury put an end to his campaign in March 1990. But his performances and goals had alerted the attention of clubs in the top flight. Rumours circulated that Tottenham, Liverpool and Manchester United were interested, though nothing concrete ever materialised. Wimbledon, also a top-flight club at the time under Bobby Gould, did make an offer. Steve accepted and signed the contract, only to later discover that the deal had fallen through after he failed the medical. 'The physio at Wimbledon thought that

Orient were just trying to get rid of me because there was an underlying problem with my groin,' Steve explains. 'But there wasn't. I never had a problem with it after that.'

Frank Clark had offered Steve a two-year deal to stay at Orient, and after the breakdown of the Wimbledon move he gladly accepted it. 'When the opportunity came at Wimbledon I wanted to take it,' he says. 'I wanted to progress as a professional footballer. But on the other hand I was in a dilemma. I was a home-town boy and I was in love with playing football at Orient. I was club captain, I was playing in the position I wanted to, I was scoring goals and I had good friends at the club. Looking back on it – and I don't mean this condescendingly – I did enjoy being a big fish in a smaller pond. So when the Wimbledon move broke down, I didn't feel as if the world had fallen between my feet. Frank Clark said to me that if I kept playing as I had been, I'd get my move in the end. And I trusted him.'

Steve admits that his feelings at the time were a reflection of his personality – that he wasn't the most fiercely ambitious of players. 'I've never been the most confident in myself. I wondered whether I was good enough to play at the top. I didn't really have any guidance either. These were the days before agents. My dad had played football at an amateur level and was quite happy with me playing for the local club and doing well there. Basically I thought, if it ain't broke, don't fix it.' As such, he was happy to pull on the Orient shirt again for the 1990–91 season. And while the team managed only a 13th-place finish, it turned out to be Steve's best season yet: he was the club's top scorer with 18 goals in 56 appearances. 'Some players would have been upset after a big move had fallen through, but I put my heart and soul into Leyton Orient,' he says, simply.

That season also brought controversy for Steve when, during a night out in November, he and two friends decided to do a runner from a Leicester Square Pizza Hut without paying. And while anti-capitalists might champion this is as a bold statement in the face of global consumerism, in Steve's case the motivation was rather more prosaic: he was drunk. Unfortunately for Steve, Leicester Square is a heavily policed area and Steve found himself being chased. A policeman – who must have had a fair bit of pace – caught up with and arrested the Orient captain.

Frank Clark wasn't impressed. 'I was very disappointed,' says Frank. 'Steve was left in no doubt that it was something that the club wasn't going to accept. We would treat it as a one-off and hope that it would never happen again. He let the club and himself down and he knew that. Steve got a bit carried away sometimes and we needed to calm him down and control him. But that was alright and he became more and more disciplined as he learned the game.'

Steve was stripped of the club captaincy and, in court, was bound over to keep the peace. 'I was a young man doing silly things, got chastised for it thoroughly and moved on,' he says. But not before the Southend fans had an opportunity to have their say. Steve's first game after the incident was an FA Cup first-round tie against the Essex side at Brisbane Road, and their travelling support rejoiced in serenading him with the ditty 'Where's your pizza gone?', to the tune of *Chirpy Chirpy Cheep Cheep*. Still, Steve had a thick crust and a perfect riposte: he scored two of the three goals that enabled Orient to win the game 3–2.

Whatever happened off the pitch, Steve could not be faulted for the huge performances he put in throughout that season. Or at least he couldn't be faulted by anyone except new assistant manager Peter Eustace. 'Peter didn't think I could play football,' Steve explains. 'He knew that I was strong and that I could score goals, but he thought I couldn't receive the ball, and would give it away. So even though I scored 18 goals that season – which is a massive achievement – I wasn't getting the recognition from Peter that I thought I deserved. I think that I could have scored 28 goals and it still wouldn't have been good enough for him.'

Steve scored 18 goals from midfield in 1990–91.

Things got worse for Steve the following season when Frank Clark moved upstairs to become managing director and Eustace took over as manager. He found himself outside the starting line up for the first two games of the campaign. 'It really knocked me,' says Steve. 'I went to Peter and told him that I felt I was lacking in confidence and that I didn't feel comfortable on the ball. He just said that was a load of rubbish and that confidence is something that's in your own hands.'

Eustace did reinstate Steve to the team for the third game of the season, and in the fourth the midfielder proved his worth with the winning goal in a 3–2 win at Hartlepool. He remained in the team, eventually scoring 11 goals in 42 starts and two substitute appearances. Yet Eustace remained unconvinced. 'My goals kept me in the team, but Peter was still desperate to replace me with what he classed as a better footballer,' says Steve. 'I felt like I was banging my head against a brick wall. I was getting scrutinised and I ended up half-believing that he was right. The enjoyment factor began to go for me and I came to the conclusion that I would probably have to leave.'

Before he did so Steve was instrumental in the season's classic game: an FA Cup third-round victory over Oldham, who at the time were flying high in the top division under the management of Joe Royle. After drawing 1–1 at Boundary Park, Orient welcomed their northern opponents to Brisbane Road for a pulsating night of football. With the scores at 2–2 the game went into extra-time, when Orient were awarded a penalty. Steve stepped up to take it – and blasted it against the bar. The gods were smiling on Brisbane Road that night, however, and the referee demanded a retake: an Oldham player had stepped into the penalty area. 'That was scary,' admits Steve. 'I tried to think whether I should put it in the same place again or change.' He put it in the same place and scored. Kevin Nugent added another late on to make it 4–2 to Orient, sealing a famous victory. Fan Mark Waters remembers the night well. He says 'There were points in that match where it looked like it was slipping away from us. But Steve Castle wasn't the sort of guy who'd give up or let his team give up.'

In the League that season, despite early promise, Orient could only manage to finish in 10th place. Steve was coming to the end of his contract and, although he was offered another two-year deal, he says that there wasn't as much enthusiasm as on the previous occasion. 'The club weren't exactly breaking their necks to keep me. I think they thought that if they could get some money for me it would help with the financial problems.' Frank Clark concedes the point, saying 'At Orient we were limited by the size of our crowd and our money. We weren't happy to lose Steve, but it was an opportunity for him to further his career.'

Everything seemed to be pointing towards Steve leaving. 'I had just turned 26 and I felt it was time for a new venture,' he says. 'I hadn't experienced any club other than Orient and I had been enjoying it less under Peter.' Although a number of clubs were interested in Steve – West Ham, Reading and Wolves in particular – only Plymouth, where Peter Shilton had recently taken over as player-manager, were willing to go to a tribunal to set the transfer fee. It was eventually fixed at £195,000 and on 2 June 1992 Steve became a Plymouth player. 'It was partly a financial decision,' says Steve. 'They offered me more money than I'd ever thought about, really. And Plymouth are a big club. My only disappointment was that having been relegated the previous season, they were in the same division as Orient, and I had wanted to push myself up a little higher.'

Steve loved his time at Plymouth, where he was reunited with his old Orient pal Kevin Nugent. His first season, in 1992–93, was beset with injury problems, though he still managed to score 11 goals and was made club captain. The next year Steve blossomed, scoring an incredible 23 goals from midfield. 'Peter Shilton said to me "There's the pitch. Just go out and play." As a footballer it was enlightening. Suddenly I could do all the things that Peter Eustace thought I couldn't. I felt like going back to knock on his door to say "Look, I scored 23 goals. I can play".'

Coventry City – then a Premier League team – came in with an offer of £800,000 for Steve, and First Division Birmingham were prepared to pay £750,000, but Plymouth, who were chasing promotion themselves, turned down both. Steve's third season at Plymouth was beset with groin problems, and he played only a handful of games. He occupied his time by dating local girl Kate, who became his long-term partner. The couple married in Jamaica in 2004.

That season Plymouth struggled and were relegated – along with Orient – to the bottom division of the League. Steve, now at the end of his contract, felt that his time was up there. 'I'd enjoyed my time at Plymouth but I had found the attention a bit suffocating,' he says. 'I wanted to move on.' Birmingham – who under the management of Barry Fry had just returned to Division One – paid Plymouth £275,000 for Steve's services. It didn't end up being a happy time for Steve. 'Barry signed me but he didn't rate me,' he explains. 'We had about 64 pros there – an abundance of riches – and I was on the periphery. Suddenly I'd gone into a massive pond and I was a very little fish.'

In February 1996 Steve went out on loan to Division Three side Gillingham, making six starts and one substitute appearance for them. On returning to Birmingham he made just a handful of appearances under new manager Trevor Francis. 'I started wondering whether Division One was a level too much for me,' says Steve. 'But I didn't actually think that it was – I just never got the opportunity to prove it.' In February 1997 – after making just 29 starts and seven substitute appearances in his two years at Birmingham – Steve received a call from Tommy Taylor, who had become manager of Orient a few months earlier. Taylor wanted Castle on loan – and Steve jumped at the chance. 'It felt like I was coming home,' he says. 'Orient was my first love and everything came flooding back.'

Steve soon slipped back into old habits, scoring in a 2–1 victory over Rochdale in his third game. His fourth game proved to be the last of his loan spell as an injury to his cartilage required surgery. It was a problem that continued to plague him. Taylor was convinced that Steve, by now 30 years old, still had a few good seasons left in him and offered him a permanent deal. But Barry Fry, in his new role as manager of Peterborough United, also required the services of the midfielder – both as a player and as first-team coach. Steve had completed his UEFA A coaching licence while at Plymouth and jumped at the chance to put the theory he had learned into practice. He signed a three-year deal with Peterborough. 'It wasn't a case of choosing Peterborough over Orient,' says Steve. 'It was just that it was my first chance to get in on the coaching side of things as well as playing. On reflection I wish I'd chosen to go to Orient because I was still playing decent football. But I did love every minute of Peterborough.'

Steve made 113 starts and nine substitute appearances for Division Three Peterborough over his three seasons there, scoring 20 goals. He was an instrumental part of their promotion season of 1999–2000, and played his last game for the club at Wembley in their 1–0 victory over Darlington in the Play-off Final that year. Peterborough wanted to retain his services and offered him a four-year deal as a coach and occasional player. But Steve, though 34 by now, still believed he had more to offer on the pitch. Tommy Taylor concurred, and offered Steve a two-year deal along with a testimonial. 'I wanted Steve for a bit of experience,' says Taylor, presumably worried that his squad of 50-odd players was not quite big enough. 'We were coming together as a team, but we didn't have a big experienced player out there. And Steve had been such a good servant to the club.'

Though Plymouth also wanted Steve back, it was to Orient he was drawn and once again he found himself rocking up to work at Brisbane Road. Unfortunately, though Steve's mind was willing, his body was less so. In pre-season, every time he played his knee would blow up. Eventually it was diagnosed as MRSA – an infection he'd picked up during a cartilage operation a few weeks earlier. Steve had to go under the knife again, and spent much of the season striving to regain fitness. 'It was an absolute nightmare,' he says. 'I had a lot of miles on the clock and I was picking up other bits and pieces like groin and hamstring problems.'

Steve did make a handful of appearances from February 2001 onwards but admits that he did not really feel part of the team. Orient were, in his absence, doing pretty well and made the Play-offs by virtue of finishing fifth in Division Three. An injury to Andy Harris, one of Tommy Taylor's preferred midfielders, gave Steve the chance to show that the old magic was still there in the Play-off semi-finals against Hull City. (And Castle certainly had the edge in goalscoring ability. Harris, as many Orient fans will recall, would have had trouble locating a barn door, let alone hitting it.)

Though Orient prevailed – losing 1–0 in Hull then winning 2–0 at Brisbane Road – the games weren't a particularly happy experience for Steve personally. 'In previous years I'd been the catalyst of the team, and I wanted to be that again,' he says. 'But my body wouldn't do it anymore. I wasn't doing myself justice and that was really frustrating.' Tommy Taylor left Steve on the bench for the Play-off Final against Blackpool at the Millennium Stadium in Cardiff, opting to start with the fit-again Andy Harris. 'As a coach I probably would have done the same thing,' Steve admits. 'But it didn't stop the personal disappointment.'

Orient lost the Final 4–2. Steve came on as a substitute but says that as the final whistle blew he still didn't feel a proper part of the team. 'I felt for people like Matt Lockwood and Dean Smith. They'd been there two years before when they lost to Scunthorpe. Losing a Play-off Final is one of the biggest psychological blows in football.'

In July 2001 over 6,500 fans turned up to see Orient play Tottenham Hotspur for Steve's testimonial – a game Spurs won 2–0. 'I was overwhelmed by it,' says Steve. 'I really appreciated all the fans turning up, and it was nice that so many people remembered me.'

Steve dearly wanted to be remembered as a great Orient player, but was beginning to feel that his final spell at the club was tarnishing his reputation. He desperately wanted to get fit for the start of the 2001–02 season and play as he once did in an Orient shirt. 'I got my head down and went for it, and I didn't think I was playing too badly in pre-season. I came on as a substitute in the first game against Cheltenham and felt that I changed things a bit. I thought that I was going to get a good run in the team. But it didn't happen. Tommy had already made his mind up that I was a liability injury-wise. It was the final nail in the coffin.'

It was Steve's last game in an Orient shirt. Finding it impossible to break into the team, Steve went on loan in September to Conference side Stevenage – where ex-Orient player Kevin Hales was assistant manager – and played in seven games, one of them as a substitute, without scoring. When he returned to Brisbane Road after two months, Tommy Taylor had been sacked and his assistant Paul Brush installed as manager. And the new boss didn't want the ageing midfielder in his side. 'Barry Hearn came to me and told me that Paul didn't see me as part of his plans,' says Steve. 'They paid me up and that was that. To be honest, I think Paul saw me as a threat. Tommy had offered me the position of youth team manager before he left, but Paul didn't want me to have that job.'

It was a pretty inglorious end for an Orient legend and one that Steve regrets. 'With the greatest respect, coming back to Orient was the worst thing I could have done,' he says. 'I wanted to play at the same

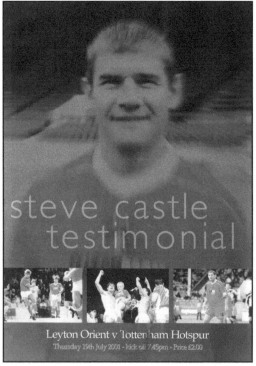

The programme for Steve's testimonial against Tottenham on 19 July 2001.

Steve with his wife Kate in 2007.

level that I had done before, but I just wasn't fit enough.' Finally, Steve decided it was time to retire from League football, leaving him a total record of 568 starts, 47 substitute appearances and 131 goals. 'It took me until I was 36 to realise I should call it a day,' he says. 'My body was saying enough is enough. I was taking anti-inflammatories to play games and it was hurting my knee to train.'

But he was in no mood to give up football completely, and in June 2002 signed for Ryman Premier League side St Albans City as a player-coach. Coaching was something that was always of interest to Steve, even back when he was an Orient apprentice. 'Dario Gradi first got me thinking about coaching,' he says. 'He was just fantastic in what he did, so I had him as a benchmark.'

Steve's old friend Barry Fry invited him to become his assistant manager at Second Division Peterborough in January 2003. In June of the same year he was made player-manager of St Albans City, where he remained until October 2005, having made 45 starts, 15 substitute appearances and scored three goals. He went on to briefly manage Essex Olympian League Division One side Tateley FC, serve as assistant manager at Conference side Cambridge United and coach the West Ham Under–13 team.

Since then Steve has been making a living from running the football youth development scheme at Oaklands College in St Albans. That and driving the taxi. In January 2008 he combined these roles with that of caretaker manager of St Albans City once again. Of the future, Steve aims to manage at the highest level possible. Orient perhaps? 'I'd love to one day,' he smiles. 'It would be a nice ambition to go back to somewhere that I gave my heart and soul to.'

No Orient fan would deny that Steve Castle did exactly that in his time at Brisbane Road, where the one-time Fancy Dan truly came of age.

# Chapter 4
# WALKING ON WATER
## Stan Charlton 1952–56, 1958–65

As memories of Leyton Orient go, there are none more stirring than that of Stan Charlton being chaired off the pitch by fans at the conclusion of the game in April 1962 that saw the club secure promotion to the First Division for the only time in its history. With a crunching tackle, driving forward runs and an apparently limitless reserve of energy, Stan was the captain who propelled his team towards the top flight and that year, for fans, he could have walked on water.

Indeed, such was the euphoria surrounding the club at the time, Charlton decided to put that very proposition to the test during the team's celebratory trip to Majorca a few days after the famous victory. He explains 'We were all sitting

Stan in 1955.

around the swimming pool and I suddenly said to the coach Eddie Baily "I bet you 100 pesetas that I can walk across it." He immediately took me up on the offer so, fully dressed, I approached the pool and attempted to walk on water. Of course, I fell straight in, and I had to hang all of the pesetas on the line to dry.'

You can forgive Stan his temporary delusions of spiritual transcendence. It had been some season, the outcome of which came down to the very last day, with promotion dependent on a victory against Bury coupled with a failure by Sunderland to beat Swansea. It gave the full-back a second chance to play in Division One, having spent three seasons there with Arsenal during the one interlude in his Orient career.

It is a time that Stan, now approaching 80 years old, remembers fondly. Age and various operations – he has had both knees completely replaced, one of them twice – have robbed him of five inches off his 5ft 10in frame and he walks with a limp, but his mind remains sharp. He lives with his landlady in Weymouth, Dorset, and after spending time with Stan it is easy to see why this dignified man is someone about whom teammate Terry McDonald once said 'No one would take liberties with Stan. We all respected him too much to let him or the club down.'

There is still a flash of fire in his eyes. Get him talking about short-lived Orient manager Benny Fenton and it's there. 'He was a joke,' he states abruptly at the first mention of the name. At other times Stan becomes quite emotional when talking about the club where he spent 11 years of his life and made 408 appearances. 'I had a terrific rapport with the Orient fans,' he says, his eyes brimming with tears. 'It brings a lump to my throat. I'll never forget them. Even now when I go back, the warmth of the people is wonderful.' The feeling is mutual. 'Stan was one of the best full-backs we've ever had,' says fan George Gatward. 'He was a brilliant tackler, he always gave 100 per cent and he was a marvellous man. And he was before his time. In those days all the full-back had to do was stay at the back and kick it up the field. But Stan was different – he invented the wing-back position, and he would tear up the pitch.' As he did so the crowd would roar him along, and fan Mickey Kasler recalls how it used to affect Stan. 'Everyone would cheer, and his whole face would go red with embarrassment,' he laughs. Stan chuckles at the memory. 'I was a shy lad,' he says.

Stan was born in Exeter on 28 June 1929 to father Stanley and mother Isabella. Within a fortnight the family had moved to South London: Stanley Snr was a footballer and was making the move from Exeter City to Crystal Palace, both Division Three South sides. The Charltons, including Stan's one sister, Edna, lived in a rented semi-detached house near Selhurst Park. While his father turned out for Palace, his mother worked in a local brewery.

Stan passed his 11+ exam, gaining him a place at one of the best schools in Croydon, John Ruskin. This, however, coincided with the outbreak of World War Two and Stan was sent up to his grandfather's house in Barnsley. On returning six weeks later, the youngster found he had been left behind in his schoolwork and, instead of attending classes, took to playing truant. 'My mother thought I was going to school but actually I'd lie under the bushes in the front garden waiting for her to go to work,' Stan says. 'Once she'd gone I'd go to a playing field and kick a ball about all day.'

Stan always wanted to be a professional footballer and follow in his father's footsteps. Yet he did not receive any coaching from Stanley Snr. He recalls 'When I was 14 I started playing for a local youth side called Spartan Boys. I would get home for my tea on Saturday after having played and my mum would suddenly say to me "You got the wrong side of the winger today – you should come back a bit." And I'd say "How do you know?" And she'd say "Your dad told me." He always used to come and watch me play, but he wouldn't let me know that he was there. He'd hide behind a tree or something. He was proud of me – he just wouldn't say it.'

For his part, Stan talks with obvious pride about his dad, pointing out that he was named as one of Crystal Palace's 100 best players in their history. The truancy meant that Stan did not last long at John Ruskin School, and he moved to a nearby secondary modern, Tavistock, before gaining a scholarship to Stanley Technical School at the age of 13. There he showed a lot of footballing promise playing for the school team, despite his lack of stature at the time. 'I was very small as a boy,' he explains. 'I took after my mother – she was only 4ft 11in.'

Leaving school at 16, Stan became an apprentice toolmaker, but it was football that remained his dream job. Through his father, he tried to get a foot in the door at Crystal Palace. 'Once, I was up there with my dad, and Ronnie Rooke, who was the manager at the time, said to me "Do you live far?" I told him I was just five minutes away so he said "Nip home and get your boots then." I did, but when I got back five minutes later he'd gone to Catford Dogs.' Feeling frustrated at his lack of opportunities, at 17 and a half years of age, Stan took a drastic step. No, not signing for Southend United, but joining the army. 'I wanted to be a footballer, but I thought I couldn't be,' he says. 'My idea was to become a driver mechanic in the army, come out and get a garage. But once I joined the army I wasn't allowed to be a driver mechanic, and became a clerk.'

Before his 18th birthday Stan was shipped out to Palestine, where he remained for the next three years without returning home. Later on he also served in Egypt. And while he continued to play football in the army, he says that the thought of eventually becoming a professional player did not enter his head once. The Suez crisis meant that eventually Stan had to serve six rather than five years in the army, and it was towards the end of his time that things began to happen that set him on the path to Brisbane Road. In 1951 he was stationed at a depot in Woolwich alongside Roy Merryfield, who went on to play for Chelsea and Millwall but at the time was playing for Bromley. He invited Stan to turn out for the Isthmian League side, and in October 1951 he played for them in the FA Amateur Cup against Barnet. 'It was a thick, muddy day,' he recalls. 'It was right up my street, and I had a hell of a game. And there were half a dozen England selectors in the crowd.'

He was picked for the national amateur side, making his debut in February 1952 against Wales in Bangor. 'It was a very proud moment,' says Stan. 'When they were playing *God Save The Queen* I had tears streaming down my face.' He wasn't the only one, for who should Stan see on the train back to London but his father. 'Once again he'd come to see me play without telling me,' he chuckles. Over the rest of that season Stan represented England another three times, including a game against Scotland at Wembley. Despite this, he still did not believe that he could make it as a professional footballer. 'I was coming up to 23,' he explains. 'I thought I was too old.'

Others thought differently. A sergeant at Woolwich was an Exeter City fan and had fond memories of Stan's father. He wrote to the club asking if Stanley Jnr could have a trial. They agreed, and Stan ended up playing half a dozen games for the reserve team. Orient manager Alec Stock, on the lookout for new players, spotted him and soon after sent chief scout Sid Hollins to visit Stan at his home. 'He brought my mother and sister some nylons and he told me that Orient were keeping an eye on me,' says Stan. That year, 1952, was an Olympic year, and in the summer Stan was selected to be part of the Great Britain football team that went to Helsinki for the games, under the management of Walter

Winterbottom. He got three weeks' special leave from the army, but did not make the team for the first game against Luxembourg. Great Britain lost 5–3, and with that Stan's Olympic flame was extinguished.

On returning, Stan found First Division Aston Villa knocking at his door, contract in hand. Surprisingly, he rejected it. 'My dad said to me that I was 23 and that I would struggle to break into their first team,' he explains. 'Besides, Orient were still interested, and it seemed that I would have a better chance of making it there.' Stan was still seeing out his last year in the army at the time, but was asked by Alec Stock to turn out for the first team for the opening game of the 1952–53 season after the regular full-back, John 'Taffy' Evans, caught an ear infection. The match was against Reading at Elm Park. 'That was a disaster,' says Stan, though he is not referring to the fact Orient lost 2–0. 'I was supposed to be taking my fiancée Shirley to a show in London that night. Alec Stock told me not to worry, that I would have plenty of time to get back to London from Reading after the match. I would have done too if I hadn't jumped on the wrong train and ended up in Bristol!'

Football-wise, Stan fared a little better. It was a strange situation he was in – he was still in the army, he had not had a chance to train with the squad and yet he was making an appearance in the first team. 'I just went out there and did what I always did,' he says. 'At half-time Alec Stock said to me "You're doing OK, but you must threaten the winger with your studs more." And the other full-back Arthur Banner came over and said in his broad Yorkshire accent "Eh, boss. You leave him alone. He's doing alright".' Perhaps Banner wouldn't have been quite so benevolent had he known that Stan would go on to take his place in the side. Stan played in every subsequent fixture that season and, midway through and having completed his time in the army, he earned himself the professional contract he'd dreamed of as a child. He was to be paid £12 a week during the season and £8 a week during the summer.

Stan says that he fitted in very well with the other players. In particular Stan bonded with goalkeeper Dave Groombridge. 'He was a Croydon boy as well and lived in Buckhurst Hill at the time. We used to go out every Friday night and have two glasses of sherry in the same pub.' These wild nights out stopped in 1953 when Stan married Shirley – who had lived across the road from him in Croydon – and the couple moved first to a rented flat in Brixton and then to a house owned by the club in Woodford Green.

In both the 1952–53 and 1953–54 seasons Orient finished mid-table in Division Three South. Stan was virtually ever present throughout both seasons, though was dropped by Alec Stock for one game. Unusually, Stock asked Stan to go to Chester on a scouting mission rather than turning out for the reserves. Stan recalls 'I said "What's all this, boss?", and Alec asked me if I'd ever played in the reserves. I said that I hadn't, and he smiled and said "Well, I didn't want to spoil your record." I was gobsmacked.'

The Orient side that finished runners-up in Division Three South in 1954–55. Stan is in the back row on the far right.

The next season of 1954–55 saw Orient pushing for promotion. They recorded some memorable victories as they did so, including a 7–1 mauling of Exeter City at St James Park in which Stan scored his first professional goal. 'I clonked it with my left foot from about 25 yards, and it screamed into the top corner,' he recalls. 'I came off the park and Nick Collins the trainer said to me "Stan, you'll never ever score another goal like that. Make the most of it." I actually did score one more that was very similar against Birmingham in the FA Cup when I was at Arsenal, but the one for Orient was pretty special.'

But the team's bid to get out of the division was hampered by the fact that only one side were promoted at that time, and Bristol City, rather than Orient, clinched the top spot. 'Alec used to offer us an extra bonus of £5 each to win games,' says Stan, 'but I would say to him "It doesn't make any difference. I can't play any harder. I'm giving you everything I've got."'

From left to right: Vic Groves, Phil Woosnam and Stan in the 1954–55 season.

Stan is full of nothing but praise for Stock, the manager who gave him his first professional contract. 'He had the knack of getting the best out of people. He helped me an awful lot.'

Stan would have further cause to thank Stock in the 1955–56 season. Orient had made a fantastic start, unbeaten in their first seven games, and suddenly the papers were rife with rumours that First Division Tottenham, under the management of Jimmy Anderson, wanted to buy Stan. 'I felt elated,' he says. 'Spurs were a lovely push and run side then.'

By October, Spurs had made a firm offer, but Tottenham believed they were owed money from a previous transfer between the clubs and the deal fell through. 'I was broken-hearted,' says Stan. 'But Alec Stock called me into his office and said "Don't worry, Stan, I'll find you a better club before the end of the week." I didn't believe him. I thought, what better club is there than Tottenham?' Yet by Friday I was at Arsenal.' Scouts from Arsenal had been paying regular visits to Brisbane Road that season, and not just because they'd got lost on the way to West Ham. They were primarily interested in the young striker Vic Groves, and on the Friday in question the North London club made a £30,000 bid for both him and Charlton. 'I'd come in that day and Alec told me we were going to see the chairman Harry Zussman in his warehouse,' Stan recalls. 'I signed the forms there and then and that was it – I was an Arsenal player. There was a maximum wage, so I got a £10 signing on fee and a salary of £12 a week, the same as I was on at Orient.'

Orient training at Brisbane Road during the 1955–56 season. From left to right: Stan Charlton, Johnny Hartburn, Pat Welton, Jimmy Lee and Jimmy Smith.

Stan says that he would quite happily have stayed at Brisbane Road, but that the chance to play for Arsenal, under the management of Tom Whittaker, was too good to turn down. 'I never thought about moving clubs until the offer came in,' he says. At Arsenal, Stan forced his way into the first team by Christmas, and once there he remained a regular feature, adapting to Division One football easily. His excellent performances led to rumours in the press of an England call-up. 'I didn't care that much at the time,' says Stan, surprisingly. 'I just never thought I was good enough. There were other fantastic full-backs around at the time, like Alf Ramsey.'

It was during that first season that Stan and Shirley's first child arrived, a boy by the name of Gary. Stan continued to perform for Arsenal in the 1957–58 season, when the Gunners finished 12th in Division One. He featured in the famous 5–4 loss to Manchester United in February 1958 – the game that preceded the Munich air crash. The next season brought a change of manager and trouble for Stan. George Swindin was appointed, and Stan found himself playing in the reserves. His place had been taken by Len Wills, who in the past had lined up alongside Swindin in the manager's playing days. 'It wasn't at all justified,' says Stan. 'I'd kept Len out of the side for three years, and now he was supposed to be better than me? George put him in the side because they were big mates.'

Stan vowed to stay and fight for his place, but by December he was still playing reserve football. On Christmas Eve 1958 Stan was paid a visit. Not by Santa Claus, but by someone bearing a gift that could trump anything the bearded fellow from Lapland might have in his sack. Stan explains 'I was putting some draught excluder up around my front door when I saw Alec Stock walking up my front path. He said "Hello Stanley, you're coming home," and handed me a contract that would make me an Orient player again. I signed it there and then on the doorstep, Alec walked back down the path and that was that. There was no signing-on fee, but the wages had gone up to £20.'

He was joining an Orient team that, like in so many seasons before and after, were flirting with relegation. 'It felt like I had come home,' Stan laughs. Goals from Tommy Johnston and Eddie Brown ensured that Orient remained in Division Two, though that season did see the departure of Alec Stock for the final time. His able assistant Les Gore became the permanent manager of the side. 'I got on with Les very well,' says Stan. 'He was much quieter than Alec and perhaps his knowledge of the game wasn't as great, but he was a good manager and was well respected.'

The next season of 1959–60, much of which Stan missed through a groin injury, saw Orient just achieve mid-table mediocrity. Fans need not have found anything too amiss, for in the 1960–61 season it was business as usual at Brisbane Road as relegation beckoned once again. Still, Stan was never shy of going into battle, and he excelled under pressure. In a 2–1 loss at home to Lincoln City in October wind, rain and mud, the *Walthamstow Guardian* wrote of him 'The going was just to burly left-back Stan Charlton's liking. He ploughed his way through the mud like a highly mobile

Stan (right) gets some post-match refreshment, along with coach Joe Mallett (left) and goalkeeper Dave Groombridge (centre).

tank, splaying passes to all the forwards. Such was Charlton's supremacy that this was a game Lincoln's right-winger will want to forget.'

Stan says that despite the struggles on the pitch, there remained a great spirit at the club. Since the birth of Kevin in 1958, he had been the father of two children but he still enjoyed socialising with the other players. Living near to Stan's Woodford Green home were Sid Bishop, Dave Dunmore, Ronnie Foster and Terry McDonald, and the group would often meet up on Sundays for a drink – Makeson's milk stout or Guinness were Stan's tipples. Stan would play nine holes of golf with Dave Dunmore on the morning of games, and after the match would join some of the other players in the Supporters' Bar. Mixing with the fans was important to him. 'We wouldn't miss a supporters' club do, that's for sure,' he says.

Not that Stan was exempt from a spot of banter from the fans. He had, however, a useful riposte should any get a bit too chippy. 'I'd lob the ball up onto the corrugated iron roof that used to be over the stand, and all the rust would fall down on the fans' heads,' he laughs. Opposition supporters weren't always so friendly, as Stan discovered in a match against Sheffield Wednesday. 'I tackled a young lad and swept him off the pitch,' Stan recalls. 'As I was getting back on my feet a woman shouted "You dirty bugger!" and smashed her umbrella over my head! Later on I was over

Why have one drink when you can have two? From left to right: Dave Groombridge, a fan, Sid Bishop and Stan Charlton at a Supporters' Club do.

there again and she apologised. I said "Don't worry, you couldn't have hit me any better place than that!"'

On away trips, Stan would play cards – brag, mostly – to pass the time. 'One time coming back on the train from Preston I was having a bad run of cards and had lost all my wages,' he says. 'To carry on playing I borrowed £10, which was quite a lot. But I kept losing and was down to my last £2 when there was a signal failure just outside Euston. In the time it took for the train to get going again I'd paid back what I borrowed, got all the money back that I lost and was owed money. If the train had got in on time I'd have been seriously out of pocket.' In those days footballers were hardly rolling in it. Stan had to supplement his Orient salary by coaching at boys' clubs in the evenings. He also took a job as a PE teacher in Romford, taking lessons every afternoon after training. The abolition of the maximum wage in January 1961 helped, though Orient, unsurprisingly, were not in a position to improve their players' salaries by much. 'My biggest wage at Orient was £43 and 10 shillings,' Stan recalls.

At the beginning of the 1961–62 season, fans – and, Stan admits, the players too – expected nothing more than a continued battle against relegation. New manager Johnny Carey, brought in to replace Les Gore, apparently felt much the same, saying at the time 'There's not a class player here. I will be satisfied if we get into the top half of the table.' It was a surefire way to inspire confidence in his team. Stan, though, is complimentary about his former boss. 'I was sorry to see Les Gore go, but Johnny had quite a reputation,' he says. 'He was a quiet man, and he always had a pipe in his mouth, whether it was lit or not. But he was a nice bloke and I got on with him personally. He'd always say "Just keep playing football, just push it around."' But whoever takes the credit for it, something began to go right for Orient that season. After five wins in six games during August and September, players suddenly started to believe. 'The whole attitude changed,' says Stan. 'We started to think that we could beat anyone.'

That season Stan had been made permanent captain of the side, after the retirement of previous skipper Ken Facey. It was a role to which he was well suited. 'I was a hands-on captain,' he says. 'I wasn't authoritative. I was still one of the lads. I led by example.' In blistering form himself, he was some example, and from late November to early January the team posted nine wins in a row. It put Orient in second place in the table, just one point behind Liverpool.

January also brought a fourth-round FA Cup tie with Burnley, at that point top of Division One. In front of nearly 40,000 fans, Orient secured a 1–1 draw at Turf Moor. The replay at Brisbane Road drew a crowd of 31,000 and saw Orient launch wave after wave of attacks, only to be undone by a cruel goal after goalkeeper Frank George accidentally punched defender Eddie Lewis in the face during a corner. 'We should have won,' says Stan, ruefully. 'I was absolutely sick. We were the better side that day. I don't think their manager saw a ball kicked in the second half – he was in the dressing room as he couldn't bear to watch.'

In the penultimate game of that season, on Easter Monday, Orient beat Luton Town 3–1, leaving them in second place, two points clear of Sunderland, who were playing their penultimate game at Rotherham the next day. This gave director Les Grade an idea. Stan explains 'Les asked me how well I knew the Rotherham skipper Roy Lambert. I told him that I knew him well. Then Les said that he'd give me and another player of my choice £100 expenses to travel up to Rotherham to offer Roy £1,000 for him and the team if they beat Sunderland. It wasn't a bribe, of course, just a bonus for the players. I went up to Millmoor with Dave Dunmore, met up with Roy Lambert and told him about the money. Then Dave and I stood on the embankment to watch the game, and we had our caps and ear mufflers on, but still two kids recognised us and asked us for our autographs. Anyway, it was all a waste of time because Sunderland won 3–0.'

This meant that in the final game of the season, Orient needed to beat Bury and hope that Swansea, who at the time were sitting near the foot of the table, could take a point or two off of Sunderland at Vetch Field. 'We thought we'd blown it,' says Stan. 'I don't think anyone was expecting Swansea to get anything from Sunderland. But we knew that we had to win to give ourselves any chance at all. The dressing room before the game was the most tense I have ever been in.' Malcolm Graham settled Orient nerves with a goal after 14 minutes, and the score remained at 1–0 until half-time. Early in the second half, word filtered through that Sunderland had gone 1–0 up at Swansea. But soon after, a huge cheer went up from the crowd: Swansea had equalised. 'Of course we realised what had happened,' Stan recalls. 'After that I don't think Bury would have scored that day. It would have to have been over dead bodies.' Another goal from Malcolm Graham secured the victory, Swansea held out against Sunderland and Orient had gained promotion to Division One for the first time in their history, sparking a pitch invasion by the 21,000 fans. 'It was tremendous,' Stan recalls, emotionally. 'It was the most wonderful feeling, you just couldn't feel any better.' Stan was chaired off the pitch by fans and spent the evening celebrating. 'We all got a bit drunk that evening,' he confesses. 'We went to the local fish and chip shop in Leyton and we just carried on from there.'

Stan puts the success of that season down to the attitude of the team. 'We knew we weren't the best footballers in the world, but that year no one could match us for fighting spirit,' he says. That summer Stan could look forward to playing in the top flight with Orient, but he almost ruled himself out after a nasty car crash. Stan had been one of the first players to own a car in the late 1950s – a 1939 Vauxhall 10 – but by 1962 he was driving an A35 van. 'I'd just been down to Eastbourne to pick up my mother from a holiday and dropped her off at the pub and had a couple of drinks,' Stan recalls. 'As I was driving home across Clapham Common I fell asleep at the wheel and hit a bollard. The next thing I knew I'd gashed my eye open and cut my chest and my knee.

'An ambulance arrived to take me to hospital, and just before it left a policeman jumped in. Obviously I was worried because I'd been drinking. The copper said to me "Here's the contents from your van. There's a picture of Orient here." I told him I was the skipper, and he said that he played for the Metropolitan Police. He asked me what had happened and I told him that I'd fallen asleep at the wheel. He said "Are you sure you want to say that?" I said "Well, that's the truth." But I heard no more about it. I could have been in a lot of trouble were he not a football fan.'

In preparing for Orient's first-ever season in the top flight of English football, Johnny Carey had a theory. 'My main task will be to convince the boys that they are every bit as good as the other players in the First Division,' he said. 'There is no question of rushing out and buying new players.' Did captain Stan Charlton agree? 'No,' he says emphatically. 'We needed more goals. We needed to sign someone to give Dave Dunmore a bit of assistance up there. There was an inside-forward at Southampton at the time called George O'Brien, who eventually did come to Orient in March 1966, and I badly wanted Johnny to sign him. I think he would have made the difference.'

As it was, Orient began the season with the same squad with which it ended the last, and immediately began to struggle. 'It was tough,' Stan recalls. 'A few players had played in Division One before – myself, Dave Dunmore, Eddie Lewis – but we weren't that experienced a side. I did think we might be able to hang on – we lost a lot of games by the odd goal – but we weren't good enough, for sure.'

There were memorable moments – victories against Everton, Manchester United and West Ham in the space of 12 days, for example – but ultimately it was a season during which Orient were destined for relegation pretty much from the outset. Stan says that despite this, the team spirit was good. 'We never got downhearted. We enjoyed being in the division – the grounds we went to, the crowds. Some of the lads had never played in places like that. It was a wonderful experience.'

The last game of the season, by which time Orient had long been consigned to relegation, was against Manchester United at Old Trafford. It was a game the opposition needed to win to avoid relegation themselves. Football fans would not be surprised to learn that it was two goals by a man named Charlton that helped Manchester United win the game 3–1 – though in one of the cases it was not Bobby's name on the scoresheet. 'I scored an own goal,' admits Stan. 'Bobby Charlton took a corner, I went to head it at the near post, and I didn't quite catch it right. It went straight in the back of the net. I laugh about it now, but I was sick at the time.'

Orient found themselves back in Division Two for the 1963–64 season. It was a campaign they would have to negotiate without Johnny Carey, who left to take over Division One side Nottingham Forest. In November a new manager arrived from Colchester United: Benny Fenton, brother of ex-West Ham manager Ted Fenton. Stan scoffs at the mention of his name. 'He was a vain person,' he says. 'One of the first things he did was to have a big mirror put up near the door in the dressing room. He said that it was to make sure we were dressed properly before we went out on the pitch. But the only person to look in the mirror was him. He was not popular with the players.'

Stan objected in particular to his coaching methods – or lack of them. 'A training session one day consisted of us learning to tie our boots properly,' he says, incredulously. 'It wasn't a punishment. He genuinely wanted us to do it. I said "I've only been tying my boots up for 10 years."' And Stan was no more impressed with Fenton's tactical nous. 'One of his first games in charge was against Rotherham, and he said to me "Every time you get the ball, play it up to Dave Dunmore. Cut the midfield out." And Cyril Lea and Malcolm Lucas turned around to me and said "What the bloody hell are we going to do then?" I told them that we would just go out and play the way we always did. We won the game 4–2 and afterwards Benny said "I told you hitting long balls would work." He didn't even realise we hadn't done it. That shows you what sort of man he was.'

In the League, Orient did no more than survive – finishing in 16th position, just four points clear of relegation. The heady days of Division One seemed a distant memory. Things got worse for Stan when, after a handful of games at the start of the 1964–65 season, he found himself dropped by Fenton in favour of a young David Webb. Though Stan had just turned 35, he says that he still felt fit and had no intention of ending his career. 'I was out of the side because I'd answered Benny back about having to tie up my boot laces,' Stan contests. 'It all came back to that.'

In December, with Orient languishing near the bottom of the table, Fenton was sacked. 'I remember it well,' Stan laughs. 'I wasn't in the side for the Boxing Day game against Charlton, so on Christmas Day I was supposed to be going to a party at my sister's place. Then Les Gore phoned me up and told me that Benny had gone and that I was back in the side. So that was the party gone.'

Unfortunately for Stan, his spell back in the first team was short-lived, and in January former Orient player Dave Sexton arrived as manager. Once again, Stan didn't see eye-to-eye with his new boss. 'Dave had all these modern ideas,' Stan explains. 'He came in with a big graph and said there was going to be a new bonus scheme. Anyone scoring a goal would get a pound. Anyone making the last pass before a goal would get 10 shillings. If the goalkeeper kept a clean sheet there would be a silver collection for him. I said "Boss, could you explain to me where I come into your bonus scheme? I'm a full-back. If I make two or three assists in a season that would be it and I rarely score a goal. The way I feel at the moment I'd rather head one in my own net than give money to a silver collection." I don't think that went down well. He tore the graph off the wall and I'd made an enemy for life.'

Stan found himself dropped again and, at the end of the season, transfer-listed. 'Harry Zussman told me that there was a job for me looking after the reserves, but I didn't want it,' says Stan. 'I was coming up to 36, but I still wanted to play.' There was interest from Southern League side Hastings United, who were looking for a player-manager. It did not quite work out. 'I was stitched up by my supposed best friend Sid Bishop!' laughs Stan. 'We were at a supporters' club dance in Stratford, and I left to run Phil White home in my car. While I was gone, the chairman of Hastings came in to the bar to ask for me. Sid told him I wasn't there and asked if there was anything he could do to help. The chairman told him that he was looking for a player-manager. Sid said "Well, I'm free" and took the job. Some friend he turned out to be!' (Sid, incidentally, denies this version of events, claiming that he was asked by a different member of the Hastings board to take the job.)

Thankfully there was another offer in the pipeline, from another Southern League side, Weymouth, and this time Stan managed to secure the job. He had no qualms about dropping down into non-League football. 'I did have an offer from Third Division Gillingham but I didn't like the terms they were offering me. I was happy to go to Weymouth and carry on playing football.'

That same year of 1965 Stan and Shirley had their third child, a daughter they named Carol. But sadly for Stan, a cartilage operation curtailed his playing career after just 18 appearances for

Weymouth, though he continued as their manager until being given the boot in 1972. 'One thing you know as a manager is that eventually – whenever it is – you're going to be sacked,' Stan smiles. There was to be one last appearance at Brisbane Road for Stan. In 1970 the club, with the best intentions, organised a benefit match for their former captain. 'It was good of the club to organise it, but it was a disaster,' says Stan. 'I'd been away for too long. I only got £995 and that week I found out that my father was £800 in debt, so I paid that off for him. That was my benefit.'

After leaving Weymouth FC, Stan went on to work for Vernons Pools for seven years, and then for Gross Cash Registers, selling tills. In 1988 he went back to Weymouth FC as club secretary until he retired in 1992, when he was made a life vice-president of the club, and he continues his involvement with the club to this day.

Stan and Shirley divorced in 1984 and two years later Shirley passed away after battling motor neurone disease. Stan never remarried, but he now has the pleasure of regularly spending time with his 12 grandchildren. Asked to describe himself as a footballer, Stan shoots back 'Rough and ready.' He's quick to point out, however, that he was never booked at Orient and only had his name in the referee's book on one occasion during his whole amateur and professional career, in a game for Arsenal. 'I was a tough tackler, but I was always fair, and I never went in over the top,' he says.

He looks back on his career with justifiable pride and has no regrets. 'I don't think there's anything I could have done differently,' he says. 'I always gave 100 per cent every time I played, everything I did. I put the effort into every game, I never stopped. I thought all players were like that. It was only when I became a manager that I realised that they weren't.' Had Orient possessed a few more players that boasted Stan's commitment then perhaps there would have been more seasons in Division One, more memories of triumphant captains being paraded around Brisbane Road, more glory. It was not to be, but for a while at least, Stan Charlton had Orient fans believing. To them, he walks on water to this day.

# Chapter 5
# A GOD-GIVEN TALENT
## Alan Comfort 1986–89

Alan playing for Orient in 1987.

To anyone who saw Alan Comfort on the ball – jinking, shimmying, confounding – it was clear that this was a footballer with a God-given talent. Quite literally, as far as the man himself is concerned, because these days Alan Comfort is the Reverend Alan Comfort, and he firmly believes that his skills were bestowed on him from above.

Football and religion went hand-in-hand for the left-winger and, indeed, his journey to Leyton in March 1986 was his very own Road to Damascus moment – except in this case the carriageway was the M11. Around a year earlier, Alan had converted to Christianity while at Cambridge United – a club that would drive anyone to seek some sort of spiritual solace – and, according to him, his transfer to the Os was part of the sea change in his life. 'Driving down the M11 from Cambridge to Orient was like being set free,' he explains. 'Things hadn't gone that well for me there, but as I headed towards Leyton it felt like I was coming to the place that I was always meant to be. Once I arrived at Brisbane Road I thought, this is me. This is where I should be. This is where I want to be. And that never changed while I was at Orient.'

In his three and a half seasons at the club, from March 1986 to June 1989, Alan made 174 full appearances and scored 50 goals – quite some record for a midfielder. Yet over and above that, and the fact that he was the creator of many more goals, Orient fans remember him for his ability to bring a game to life. When the winger got on the ball the crowd would edge forward on their seats as one with a collective intake of breath. And if Orient ended up losing a game, which, let's face it, was more often than not, supporters could at least rest in the knowledge they had seen a pure footballer in action, a player who lit up the dark days of Division Four at Brisbane Road. Such is the esteem in which Alan is held that in a 1999 poll to discover Orient's greatest players of all time, he was second only to Tommy Johnston.

Alan's final game in an Orient shirt was the Play-off Final victory against Wrexham in 1989, and the day was a double celebration for him. Exiting the game on the final whistle he travelled from Brisbane Road to Newtownards in County Down, Northern Ireland, via helicopter, two planes and a speeding car to make it in time to be married to Jill. Two weeks later he signed for Second Division Middlesbrough but, tragically, after just 18 appearances for the club, suffered a career-ending knee injury. After joining the clergy in 1990, Alan is now vicar of St Mary's Church in Loughton and serves as Leyton Orient's club chaplain.

Quietly spoken, though never short of things to say, Alan does indeed sound like a vicar rather than a footballer. His accent hails from Hampshire, where he was born in Aldershot – better known for its enormous army base than the quality of its football team – on 8 December 1964. His father, George, was a printer, producing local newspapers; his mother, Shirley, stayed at home to bring up Alan and his three elder sisters, Debbie, Donna and Sharon. 'I was very quiet as a child,' says Alan. 'I was probably quite shy. My sisters always treated me like the baby of the family – they still do!'

Dad George played Saturday and Sunday football for local amateur sides, though the Comforts were by no means a die-hard footballing family. 'You can't really say I was born into football by nature,' laughs Alan. 'I think I'm a bit of a freak.' He certainly had a freakish talent, and by the age of just four Alan was playing in an under-7s team. 'As a kid, playing football came with ease,' he says. 'Off the pitch I was very quiet, but on it I came alive. I dominated that world I was in.' And while Alan says that his parents never pushed him into anything, all he wanted to do was play football and, like many kids, he dreamed of one day making it as a professional. On entering primary school Alan made the district and county teams two or three years above his own age. Playing centre-forward at that stage, he would regularly score four or five goals. 'I must have been awful to play with,' Alan admits. 'Generally I'd get the ball, run from one end to the other and score. I had a talent that was very noticeable.'

When Alan reached 13 years of age, Chelsea came calling. 'I remember the phone call,' he says. 'My dad was so excited. They asked if I wanted to go and train at their ground. It was an amazing feeling to know that a professional club wanted me. The first week I went there they had a practice match and I scored three goals in five minutes. As soon as the game ended they were trying to get me to sign forms.'

They were not alone, and Alan also received offers from Manchester United, Fulham, Crystal Palace...in fact, as a 14-year-old he could have signed for pretty much anyone. In the end he chose Queen's Park Rangers. This is not as bonkers as it may sound, as at the time the west London club were doing well in English football's top division – they finished second in 1975–76. To shy, quiet Alan, anxious not to have to leave home, QPR seemed a perfect choice to him. 'I used to take a day off school a week and train with the first team, with the likes of Stan Bowles, and I was playing in the reserves at 15,' he says.

At this point, says Alan, things got harder. He could no longer run around everyone on the pitch and score at will. There were other good players around him. The issue of unfulfilled potential rears its head. It is something that Alan returns to again and again; the notion that, given his precocious talent as a youngster, he should have made even more of himself as a footballer and should have reached the very top. It is not something that Alan has easy answers for. QPR manager Tommy Docherty referred to him as 'the best 15-year-old I have ever seen in my life'. He was also regarded as a certainty to play for England Schoolboys and yet, at 15, did not make the final cut. 'It was a shock to everyone, myself included,' says Alan. 'The truth was that the pressures changed. You had to perform at the right time, and I guess at the moment that it mattered, I didn't pull it off.' He finds it hard to explain why. 'I don't think my career was fraught with a lack of confidence. But some players have a brilliant way of thinking where they should be – I should be in the first team, I should be playing for England – and I didn't have that.'

Two years later, when he was 17 and had left school with five O Levels to his name, Alan did finally get to wear the three lions on his shirt when selected for the England Youth Squad to play in an international tournament in the south of France and again for a tournament in Norway. At 18, QPR rewarded him with a three-year contract, yet he found breaking into the first team impossible. 'There were players like Mike Flanagan, Ian Stewart, Wayne Fereday and Steve Burke who all played on the left wing and were all ahead of me in the queue,' says Alan. 'I should have been thinking, I'm better than all of them. But it just wasn't in me. I'd just think, wow, they're all really great players.'

In September 1984, at the age of 19 and still without a first-team appearance for QPR, Alan went on loan to Third Division Cambridge United. He did well, and in October was offered a three-year contract by the club. He signed it, with Cambridge paying £15,000 to QPR. 'It was a foolish decision,' says Alan. 'There is no reason why I should have signed for them. It was absurd. I still had two years of my contract at QPR left and I should have fought for a place in the side. But Cambridge wanted me and offered me, a 19-year-old, the highest salary in the whole club. I revelled in being a top player and I signed.'

The decision was an absolute disaster – 'football suicide', Alan calls it. That season Cambridge won only four games and were relegated to Division Four. And yet Cambridge was the place where Alan's life was changed forever. The catalyst was Graham Daniels, a committed Christian and ironically the man Alan was bought to replace. It seemed Daniels, then just 24, was finished in football, and yet he insisted God would look after him. 'Seeing Daniels, I think I realised that there was something more important than even football,' says Alan. 'It was life – how you actually live your life.' The pair became friends (Daniels went on to be Alan's best man at his wedding) and, after attending his first ever prayer meeting at a church in Cambridge in December 1984, Alan's life came sharply into focus. 'The peace I had seen in Graham started to make sense. I found myself asking God to forgive me. Immediately I felt free, as if a huge burden had been lifted from my shoulders.'

There were huge changes going on in Alan's personal life. Around the same time Alan also split up with Sue, his fiancée he'd been with for five years. And he admits that towards the end of the 1984–85 season his football suffered – he was in and out of the team. Things picked up the next season under new manager Chris Turner (the ex-Peterborough player, rather than the identically named Orient manager), though when in January 1986 the boss decided he needed to trim the wage bill, Alan – as the club's highest earner – found himself in the firing line. Turner asked him to take a pay cut. Alan refused – 'No one else had to take a cut,' he explains – and Turner decided he wanted him out. He questioned Alan's commitment. The player had a day release written into his contract as he was studying business studies and then accountancy at college every Wednesday – something he continued during his time at Orient. Turner also accused him of not being available on Sundays because of his faith. But Alan maintains this wasn't true: he always played on Sundays and trained too, if asked. 'Eventually he said to me – and this is the bizarre bit – "Who's more important to you, God or me?" I replied "You've got no chance." He then told me to see the door and not to ever come back. He also said that he was going to ring every single other football manager and tell them that I was a Christian and that I was bad news, and that I was finished in football.'

For a while, Alan feared that Turner might be right. But he says 'I'd rather have been finished in football than have to give in to a man like that. It was all about control and his ego.' Thankfully for Alan – and for fans of Orient – Turner's influence did not reach as far as Brisbane Road, and four weeks later, in March 1986, Orient manager Frank Clark put in a bid of £10,000 for the player. Alan left Cambridge having made 61 full appearances and scored five goals. Frank Clark says 'I could see at Cambridge that he was a very skilful player. I thought there was something in him that we could adapt and use to improve our team.'

Alan was only too happy to come to Orient – and not simply because it was the only club that came in for him. 'Frank Clark is the gentleman of football,' he says. 'After my experience at Cambridge I needed a man like him. And as I walked out onto the pitch at Brisbane Road I thought, this is where I want to play my football. I felt like I was at home.' The 1985–86 season was Orient's first-ever in the Fourth Division of the Football League, having been relegated – along with Cambridge – the season before. But they were flying high, thanks to the likes of Ian Juryeff, John Cornwell and the three Kevins: Godfrey, Hales and Dickenson. 'I knew some of the lads because I'd played against them, but I was still nervous going into the dressing room that first day,' Alan recalls. 'I was wondering who I'd be sitting next to. As a number 11, I thought I might be next to Kevin Godfrey or Chris Jones maybe, but when I arrived I saw my shirt hanging up next to John Sitton. And he was just sitting there with that intensity he has. I thought I had to be the unluckiest guy.'

But Alan soon had call to thank his new teammate. 'During one game the full-back kept kicking me again and again,' he says. ' I never usually said a word; I'd just get up and carry on. But this time, in the end, I turned to him and said "I wouldn't do that if I were you." He asked me what I was going to do about it. He could see I wasn't a fighter. So I said "It's not me you need to be scared of, but see that guy there – he's going to kill you in a minute." And John was standing five yards away, growling, and he gave the full-back his look. And the life just fell out of this guy's face. John was quite frightening.'

Alan with Terry Howard in the 1986–87 season.

Alan hit form quickly, and in the remainder of the 1985–86 season scored five goals in his 15 appearances. 'I found myself playing as I did when I was a kid,' he says. 'It just all came together. One of my first games was away at Stockport – we won 3–2, and I scored the winner. The next day I got a 10 in *Match* magazine.' Alan says his performances owed a lot to Frank Clark. 'I needed a manager who believed in me and just let me go out and play. At Cambridge I had three managers who didn't have a clue. But Frank understood me. He never got down on me in any way, and he'd always play me.' He also found that his new-found faith was helping his football. 'I'd pray before games; during games sometimes,' he admits. 'We'd be 1–0 down with 10 minutes to go and I'd say "God, we need a bit of help here." I also found that I enjoyed playing more after I became a Christian. I stopped worrying as much about what the manager thought of me or my form, and just got out there and did what I loved.'

Unfortunately, Alan's performances were not enough to drag Orient into the Play-offs that season, and they finished fifth in Division Four. It was a pattern that continued during his next two seasons at the club. In 1986–87 Orient finished seventh, and in 1987–88 they were eighth, despite scoring 85 goals. 'We weren't the ideal team to get promotions,' admits Alan. 'In all those seasons we were the best footballing side in the division, but the sides that got promoted were often really strong teams that could grind out results. We often lost against the best teams.'

Alan himself improved with each season: in 1986–87 he scored 11 goals in 46 appearances and the following year 15 in 53, winning Player of the Year for doing so. And yet he admits that he may have been one of the players who did not raise their games at the right moments – to push the side towards promotion. 'When you look back on it, I was one of the players that could win the team games. So if we weren't doing it against the better teams then I would have to say I was one of the ones responsible. But it's also fair to say that against the better teams I'd have two or three people marking me and I couldn't get the ball. We had certain flair players – like Kevin Godfrey, Lee Harvey and myself – that could win games, but if they snuffed us out the team had a problem. We needed a different way of playing.'

Off the field, Alan was enjoying his time at Orient and attests to a great team spirit at the club. 'We had a variety of good characters. Shaun Brooks looked like he was going to commit suicide every day – but was funny with it. With Paul Shinners you never knew what he was going to do next. Terry Howard was very quick. It was such a good mix of humour and melancholy.' And Alan's role in the dressing room? Inevitably nicknamed 'The Rev', he became the butt of many a prank aimed at his Christianity. 'I'd be asleep on the team coach and when I woke up there'd be a pornographic magazine on my face,' he laughs. 'Or they would put on a pornographic film and they'd pin me down and try to force my eyes open so I'd watch it.'

One imagines that it must have been pretty tough for a committed Christian in the harsh world of 1980s lower division football, where most players' idea of faith was to religiously attend the local greyhound racing track. But you get the impression that Alan – who is pretty sharp-witted – could stand up for himself. 'I would just laugh,' he says. 'I could have got offended, but I just found it funny. They'd wind me up, but I'd wind them up back. There was always something I'd say that would make them laugh. And I was always willing to laugh at myself. To be honest, they were always very respectful to me.'

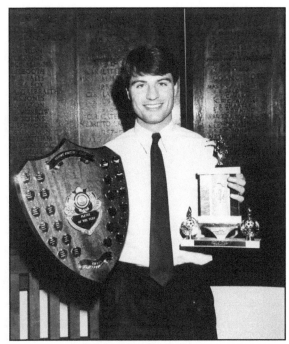

Alan with his Player of the Year award for the 1987–88 season, in which he scored 15 goals from midfield.

Far from sloping off to Bible class after matches, Alan would be out with his teammates at bars and clubs until the bitter end. Well, almost. 'I was proud of being a Christian, so I didn't need to say I don't go there, or I don't do that,' he says. 'That would have made it seem as if I was frightened to go to bars or clubs because I couldn't control myself. And besides, my teammates were my friends. I enjoyed going to bars with them and having a couple of drinks. But I never got drunk. And there was always a point towards the end of the night when I knew that it didn't matter whether I was there or not, when we were in the nightclubs and the boys started to do what boys do. And then I'd get a taxi home. By that time I don't think anyone even knew I'd gone.'

At the beginning of 1988 Alan met Jill, a social worker who would become his wife. They were introduced by a mutual friend at a church service in Guildford, Surrey. 'She was singing and she had a beautiful voice,' says Alan. 'When I talked to her she was so bubbly and enthusiastic, one of those people that makes everything brilliant. And obviously I quite fancied her.' After a whirlwind romance, the couple got engaged in the summer of 1988 and set their wedding for 3 June 1989. 'Obviously as a footballer I needed to get married in June to fit in a honeymoon before pre-season training starts,' says Alan. 'I phoned the Football League and asked what the first free date would be after the Play-off Final. They told me 3 June would definitely be OK – the Play-offs had never gone into June.'

Alan with Kevin Nugent (left) and Lee Harvey (right) in the 1987–88 season. He attests to a great team spirit at the club.

Alan in action against Crewe on 27 August 1988.

That year, however, the Hillsborough tragedy led to the football season being extended, and the Play-off Final was rescheduled for the very Saturday of Alan's wedding. It meant that should Orient reach the Final, Alan was going to have the mother of all double bookings. Not that there seemed any danger of that at the start of the season. Orient failed to win until their sixth game, were dumped out of the FA Cup by non-League Enfield and, despite thumping Colchester 8–0 in October, were nearer the bottom of the table than the top by Christmas. 'It was the same old problem,' says Alan. 'We were relying on certain players to make things happen and they weren't – myself included.'

Manager Frank Clark's position looked under threat, though he can be credited with the signing of two players who helped turn things around in the New Year: Kevin Campbell on loan from Arsenal and Mark Cooper, signed from Gillingham. 'They made the team work better,' says Alan. 'But at the same time we had some young boys that emerged as real players – Steve Castle, Terry Howard, Lee Harvey – and the experience of people like Steve Baker. We had a great side.' Alan himself began to play perhaps the best football of his life and was scoring regularly. 'They were always typical goals,' he laughs. 'The ball would come over to the far post and I'd drill it across the goal into the net. In training I'd do that every time. I could do it without thinking about it.'

Frank Clark had also changed the formation, giving his winger a role with more freedom. Alan explains 'He said to me "Just go and find the ball and play. Go anywhere to get it." It meant I couldn't be marked out of the game.' Clark himself says 'We ended up setting the team up to give Alan the best possible chance to do what he could do. We played a kind of 4-4-2 with him on the left, but we didn't want to tie him down to being out wide because he was a good finisher. So we encouraged him to come inside at the right time and move into positions where he saw opportunity. Fortunately, the other midfield players would adapt as Alan moved around to keep the balance. And it worked quite well. When Alan was on form he was unstoppable.'

Orient began to climb the table – and Jill began to worry. 'When they changed the Play-off date Jill asked me if she needed to be concerned,' says Alan. 'At that point we were near the bottom of the table so I said she had nothing to worry about. Then we started winning again and again. I'd reassure her by saying "It's OK, we always blow it at the end." But then I'd keep coming home on a Saturday night and saying "I'm so sorry. I scored and we won."'

The team lost just twice in their last 17 matches and secured a place in the Play-offs. Alan felt confident that Orient could win them. 'We had momentum,' he says. 'We were playing so well by then – we'd beaten Scunthorpe 4–1 to deny them automatic promotion in the last game of the season. We'd hit form at the right time.'

The semi-final was against Scarborough – Alan's bogey team. 'Neil Warnock was the manager at the time,' he recalls. 'He was an absolute nightmare. He'd stand on the touchline and talk to me the whole time. He hated me! He'd say to the right-back "Break his legs. Snap his legs." And the right-back would come flying in from everywhere.' Thankfully, Alan survived, as did Orient, qualifying for the Final courtesy of a 2–0 victory at Brisbane Road followed by a 1–0 loss in Yorkshire. The first leg of the Final saw them draw 0–0 with Wrexham at the Racecourse Ground. The return leg was set for 3 June, leaving Alan with the slight problem of a wedding to consider.

The ceremony was set for 3pm in Bangor in County Down, where Jill's family hail from. Invitations had been sent, guests had booked flights and hotels – there was no way the couple could cancel. But where there is a will there is a way, and just as he used to begin a mazy run towards goal from midfield, Alan embarked on a plan to get himself from Brisbane Road to Northern Ireland. With the help of his brother-in-law, a newspaper editor, Alan got the *Sunday Express* to agree to print the story and make their helicopter available on the day. They would fly Alan from Leyton to Heathrow Airport, where a plane would take him to Belfast to connect with another flight to Newtownards, near Bangor. Everything was planned with military precision, and the wedding was moved to 5.30pm. But that still did not leave time for Alan to play in the game, which was due to kick-off at 3pm. Which is where Frank Clark came in. 'I did ask Alan to move his wedding, but being the sort of lad that he was there was no way he was going to do it,' says the former Orient manager. 'So we had to figure out a way around it. I managed to persuade everyone that the game should be a lunchtime kick off. The police were keen on that idea too as they thought it would be easier to control things, so obviously we

Alan leaves Brisbane Road for his wedding after the Play-off Final victory over Wrexham on 3 June 1989.

supported them 100 per cent in that. I wanted to put out the best team I could and Alan was a part of that.'

On the day itself, the game actually kicked off 20 minutes late due to the number of fans still trying to get into the ground. Once on the field, however, Alan was focussed fully on the football. 'It was so important I never thought about getting married,' he says. The game was tense, but some good play from Alan released Lee Harvey, who put Orient 1–0 up in the first half with a great strike from 20 yards. Wrexham equalised early in the second half with a header, and the game tightened up. 'I think we were the better team,' says Alan. 'I always thought we were going to score. But as the half went on we were creating fewer and fewer chances, so I didn't know where it was going to come from.'

After 80 minutes the game remained locked at 1–1 and heading for extra-time. The *Sunday Express* helicopter was circling above the ground. 'At this point I knew I was in trouble,' says Alan. 'I had a horrible feeling I wasn't going to make it for my own wedding. I thought, I just can't do extra-time. Of course I would have played, but I was thinking, we need a goal from somewhere.' Alan, along with every Orient fan present on the day, remains eternally indebted to Mark Cooper who, with eight minutes to go, scored the goal that won the game. 'I was standing behind him when he volleyed it,' says Alan. 'He struck it so sweetly. It was a goal that was worthy of winning the game.'

As the seconds ticked down to the final whistle, Alan began to hug the touchline by the players' tunnel, and as the game ended made a break for it, unable to spare the time to join the celebrations. 'I ran into the dressing room, had a quick shower and put some clothes on,' he recalls. 'The helicopter couldn't land on the pitch because of all the fans, so I had to jump in a car to Hackney Marshes. I had a bottle of champagne in one hand and my wedding suit in the other. As we landed at Heathrow Airport I tried to help shut the door of the helicopter and it took off a chunk of my thumb, so I was pouring with blood too.'

Alan made his connection to his next flight, and was greeted by a police escort as he landed in Newtownards. 'By now the *Sunday Express* reporter was so drunk that when the police asked if he was with me, I said no,' he laughs. 'So we left him behind.' The groom had time for a quick bath in a house next to the church in Bangor, yet encountered another problem. 'The cold water had broken down,' he explains. 'I had to have a scalding hot bath, and when I got out I was bright red and pouring with sweat. During the service the minister had to keep dabbing my forehead. I was also dripping blood everywhere from my thumb.' Thankfully, the ceremony went off without any further hitches, capping what for Alan was a monumental day. 'It brought a whole lot of things together,' he says. 'Although I was exhausted, I could sit back and see that, for me, it was a point where everything I could ever want – and more – I'd got.' His one regret is that he didn't get to celebrate Orient's win with his teammates and the fans. 'I missed the moment,' he says. 'In football you don't succeed that often, so when you do you have to enjoy it. When I saw the pictures of the players celebrating I was sad that I never got to do that. But I still had the experience of getting there and playing the game, and I enjoyed that. The club deserved to get promoted, the fans deserved it, and the team was full of so many good players that they deserved to succeed. It was the moment they rose up to be as good as they could be.'

It turned out to be Alan's last game for the club. The winger was in the last year of his three-year contract during the 1988–89 season, and he says that the club never really tried to keep him. 'Towards the end they offered me a new contract, but only for £25 a week more,' he explains. 'And I'd scored 19 goals that season. I couldn't work it out.' That season Frank Clark had brought in Brian Eastick as his assistant manager, and Alan says that the new man didn't rate him as a player. 'He absolutely hated me. He used to have a chart on his wall with all the players' names and coloured dots indicating their performances in each game. Red was brilliant, blue was average and yellow was poor. All I had was yellow dots. I'd score two goals in a game and we'd win 2–0 and I'd still get a yellow dot! He said to me "If I picked the team you wouldn't play." I just replied "Well isn't it good that you're never going to get to pick a team".'

Alan does not believe that Frank Clark no longer rated him as a player, but that the club had decided it was time for him to go. He was certainly at his most saleable after scoring 19 goals in the season. On the one hand Alan says he would not have been averse to remaining at the place where his career had blossomed, yet he also craved football at a higher level. 'From a footballing point of view it was right for me to move on,' he says. 'I always knew that I could play at a higher level, I was just waiting for someone to give me a go. But if Orient had offered me something, I would have stayed.'

Frank Clark says that the club couldn't ignore the interest from bigger clubs. 'We didn't want to sell him but a club like Orient couldn't turn down that sort of money and we couldn't deny the

Alan after signing for Middlesbrough in the summer of 1989.

boy the opportunity.' Clark also disputes the notion that his coach Brian Eastick didn't rate the tricky winger. 'Brian was a bit of a perfectionist and was more intolerant of the players than I was. But it worked very well between us. Alan might think that Brian didn't rate him, but he had probably the best season of his career playing under him so he'd have to accept that Brian was good for him. Brian was demanding, but he was just trying to make Alan a better player.'

There was talk of many clubs being interested in Alan, but ultimately the player received three firm offers, from Bournemouth, Bradford City and Middlesbrough. All three were in Division Two. The idea of playing for Middlesbrough was one that seemed most attractive to Alan – although not, initially, to his new wife. 'When we drove into Middlesbrough Jill cried her eyes out,' he recalls. 'She said "This is the worst place I've ever been in my life." But when I sat in the stands at Ayresome Park and knew there would be 25,000 people there on a Saturday I thought, this is what I'm made for. This is my chance.'

Alan's transfer fee was set at £175,000 by tribunal, and he made his Middlesbrough debut in a 4–2 win against Wolves on 19 August 1989. He was playing under manager Bruce Rioch and alongside the likes of Bernie Slaven, Stuart Ripley and, until his transfer to Manchester United, Gary Pallister. For the first few months Alan excelled, scoring twice and winning over fans with his exciting wing play. But his 18th appearance for the club – a derby against Newcastle United at St James' Park – proved to be his last ever as a footballer. 'We were winning 2–1 in the second half and it was a hard, frantic game,' says Alan. 'I was chasing a ball that was running out of touch alongside one of their players. We leaned into each other – no more than that – and my studs must have got caught in the ground and as I fell I twisted my knee. Something snapped. It wasn't particularly painful, but I knew something terrible had happened. My leg just locked – I couldn't move it.'

Alan had damaged his cruciate ligament. It is a bad injury, but one from which footballers routinely recover. But Alan had complications – a rare disease behind the kneecap called traumatic chondromalacia patellae, which had been caused by the initial injury. The player saw a succession of doctors, surgeons and physiotherapists until, at a private clinic in Dublin in June 1990, he underwent an operation. When he came round the consultant surgeon asked his patient what he planned to do once he had finished playing football. 'I told him that I didn't know because I had another 10 years before I'd have to worry about that,' recalls Alan. 'But then he looked me straight in the eye and said "Start thinking about it now." It was such a shock.' Refusing to give up, Alan sought a second – and third – opinion from top surgeons. But they confirmed the diagnosis: his knee was ruined and his career was over at 25. 'I actually went through a process like losing somebody close to me,' says Alan. 'The shock of trying to cope. I had the gift to do something really special, but physically I was all washed up.'

On 21 October 1990 Jill gave birth to a daughter, Sarah, and Alan – though he received a one-off payment equivalent to a year's wages from Middlesbrough – was left facing the financial reality of having to provide for his family. He had another year of study to complete before qualifying as an accountant but says that at that point he realised it was not the career for him. 'It would have meant that, for me, my life would have been a disappointment compared to what it was,' he explains. Alan applied to do a law degree at Newcastle University. He secured a place, but found that his true vocation lay elsewhere. 'I felt like God was calling me to the Church,' he explains. 'It terrified me, the idea of becoming a vicar, because I wasn't a public speaker. I thought every day I was going to be doing things that I was terrified of. Yet it was something I really wanted to do.'

Alan was accepted to train for the Anglican ministry and in September 1991 began a three-year course in theology at a college in – ironically –

Alan becomes a vicar in July 1994. With Roger Sainsbury, the Bishop of Barking.

Cambridge. Yet, despite everything he had been told by the top surgeons, he still could not quite accept that he would never play football again, and a couple of months earlier had accepted an offer to play for Vauxhall Conference side Farnborough Town. He lasted until the second game before the ligaments in his knee went, and he spent the next six months in physiotherapy. A second comeback lasted seven minutes, and a third – for the final few games of the season – resulted in his knee ballooning up after every game. Alan knew it was over. 'I realised it was a waste of time. There were people I was playing against who I shouldn't have been on a pitch with, yet I was coming down to their level. I was destroying the reputation I'd built up.'

Alan focussed his attentions fully on his studies and completed his training in July 1994, just after the birth of his and Jill's second child, Henry, who was born on 25 February that year. He was invited to become curate at St Chad's Church in Chadwell Heath – conveniently near his old Brisbane Road stomping ground. Attending a game, Alan was invited up to the boardroom. He explains what happened next: 'Tony Wood, the chairman, said to me "You are going to come back aren't you?" I replied "OK, how about as chaplain?" And he agreed. It was that simple. They'd never had a chaplain before, they weren't looking for one, but I think they would have had me back doing anything.'

It is a role that he has held ever since, and one he combines with being vicar at St Mary's Church in Loughton, where he lives with Jill, Sarah, Henry and Ollie, who was born in April 2001. As club chaplain Alan works with players who might have problems at home, been bereaved or even suffered a loss of confidence on the football pitch. He will also conduct funerals and spread ashes on the Brisbane Road turf at the request of Orient fans. Then there are the weddings, and fans will remember that in 1995 new chairman Barry Hearn came up with the ludicrous innovation of half-time nuptials – with Alan as vicar. 'I didn't like that particularly,' Alan laughs. 'It made a bit of a mockery of marriage. The first one I did properly, but the second one I thought I'd get the bride to score a goal. I thought they'd never ask me to do it again if I did that, and thankfully they didn't.'

Alan also joins in with training – his knee can manage that, at least – every Monday. 'I try to nutmeg everyone,' he smiles. 'And I make the most of it if I do.' The skills that used to light up Brisbane Road have not totally deserted him. Occasionally – though he tries not to – Alan wonders what might have become of him were his career not cut short at 25. 'I think that I was maturing and that the older I got, the more likely I would have been to deliver,' he says. 'I think I would have shone at a higher level. At Orient I used to get clumped all over the place by maniacs. I think I could have been a star at Middlesbrough and then, after that, who knows?'

Talking about it does sadden him. 'It was an unfulfilled career,' he admits. 'When I think back to how I was as a 15-year-old, I was unbelievable. And I only ever showed glimpses of that as an adult. It was a waste of talent. I do feel that. It could have been so much more. When I went on a football pitch I had the ability to make people stop. And it was a rare gift. And I miss it, because there's nothing else in life I can do as well.'

Once again, Alan finds it difficult to explain exactly why he did not progress further; why he was not playing in the top flight, or for his country. 'There were two or three times when I knew scouts were watching me, and I didn't deliver,' he says. 'I wanted it so much I was frightened of messing it up. Some people grab their moments, but when I needed to impose myself, I didn't do it. At those crucial moments I didn't have the character. I think that I do now, but at the time I didn't. I believed that I could be the very best, but I also believed I could be the very worst. Maybe that's why I ended up playing for Orient!'

And that is something about which Alan has no regrets. 'To be one of Orient's top players in their history, well, I wouldn't swap that for anything. In a footballing sense I can look back and say that, yes, my career ended early, but how many players have the experience I did? I went to a club, I felt like I fitted in perfectly, I did well on the pitch and people remember me.'

# Chapter 6
# BLACK MAGIC
## Laurie Cunningham 1974–77

Laurie at Orient in December 1976.

Luck is not something normally found in abundance at Brisbane Road – apparently it cannot get through the turnstiles. But anyone who frequented the ground between 1974 and 1977 was blessed with the most incredible good fortune, as they got to witness a young man by the name of Laurence Paul Cunningham at work. A winger of spine-tingling speed, skill and balletic grace, Laurie sprinkled magic on that muddy field in Leyton, and the anticipation in the stadium was palpable every time he got on the ball. That he is an Orient great is unquestionable, but he is also a football great, a legend whose life was tragically cut short when he died in a car crash at the age of 33.

By then Laurie had already blazed a trail for black players in the game, becoming the first to represent England at Under-21 level and enduring unimaginable abuse and hostility to propel West Bromwich Albion to the upper reaches of Division One. With Real Madrid – who paid £995,000 to make him their first-ever British player – he once tore apart Barcelona at the Nou Camp and was given an ovation by the opposition supporters. But it is at Orient where Laurie is most fondly remembered. 'He was like no player we've ever had,' says fan Mickey Kasler. 'He was world-class. He wouldn't have been amiss in the Brazilian side.' Supporter Laurie Woolcott agrees. 'Laurie was a special player – he always shone out,' he says. 'It was his grace on the ball and his speed. He was greased lightning.' Mark Waters also had the pleasure of watching Laurie. 'When he got the ball you thought he could do something special,' he says. 'It made it worth going to see the team. He had terrific skill, a fair bit of pace, and a lot of class. He was a cut above. He could take people on, beat them and leave them for dead.' George Petchey, Laurie's manager at Orient, was no less of a fan and once said 'He has enough skill and ability to take on the top teams at their own game, and he'll come through as the most outstanding player in the world. I can't see him being anything other than a great player.'

Laurie was also an enigma. A lover of fashion, music, dancing, modelling, architecture and wine bars, he was no typical footballer. Legendary choreographer Arthur Mitchell, the director of New York's Dance Theatre of Harlem, wrote to Orient to say Laurie had a future in dance should he fail at football. 'Suppleness?' Laurie once said in response to a reporter marvelling at his dexterity. 'That comes with dancing. I love soul music.' But his off-field interests got him into trouble at Real Madrid when he was caught in a discotheque the night after having an operation on his toe, and his career began to drift. He had spells at Manchester United, Leicester, Wimbledon and clubs in France, Belgium and Spain, but he never again produced the magic of his early career under the Orient management team of George Petchey and Peter Angell. Indeed, it is perhaps Orient fans who got to see Laurie's talent at its very purest. It is something with which Laurie, towards the end of his life, concurred. 'I don't think I have ever fulfilled my true potential,' he said. 'All the coaches I've had, with the exception of Petchey and Angell at Orient, have never appreciated what I can do.'

Laurie was born in Archway, London, on 8 March 1956, the son of a Jamaican racehorse jockey. He believed the incredible ball control he had in his later life was bred in his childhood. 'I was always around black guys,' he explained. 'We knocked the ball around in streets. English kids seemed to rush around a shade too fast.' He played for the Haringey and South-East Counties schools football teams and was signed on schoolboy terms by Arsenal, alongside another Orient player-to-be, Glenn Roeder. But the north London club were not convinced by Laurie – George Petchey later claimed that it was his lack of punctuality, rather than his lack of skill that did for him – and he was released at 15 years of age.

Still, Arsenal's loss was Orient's gain, and scout Len Cheesewright invited Laurie to Brisbane Road. Orient full-back Bobby Fisher, who played in the same youth team as Laurie, recalls the winger's first day at the club, when he turned up for a trial match. 'Everyone else was waiting – the first-team players, manager, reserves – and suddenly Laurie just strolled over. The rest of the guys said he must be either very stupid or he must be one hell of a player. It turned out to be the latter.'

Laurie was signed as an apprentice in August 1972 and played in a youth team that also featured Tony Grealish, Glenn Roeder and Nigel Gray. On the pitch, Laurie impressed immediately and in his first season in the youth team was voted Player of the Tournament in an international competition held in Holland. In the second year of his apprenticeship he helped the team finish runners-up in the South-East Counties League and win the London Youth Cup. Off the pitch, things were a little more complicated. Laurie was unconventional, and his dislike of authority was matched only by his contempt for punctuality. 'We had one or two problems with him in the early days,' admitted Petchey. 'There was a time when Peter Angell and I wondered if we could win Laurie over. He had to struggle in life and was the sort of youngster who was used to living on his wits. He was suspicious of people outside his own circle. He took a long time to trust other people. He often turned up late for training, the eyes flashed when we fined him, but for all that I loved the spark that made him tick.'

Looking back later in his life, Laurie recognised that he was a problematic youngster. 'At first I must admit I was not the sweetest person to be with,' he said. 'Nothing stirred me, I was just a dreamer.' Yet he also revealed that it was his coaches at Orient who helped him to focus, saying 'It was George Petchey and Peter Angell who showed me that the only person who could make my dreams come true was, in fact, myself.' As such, he began to practise religiously. 'He was fanatical about kicking balls with his left foot against the wall underneath the stand,' recalls fellow youth teamer Tony Grealish. 'Every time we had a 15-minute break the rest of us would sit down, and he'd be out the back.' And George Petchey said at the time 'If I don't call him in he'll keep it up all afternoon.'

By the beginning of the 1974–75 season, Petchey was ready to give 18-year-old Laurie his first-team debut. It came in the Texaco Cup – the short-lived tournament involving teams from the UK and Republic of Ireland – in a game against West Ham at Upton Park on 3 August 1974. Though Orient lost the game 1–0, Laurie impressed manager George Petchey, who said after the game 'It took him a little time to get adjusted to the pace of the game, but I was delighted by the way he played from then on. He has a natural talent. He has the speed and agility to take on men. He never gives up. There's a big future ahead for him.'

Laurie made his League debut two months later in a 3–1 victory against Oldham, and once again caused havoc with his pace and skill. He was joining an Orient team that were struggling. The previous season they had suffered the heartbreak of missing out on promotion to Division One by a single point and the subsequent hangover was a long and nagging one. The biggest problem was goals – or the fact that Orient's strike force of Mickey Bullock and Gerry Queen were not actually scoring any.

Laurie was selected to play against Millwall at the Den on 7 December, a game that introduced him, in the harshest way possible, to the plight of a black footballer in the mid-1970s. It was a time of simmering racial tensions, with widespread opposition to immigration policies and the far-right group the National Front claiming over 20,000 members, and you were about as likely to find a black player in a professional football team as you were a blade of grass on Orient's mudbath of a pitch. In fielding Laurie alongside Bobby Fisher and Bombay-born Ricky Heppolette, Orient were ahead of their time. It meant that the game against Millwall – smack in the heartland of the far right – was always going to be one with the potential for trouble. When the team arrived at the Den they were met by National Front activists distributing racist propaganda. Inside the ground the players emerged into a cauldron of hatred, with the opposition fans spitting a torrent of abuse at Laurie and Bobby Fisher. Objects – including bananas and a six-inch carving knife – were thrown onto the pitch. 'Me and Laurie did the black power salute a couple of times,' Bobby Fisher recalls. 'To be honest, we didn't properly understand the significance. All we knew was that some black American athletes had done it at the Olympics, and that was good enough for us.'

The game was drawn 1–1 but was significant in that it gave Laurie a bitter taste of the racial prejudice he would face for much of his career. And while he was not particularly politically motivated, he did recognise that he was potentially paving the way for more black footballers to come into the game. 'I can't let it get to me,' he said of the abuse at the time. 'If I can get through this, maybe it will lead to others getting a fair chance.' And he intimated that it was less the hostility from the crowds that bothered him than the abuse he experienced from those within the game – he'd routinely hear managers instructing his players to clobber the 'black coward'. 'First and foremost I'm looking for respect from professional players,' he said.

Looking back a few years later, Laurie reflected on his feelings about race during his spell at Orient. 'There have been times when I've been mixed up about the race thing. A couple of years ago I thought that to be black in England was to be a loser. You know, back of the queue for decent jobs, suspicion on you before anyone knew what you were about. I did have a feeling for "black power". It seemed to meet the mood of frustration. It could give you some pride. Then I changed. It sort of struck me that the great majority of people, black and white, are in the same boat, fighting for a decent living. It also struck me that down at Orient I was getting a very good break. I got on well with George Petchey. It didn't matter to him whether I was black, white or Chinese just as long as I could play.'

After the Millwall game Laurie had another short spell out of the team, though he did appear as a substitute for two games in January. Fan Alan Harvey remembers bumping into Laurie's mother Mavis on one occasion that her son was named on the bench. He says 'I was standing outside the entrance to the Double Os club and there was a dear little black lady waiting outside. She asked me "I am allowed to go in here?" I said "Yes, of course you can." She told me that her son was Laurie Cunningham, and I told her she'd be very welcome. So we took her into the bar. But this little black woman must have been very, very nervous coming into the culture of football.'

By March, Petchey was ready to give Laurie an extended run in the team at the expense of the fading Barrie Fairbrother. In his second game back, against Sheffield Wednesday at Hillsborough, Laurie set up the goal for Gerry Queen that gave Orient a 1–0 victory. 'Laurie Cunningham's eye-catching skills must have been the envy of many rival managers,' said teammate Peter Allen at the time. Following this, Laurie started each of the remaining nine games of the season and continued to sparkle. But there was one thing still missing – goals. Before the final game of the campaign, a home match against Southampton, Laurie turned up late at the stadium. No surprise there, but an irked George Petchey told him that if he did not score he would be heavily fined and suspended.

Laurie duly obliged. 'Cunningham picked up Bullock's headed pass on the halfway line, out-paced three defenders and then nonchalantly eased the ball past the advancing keeper from just inside the penalty area,' wrote the *Walthamstow Guardian*. 'Arguably Orient's outstanding goal of 74–75.'

It was Orient's 28th and last League goal of the season, the lowest haul in their history, and it left them in 12th position in the table with a sleep-inducing 12 goalless draws to their name. Apparently seeking to address this, they began the next season with a novel approach – letting the opposition score for them – and the first game of the season produced a 1–1 draw against Blackburn in which Rovers defender John Waddington netted Orient's only goal. It did not last, and the next eight games yielded only four goals. Strikers Mickey Bullock and Gerry Queen looked past their best, begging the question of what the club could have achieved had a Johnston, a Kitchen – hell, even a Gary Alexander – been on the receiving end of some of Laurie's dazzling approach play.

In October the *Walthamstow Guardian* reported that Laurie had England legend Bobby Moore 'in all sorts of trouble' when Orient played Fulham at Craven Cottage, and the winger was rewarded with a 24th-minute goal. A few weeks later Laurie was kicked all over the park by Southampton defender Jim Steele in a 2–1 victory over the south coast side. Indeed, he was regularly clobbered whenever he played. 'He used to run down the wing, and he'd get kicked over the touchline three times out of four by the big lumbering full-backs that used to populate the Second Division in those days,' recalls fan Mark Waters.

In January Laurie's goal gave Orient a 1–0 victory over Hull City and the *Walthamstow Guardian* reported 'Laurie Cunningham's excellence lifted him above the other players and left Hull City gasping. He scored a marvellous goal and conjured up several more chances. The home side were anxiously searching for a breakthrough when Cunningham pulled out one of his many tricks in the 34th minute. He took the ball from Bill Roffey, controlled it on the edge of the box, looked up and chipped it precisely into the far corner over keeper Jeff Wealands' head. It was a goal that would have graced any ground in the country.' George Petchey added 'If that goal had been scored at Liverpool or Leeds it would have brought the house down.'

All this was getting Laurie noticed outside of east London, and Petchey found himself constantly having to deny that he would have to sell him. The trouble was, Orient were in pretty dire financial straits at the time and owed the bank around £90,000. Everyone knew that at some point the club would be forced to take a big fat cheque for their talented winger. Even Laurie himself realised this and said in February 'If the day comes when I have to go, it will be with regret. I'd always be coming back to see George and the lads.'

Back on the pitch, Laurie scored in a 2–0 win over Fulham in February. But it was his goal in a 2–0 victory over Chelsea at Stamford Bridge on Easter Monday that will live longest in fans' memories of that season. He had missed the two preceding games after knocking himself unconscious on a train door – this sort of thing tended to happen to Laurie – but it was the Chelsea defence who were left feeling woozy when he returned. Fan Mickey Kasler recalls it well: 'The Chelsea fans were giving him some real treatment that day – racial abuse. In the second half he picked up the ball on the halfway line and dribbled at pace, side-stepping and swerving. Then he smashed it into the top corner from about 25 yards. It didn't half shut the Chelsea fans up.'

Laurie actually finished that season as Orient's top scorer with eight goals, which perhaps says more about the club's strikers than it does about Laurie. The team finished in an uninspiring 13th position in Division Two. In September of the next season, Laurie scored two goals in a 3–0 thrashing of Cardiff City,

Laurie takes a corner in Orient's match against Bristol City on 14 February 1976.

after which Petchey drooled 'I've never seen anyone like him. No young winger in the country, and I include Steve Coppell and Peter Barnes, has his flair and electrifying pace.' Soon after, reports in the national press claimed that Leicester and Ipswich were interested in the player and that both West Ham and Norwich had put in bids. Petchey denied it, saying 'Clubs may be sending their scouts to look at Laurie, but no one has asked me about his availability.'

In December Laurie was widely expected to be named in Don Revie's England Under-21 squad. He was not, which left George Petchey aghast. 'I am disappointed for the boy rather than for myself or the club,' he said. 'Without disrespect to the lads in the squad, it is obvious that Laurie is better than many and certainly he has more experience. Perhaps the England manager hasn't watched Cunningham this season.'

Early in March 1977 West Bromwich Albion – at the time making a good account of themselves in Division One under manager Johnny Giles – bid £75,000 plus two players for Laurie. Orient turned them down, with Petchey saying 'Laurie has made it quite clear that he wants to stay with the club and help fight relegation.' But even Petchey must have realised that by then he was fighting a losing battle to keep hold of the player he'd brought to the club as a 15-year-old. Attendances at

Brisbane Road were at an all-time low, the pitch was a quagmire and the club needed money. First Division clubs waving cheques were hard to turn away. Figuring the game was up, Petchey tried to persuade the managers of four London clubs to take Laurie, though, surprisingly, none were willing to take the plunge. 'It's their loss,' said Petchey petulantly. 'I guarantee he'll play for England.'

SV Hamburg, St Etienne and Anderlecht were reportedly interested, but eventually it was West Bromwich Albion, with an improved bid of £110,000 plus Joe Mayo and Allan Glover, who secured the signature of Laurie on 6 March 1977. 'I did not want to sell him, but we were over our limit at the bank, and West Brom were ready with a cheque,' said Petchey at the time. 'Obviously I'm very disappointed at losing a player who I have seen progress from the age of 15, and I think he was as reluctant to leave as we were to see him go. But it was an offer of First Division football which he could not refuse.'

Laurie was perhaps not quite as reluctant as Petchey thought, and he said later 'I jumped at the chance of moving into the First Division with West Brom. It was progress as far as I was concerned, and I was impressed with Johnny Giles's approach to the game.' He was joining a team sitting in 10th position in Division One after clinching promotion the season before. To many they were over-achieving, but with players such as Bryan Robson and Scotland international Willie Johnston, the club was embarking on what would turn out to be one of its most successful eras. Laurie made his debut in a 2–0 win over Tottenham at White Hart Lane on 12 March and appeared at the Hawthorns four days later in a 4–0 win over high-flying Ipswich. He bagged one of the goals himself and became an instant hero, nicknamed 'the black flash' by the local press. 'The First Division suits me fine,' he said. 'I was surprised how easy things were. The pace wasn't as quick as I imagined, and there were few tackles. I expected it to be a lot more physical, but it wasn't. I believe I can play for England now. I know I have to work hard, but if I do nothing can stop me.'

Laurie was West Bromwich Albion's first-ever black player, and the most high-profile playing in Division One. It turned up the heat on the hostility he had received from opposition fans, no more so than when the Baggies played Manchester United at Old Trafford on 23 March. Laurie was subjected to intense abuse from home fans – tens of thousands of people in racist unison – whenever he went near the ball. And yet, by all accounts, he played a blinder. 'Have you seen a player, tightly marked, perform an exuberant aerial split three feet off the ground and, disturbing neither rhythm nor balance, flick the ball on behind him with the outside of his boot into a measured and enticing pass for his winger?' wrote the *Sunday Times* the next day.

After the game, Laurie was measured in his response to the treatment he had received from the fans. 'The Manchester jeering wasn't as bad as I expected,' he said. 'I'm the natural target, but I don't let it get to me. I'd be doing what they want. There's no way I'd ever be ashamed of being black, but it's more important that other professionals seem to have stopped calling me things.' Laurie went on to score six goals in his 13 appearances for West Bromwich Albion that season, helping them to a highly impressive seventh in the table. Johnny Giles was proving to be a big influence on the young winger. 'He talks about Pelé,' said Laurie at the time. 'Johnny says Pelé is the perfect pro; he does the simple things to the ultimate and saves the sensational stuff for the goalscoring. I'm learning from that. I know I have a special gift. But I've got to prove it, and go on proving it.'

But some of Laurie's problems persisted, not least his inability to actually get anywhere on time. Two months into his stint at West Brom he was dropped and fined for failing to turn up to training. 'I saw him later, and he said he had one or two things to do,' said Giles, presumably flummoxed by this typically Laurie response. Laurie at least seemed to recognise that his lackadaisical approach to punctuality probably was not the best way to ingratiate himself with his new manager and said at the time 'I would be mad not to admit that I have things to learn. I've made mistakes which I won't ever make again. When you are 21 and in your first year of First Division football you have a lot of things to sort out. I'm sorting them out now. Don't worry, I'll make it.'

That season, just a month after leaving Orient, Laurie was finally selected for the England Under–21 squad. It was presumably no coincidence that it took a move to a Division One club for him to be deemed worthy of a place. On 27 April 1977 Laurie became the first black player to represent England at any level, and scored with a downward header in a 1–0 win over Scotland at Bramall Lane. He joined the Under–21 squad for a trip to Finland and Norway that summer, though courted controversy when he behaved disrespectfully during the Finnish national anthem before a game. The spectre of racism also reared its head again, and reports in the press suggested that he had been refused entry to restaurants and bars because he was black.

Laurie also spoke of some of his frustrations of playing for the national team, where he was asked to play as an out-and-out winger rather than cutting inside, as he'd done at Orient and West Brom. 'I attempted to adapt to tactics in a relatively strange position,' he said. 'The restrictions imposed while I was playing for England really upset my game.' That summer, before departing West Brom, Johnny Giles bought a young black electrician-cum-part-time footballer by the name of Cyrille Regis to the club from non-League Hayes. Born in French Guyana and raised in London from the age of five, Cyrille was to play a significant part in Laurie's life – and in the fortunes of West Brom. He recalls first meeting the teammate who would soon become his partner in crime, on and off the pitch. 'My first impressions of Laurie were that he was a very nice guy,' says Cyrille. 'From a personality point of view he was misunderstood. He was fairly shy, but people used to see an arrogance about him. Sometimes if you're quiet and shy people mistake that for being aloof and distant. But we just hit it off. We were two Londoners, two black guys in West Brom, where there were no black guys at all. We became friends quite quickly. '

Laurie with best friend Cyrille Regis in the 1978–79 season.

Football affords its players plenty of spare time, and Laurie and Cyrille spent much of it together. 'We'd walk the streets, buy clothes, have a beer, chat,' says Cyrille. 'We used to go to wine bars – a bit more sophisticated than going and swilling 10 pints in a pub. Laurie wasn't your typical footballer. He was very creative in his thinking, was very much into his clothes and loved going out. He was a fabulous dancer and he loved his music. I think the fact that we got on so well together socially was a key element as to why we got on so well on the pitch.' Cyrille made an instant impact, but puts much of his success down to the efforts of his new teammate and friend. 'It was kind of embarrassing, to be honest, because all my goals came from Laurie running down the wing, beating two or three players and putting the ball in,' he says. 'He had pace, grace and style. He was the most watchable player ever.'

In December 1977 Ron Atkinson was made manager of West Bromwich Albion. The former Cambridge Town boss brought Grenada-born defender Brendan Batson with him, and West Brom became the first top-flight club to simultaneously field three black players. Atkinson, never one to shy away from publicity, dubbed them 'The Three Degrees' after the Philadelphia soul trio touring England at the time. He arranged a photo shoot with the black American singers in which they wore West Brom shirts and his three players wore fur coats. Laurie, one would imagine, must have loved this collision of a number of his passions: football, music and clothes.

But while West Brom were enjoying the spotlight of media attention, the fact there were now three black players turning out for the club meant that the racial taunting intensified. 'They were hostile environments,' says Cyrille. 'At some grounds you'd get 10,000 people shouting racist abuse at you – singing monkey chants, throwing bananas on the pitch. There'd be people handing out National Front leaflets in the crowd. We'd get letters through the post, death threats. But Laurie handled it like we all did. He internalised the hatred and aggression and turned it into performance. Of course, sometimes he'd get angry and react to the crowd, but in the main he'd take the negative reaction and try to turn it into something positive.'

Laurie (left) with Cyrille Regis (centre) and Brendon Batson (right) – West Bromwich Albion's legendary 'Three Degrees' – in the 1978–79 season.

Back in 1977, Laurie said much the same thing. 'I haven't got a fiery temper and maybe that helps because I'm able to walk away from explosive situations. It takes a lot to get me to lose my rag, and so far I've been more interested in getting on with the game than looking for trouble. It's always better to keep cool and maintain your concentration, otherwise you can be a menace to yourself – and the rest of the team. Since arriving in the Midlands and the First Division I've been conscious of the encouragement we can generate among black kids in the area. A lot of nonsense has been talked about black players not having enough heart for the game when the going gets tough. Well that's a theory that has quickly been dispelled. More black players are coming into the game all the time, and that can only help others to try their luck. I want to tell a lot of those black kids out there that the same thing can happen to them.'

That season West Brom finished sixth in Division One and reached the semi-final of the FA Cup, where they were knocked out by Ipswich. And while Laurie was immense in some games, he was anonymous in others, and he began to attract some criticism for his inconsistency. Cyrille defends his friend: 'Part of the problem is that when you're so gifted and so young people want you to be 10 out of 10 every game, which is impossible. So at times he could be inconsistent, which wound up the fans and wound up the manager. But in spells – for months and months – he was fantastic.'

He also continued to be dogged by rumours in the press about his playboy lifestyle, prompting boss Ron Atkinson to have a one-to-one with his young winger. Laurie said afterwards 'It was great of the boss to discuss the rumours with me, rather than believe them. They have been getting me down. I don't have much of a social life anyway.'

In the 1978–79 season West Brom finished in third place in the League, their highest position ever, and Laurie was very much part of the success story. The club also went on a fantastic UEFA Cup run, eventually reaching the quarter-finals. It was in their third round tie, away at Valencia, that Laurie had what many consider to be the defining game of his career. The Valencia team contained World Cup stars Mario Kempes and Rainher Bonhof, but it was Laurie who stood out, scoring the goal that gave West Brom an unlikely 1–1 draw. 'He was awesome,' says Cyrille. 'Honestly, everything he did that night came off.' Ron Atkinson said 'He virtually destroyed them. I thought Laurie looked like George Best out there.'

In January Laurie was called up to the full England squad for the first time, though he did not make the pitch. 'The growing recognition of black players is tremendous,' he said at the time. Four months later he was called up again for the Home Championships. 'This season has been my most consistent since I've come into the game,' said Laurie. 'I've got 17 goals, which is not bad for a winger, and now I want to show I can do it at the highest level.' England manager Ron Greenwood was excited at the prospect of having such an exciting talent at his disposal and said of Laurie 'He's got that electrifying ability to go past people. Wembley is the perfect platform for him.' This time Laurie did get on the pitch, making his full international debut in the 0–0 draw against Wales on 23 May 1979. It made him the second black player – Viv Anderson was the first – to appear for the senior England team. He made two more appearances for the national side that season – against Sweden and Austria – though did not manage to convince manager Ron Greenwood that he should be preferred to either Steve Coppell, which is possibly fair enough, or Manchester City's Peter Barnes, which possibly isn't. Many commentators at the time believed that had Laurie been playing for a club more fashionable than West Brom (and, let's face it, most are) he would have been a shoe-in to the England starting XI. As the 1978–79 season ended, Laurie became frustrated with West Brom. 'I know he wasn't getting paid enough,' explains Cyrille. 'That was winding him up. I heard when he left he was on £150 a week.'

Laurie's eye-catching performance against Valencia earlier in the season had brought him to the attention of Real Madrid. He decided that the Spanish club was the right place for him and, to hurry the process along, Laurie flew out to Madrid, knocked on the door of the Bernabeu and asked if they wanted to sign him. These days it seems an incredibly audacious thing for a footballer to do – even then it was pretty ballsy. But it was Laurie all over. Real Madrid were flattered, but general secretary Fernando Trigo said at the time 'You can imagine our surprise. Of course, it is very satisfactory to have an international player of such class come and offer to play for us. But Real Madrid is a serious club and we told him that we must do the correct thing and contact West Bromwich Albion.'

They did exactly that, and Ron Atkinson relates the story of how the two clubs came to agreement over the transfer fee: 'The Madrid president, a charming man called Senor Calderon, arrived at my home in Sutton Coldfield, with the club secretary. Senor Calderon pronounced "I think Cunningham is worth £300,000." My dog growled. "He doesn't like that figure," I said, and the Spaniards laughed. I picked up an old brown envelope and suddenly negotiations became serious. They wrote down 400,000 on the back of an envelope and I replied with my figure of 1.5 million. In turn we crossed out each other's figure until we reached something like £995,000.' With that Laurie became Real Madrid's first-ever Englishman. 'I've thought about the move for some time now and I feel that I must learn more about the game,' Laurie said. 'I decided it was time I did something different. They will be able to show me a few tricks I don't know.' Though he received a £150,000 signing-on fee, he railed against the idea that it was the money that was the driving factor in his move, saying 'I was thoroughly depressed by my long-drawn-out negotiations with Albion. People in England think I was trying to act the big star. Nothing could be further from the truth. I did not come to Madrid just for the money. I wanted to see what the Spanish way of life was like.'

According to the *Daily Telegraph*, over 20,000 people turned up to watch Laurie's first training session. Spanish football writer Guillem Balague says 'He was adding something that there wasn't much of at Madrid at the time – loads of skill. You tend to relate Spanish football to skill, but they were much more defensive than they are now. They didn't have much glamour. He added that glamour.' Initially Laurie didn't disappoint, scoring one and making two assists in his debut at the Bernabeu in a 3–2 win over Valencia. His skill and ability shone in the Spanish sun, and he added a new party trick to his repertoire – shooting directly from corners with the outside of his right boot. He went on to help the side achieve a League and Cup double in that 1979–80 season. One match in particular stood out: the match between Spain's fiercest rivals, Real Madrid and Barcelona, at the latter's imposing stadium, the Nou Camp, which Real won 2–0. Guillem Balague explains: 'There have been only two players in the last 30 years that have been clapped by the opposite set of fans in Spain – Diego Maradona at the Santiago and Laurie Cunningham at the Nou Camp by the Barcelona fans. He had a fantastic, extraordinary match.'

For the most part, opposition fans were not so complimentary. He was the only black player in Spain at the time, and once again he was subjected to terrible racial taunting. There was also disappointment on the international front – Real Madrid refused to allow him to play in England's European Championship qualifier against Denmark in September 1979, and then Laurie was overlooked for the tournament itself in 1980. Few players plied their trade abroad in those days and

Laurie's case was certainly one of out of sight, out of the England squad. But, in that first season at least, Laurie seemed happy in Spain. His long-term girlfriend Nikki Brown – they had been together since he was 17, she 15 – had accompanied him, and they lived just outside Madrid. 'It was a lovely house,' says Cyrille, who visited Laurie every summer. 'He and Nikki had a couple of dogs, and they'd go out after training, buy clothes, go and eat, visit friends. It was very much a café society. It suited Laurie.'

Laurie himself said at the time, 'The most significant thing of all is that I needed to leave England before finally feeling at home as one of the lads. I could not be happier. The Spaniards are much more open in their feelings than they are in England, and I have been made welcome.' It was in Laurie's second season that things began to unravel. In October 1980 he was called up to the England squad again for an away match against Romania, though he contrived to miss the flight and had to join up with his teammates later. 'It's all been a bit of a mix-up,' he said in true Laurie style.

In November he injured his big toe when, he claimed, a defender deliberately stamped on his foot while play was at the other end of the pitch. In December it was operated upon, and the surgery went so well that Laurie decided to go straight from the hospital to a nightclub. 'I was just happy I did not have any pain after the operation,' he said. 'I decided to go and have a few drinks. I was celebrating the success of my operation.' Real Madrid were distinctly unimpressed and hit Laurie with a £6,000 fine – the biggest they'd ever handed out – and a month's suspension. 'I've accepted the punishment. All I want to do now is put it behind me and get back to playing for Real again,' said a contrite Laurie, before adding cheekily 'It turned out to be the most expensive night out of my life. But I meant no harm.'

Laurie sat most of the season out and had to have another operation on the toe in March 1981. But he did manage to appear in that season's European Cup Final against Liverpool. He struggled to create an impact on the game and Real Madrid lost the game 1–0. There was more injury heartbreak the next season. He severed a tendon during the summer and then, when recovered and about to return to

Laurie before England's World Cup qualifier against Romania on 15 October 1980.

first-team action, was crocked again by an over-the-top tackle in training that left him with torn ligaments. Laurie claimed it was pre-meditated and that the players and staff had grown to resent him, upset that one of the highest-paid members of the team was supposedly spending all his time in discos.

Stories had long been circulating in the Spanish press that Laurie was a heavy drinker. But according to his friends it was far from the truth. They concede, however, that his love of music and dancing meant that he was often to be found in nightclubs. 'He probably strayed there too much,' admits Cyrille Regis. 'But then again, what are you supposed to do if you're injured? Sit down all day? His trips to nightclubs got blown out of proportion in the press. He was like David Beckham at the time, a superstar, so there was a lot of mileage

Laurie before a Real Madrid game in September 1982.

in it for them. He was labelled. But part of Laurie's make-up was to say, you can write whatever you like about me, but I'm still going to go out. I'm not going to lock myself in my room.'

With injuries lingering on – a cartilage operation gave him continuing problems – he made only intermittent appearances in that 1981–82 season. Although he was called up to the England squad for a friendly against Atletico Bilbao, Real Madrid refused him permission to leave. In March 1982 there were rumours that Laurie might be returning to West Brom. 'At the moment it's a sea of politics at Real,' he said. 'If an approach is made I might be interested and I might be keen.'

Soon after, Laurie split up with Nikki and married a Spanish woman, Sylvia, with whom he went on to have a child, Sergio. By October 1982 he believed that he was nearing full fitness again. 'It's been two years since I got in a regular run of games,' he said. 'I've been terribly unlucky with injuries, and I suppose as far as Real are concerned I've gone down the drain. But I've still got plenty to offer.'

He did play a handful of games but failed to reproduce anything like the form of his earlier career. By March 1983 Real Madrid were frustrated enough with their English enigma to send him out on loan. Ron Atkinson, then manager of Manchester United, believed he could still get something out of his former player and brought him to Old Trafford. But Laurie was far from fit, and made only three full and two substitute appearances for the club, although he did score in a 2–0 win over Watford on 23 April 1983. Manchester United reached the FA Cup Final that season and Atkinson wanted to name Laurie as a substitute. It was Laurie himself who declared himself unfit, saying 'It seemed too good to be true for me to go from playing for Real Madrid to a month later being in a Cup Final for the next greatest team in the world. I felt like I was taking someone's place.'

Real Madrid farmed Laurie out on loan for the 1983–84 season to fellow La Liga side Sporting de Gijon, where he managed a relatively stress-free, if unspectacular, season. 'I came through this season fairly OK, and I hope my injuries are a thing of the past,' said Laurie. In the summer of 1984 Real Madrid were finally done with their wayward star and released him on a free transfer. It was a sorry end to something that had begun so promisingly. What had gone wrong? How had a player who had captured the imagination of the hard-to-please *Madridistas* in his first season drifted so aimlessly through the next few years? Cyrille Regis believes that Laurie should not have gone to Spain at such a young age. 'He wasn't mature enough at 22. There wasn't the support system around him that you would have nowadays – you'd have your agent, language lessons, that sort of thing. There was a lot of pressure on Laurie because of the money that Real Madrid had paid for him, and he wasn't equipped to deal with it. The weakest part of a player at that age is their mental strength. Criticism hurt him, and when things weren't going well he was lonely.' Cyrille also reveals that Laurie confided in him that he'd been having problems with the club. 'He was fighting them. They weren't paying him as much as they had agreed. He thought there was a conspiracy, and he didn't have an agent to fight his case.'

Finding himself clubless, Laurie considered his options. 'Maybe this is the time to consider returning to England,' he said – before signing for French First Division side Marseille. It did not turn out to be a happy experience, and in May 1985 he was transfer-listed. 'I'm shocked by the decision, stunned and hurt,' he said, upon finding out. 'Perhaps it's time to come home. I'm homesick. The soccer in Europe has changed, although I've been pleased with my form. I'm completely free of injuries now. I've also found Marseilles not as ambitious as they said when they persuaded me to sign. They play me at number 10 as an attacking inside-forward. Everyone in England knows I'm a winger. English soccer seems to have improved so much, while European clubs seem to want technical ability first. It used to be the other way round.'

He got his wish, for in the summer of 1985 Leicester City, then a Division One side under Gordon Milne, took him on loan from the French club. 'I'll be back on my glory trail,' said Laurie optimistically, but it wasn't to be. He made just 15 appearances for the Midlands club and was clearly distracted. In an interview with the *Sunday Times* at the time he talked of the 'plots, betrayals, racism, injuries, official ineptitude, cultural clashes, bad playing systems, bad doctors, bad fans, bad press, bad management' that had dogged his career. Returning to Europe, Laurie spent the 1986–87 and much of the 1987–88 season at Belgian First Division club Charleroi. He did return to England one last time, joining Wimbledon at the height of the Crazy Gang era and playing 30 minutes in the famous 1–0 FA Cup Final defeat of Liverpool in 1988. The winners' medal was the only honour he received in English football.

Laurie returned to Madrid to play for Second Division team Rayo Vallecano for the 1988–89 season, and scored the goal that secured them promotion to the top flight. Days later he was dead. Cyrille spoke to his long-time friend a few days before the fatal accident. 'Laurie was going to come and visit me. He seemed fine. You know what men are like – even if he did have problems he gave the impression everything was OK. I think he had frustrations. He was 33 by then and was more reflective, looking back on where his career had gone. Like any footballer he would think, did I maximise who I was as a footballer? And, for him, given he had so much talent, if the answer was no, then there would have been a sense of frustration.'

Laurie was killed just before dawn on 15 July 1989. He'd been driving along a main road, 15 miles north of Madrid, with an American friend, Mark Cafwell Latty. According to newspaper reports, the car, a Seat Ibiza, had skidded, hit a lamp-post and overturned. Latty staggered from the vehicle with only minor cuts and bruises. Laurie, who hadn't worn a seatbelt and was thrown against the windscreen, was dead on arrival at hospital. Cyrille Regis says 'I had a call that Laurie had died in a car crash, and it broke my heart. He was a very loyal friend and we had become like brothers. His death had a deep effect on me.' In an obituary, Laurie's former boss Ron Atkinson said 'He was the greatest natural talent unearthed since George Best. He was as talented a player as I have ever worked with. Injuries stopped him becoming the world star I thought he would be.' He added 'If he ran on snow, he wouldn't leave any footprints.'

In September 1989 a memorial service was held for Laurie at Southwark Cathedral in London. Over 250 people attended, including Bobby Robson, Ron Atkinson, Bryan Robson, Brendan Batson and sports minister Colin Moynihan. Orient fan Laurie Woolcott was also there to pay his respects. 'It was so sad,' he says. 'It seemed to be such a waste of a life.' It was a tragic end to the life of a supremely gifted footballer – one who was all too often misunderstood. 'I was never a rebel,' he said before he died. 'People thought I had a chip on my shoulder because of my colour. But that's wrong. They thought I was always raving it up at discos. That was wrong.'

But Laurie has a legacy. You can see it when Rio Ferdinand trots out onto the Old Trafford pitch. When Shaun Wright-Phillips scores for England. When Micah Richards makes a last-ditch tackle at Eastlands. When Emmanuel Adebayor cannons in a header for Arsenal. Back in his Orient days, the young Laurie, with remarkable prescience, once told a reporter 'If I made it, a lot of managers might change their minds about us.' By 'us' he meant, of course, black players, and the fact that Laurie did have such success paved the way for the likes of Ferdinand, Wright-Phillips, Richards, Adebayor and the hundreds of other black players who can now play professional football in Britain without enduring the vicious racial hatred that dogged most of Laurie's career.

In the same interview Laurie added cheekily 'Anyway, the greatest player in the world is black, you know.' Naturally, he was referring to Pelé, but for those two and a half seasons at Brisbane Road, for those fans lucky enough to witness him in action, it felt like it was Laurie himself.

# Chapter 7
# SHAMROCK WARRIOR
## Tony Grealish 1974–79

'Anthony will never make anything of himself in life walking around with a ball under his arm.'

So said the school report of a young Anthony Patrick Grealish who, just a few years later, was sitting on the bench at Brisbane Road waiting to make his debut as a professional footballer. 'At that moment I wanted to tell the teacher who wrote that I'd never make anything of myself that, well, I did actually,' he says. Tony remains one of the most exciting, committed and talented young footballers ever to turn out for Orient. As a midfielder-cum-utility player, he made 192 starts and three substitute appearances for the club between 1974 and 1979, scoring

Tony in his Orient Days.

10 goals and starring in the famous FA Cup run of 1977–78. He represented the Republic of Ireland 45 times, went on to play in Division One for many years with Brighton, West Bromwich Albion and Manchester City and featured in the FA Cup Final of 1983. And, aside from all that, for many years he sported a beard that could be considered an achievement in its own right.

Tony, though born in Paddington and blessed with a north London accent, is Irish through and through. Born to parents from the Emerald Isle and brought up on a diet of Gaelic football and hurling, he seemingly hasn't just kissed the Blarney Stone – he's positively snogged the damn thing, for he can talk for Ireland and England put together. He speaks with great fondness about his time at Orient – and even now he appears wide-eyed with excitement about the fact that he was earning his living as a footballer. And while Tony undoubtedly enjoyed his life off the pitch – 'beer was part of the game back then,' he chuckles – no supporter could ever accuse him of being anything less than 100 per cent committed once on it. 'He was a brilliant hard-tackler,' says fan Alan Harvey. 'He was a ball-winner and had loads of energy. Orient could do with someone like Tony Grealish today.'

Tony was born on 21 September 1956. His father, Patrick, and mother, Nora, both hailed from Athenry in Galway. Patrick was a stonemason who'd moved to London in the early 50s looking for work; Nora was a professional Irish dancer. Aside from Tony they had three other children, Brian, Christine and Anne. Growing up in Kilburn – a part of London that was home to many Irish emigrants – Tony describes himself as a 'rowdy' child. 'I was very industrious. At every opportunity I'd be out on the street playing football or making go-karts with a couple of pram wheels and a plank of wood.' He played Gaelic football and hurling as a young lad, but it was at football that he began to really excel, playing for his school, Rutherford, and making the west London under-11 district side. Though he made a career out of soccer, he believes he could have made it as a Gaelic footballer should he have chosen to. 'Initially I preferred it, but I'm glad I chose soccer in the end, because Gaelic football is a tough old game,' he says. As a teenager Tony played for Beaumont Boys Football Club and, while there, had trials at Queen's Park Rangers and Tottenham. He was rejected by both for being too small.

Many of the Beaumont boys – including Nigel Gray and Gary Hibbs, who also went on to play for Orient – would travel over to Leyton by tube on Tuesday and Wednesday evenings, accompanied by chief scout Len Cheesewright, to train at Brisbane Road. Tony was won over by the charm of the club. Or rather, its food. 'We used to have tea and sandwiches after training and, I know this sounds daft, but it was lovely,' he says. 'We were easily bought in those days.'

In May 1972, a month before 15-year-old Tony was due to leave school, Len Cheesewright and then Orient manager George Petchey visited Mr and Mrs Grealish to offer their son a two-year apprenticeship. They didn't need to ask twice. 'It was either football or the army,' says Tony, somewhat surprisingly. 'I'm glad the football worked out, because I think there could have been a lot of problems in the army with my parents being of Irish background.' In June, after leaving school – 'I enjoyed history, geography and PE, but I was never big on maths and science,' he says – Tony spent his first day as an Orient apprentice. 'What a bloody eye-opener that was,' he laughs. 'When the senior pros came in they looked huge and they were all telling stories and taking the mickey out of you. People like Tom Walley, Mickey Bullock, Mark Lazarus, Gordon Riddick. They didn't take any prisoners in those days. If you walked into the dressing room when you weren't supposed to, you'd get a right bollocking.'

As an apprentice Tony was paid £7 a week plus a Tube pass, and he is not shy of relating just how hard he had to work to earn the cash. 'It was a long day. You'd have to get there for 9:30am. We had to clean the dressing rooms, the floors, the steps, the corridors, sweep the terraces and whatever. Peter Angell was in charge of us, and he was such a stern disciplinarian. He was like a typical old soldier from the 1950s. He'd run his finger over the pipes and over the cupboards and no one could leave until everything was done.'

Though signing principally as a right-back, Tony was soon moved to midfield at the behest of manager George Petchey. He retained the ability to play in both positions – and could fill in at left-back too if he was needed – throughout his career.

As an apprentice he did not have too much contact with Petchey, although on one occasion Tony did incur the manager's wrath. The youngster had continued to play hurling and Gaelic football and one day turned up with an injury. 'I had a big scar and three or four stitches across my eyebrow,' he says. 'I'd been playing hurling. I didn't realise that you weren't allowed to play any other contact sports. But George didn't believe me and assumed that I'd been out fighting on the Saturday night, so he fined me £10. I had to pay a pound a week out of my wages for the next 10 weeks. I'll never forgive him for that because I was telling the truth – I had been playing hurling. But that was the end of my days of playing Irish sports. It says in your contract that you can't do that so they have you by the short and curlies. It was fair enough though, because even though you're so fit when you're 16 or 17, your legs used to get battered. And the side of your head too.'

In the second year of his apprenticeship Tony was part of the talented team that won the London Youth Cup and finished runners-up in the South-East Counties League. After a number of trials, he was also selected for the England Under-18 squad for an international tournament. But the week before he was due to go, he was approached by Republic of Ireland coach John Jarman in the tunnel at Brisbane Road after a reserve game and asked if he would like to go along for a trial for the Ireland youth team. Tony sought the advice of both his father and George Petchey. 'My dad loved the idea,' he says. 'He wasn't a huge football fan as he was very much wrapped up in Gaelic football and hurling, but he was an armchair Everton supporter. But I thought that playing for Ireland would have made him very proud. And George told me that, with all due respect, I'd have a much better chance of playing for Ireland than I would England. He said that for England there are hundreds of players like me and that I might end up only getting two or three caps. And as soon as he said that it wasn't a problem for me. I just changed straight away.'

It was an easy decision for Tony. At the root of it was the fact that he always felt more Irish than English. 'It's always been in my heart,' he says. 'The area I grew up in, the Gaelic football...even to this day my mum runs a pub that's full of Irish.' And, looking back, he says it was the right decision. 'George was absolutely correct. There would have been hundreds of players in my position for England.' Tony ended up playing for Ireland – alongside the likes of Liam Brady, Frank Stapleton and David O'Leary – in the very same youth tournament for which he was due to represent England. 'I got some s**t from the lads,' he laughs.

Back at Orient, Tony was made a professional footballer in the summer of 1974, still shy of his 18th birthday. He had to wait until 28 September and a home League match against Sheffield Wednesday to get his chance to prove himself in the first team. The call-up came as something of a surprise. 'On the Saturday of the game I was told I'd be on the bench,' he says. 'I nearly crapped myself. There were players like Tom Walley, Gerry Queen, Mickey Bullock, Terry Brisley, Phil Hoadley… They were all big guys. Then there was me, a little dwarf stepping in. I didn't know what to do. But they make you welcome.' Tony got about 10 minutes on the pitch, coming on for Barrie Fairbrother and helping see out a 1–0 victory for the Os. To this day, it stands out as the highlight of his Orient career. 'I know it sounds daft but sitting on the bench there waiting to come on was the greatest thing,' he says. 'I'd become a professional footballer.'

On 30 November Tony made his full debut against Nottingham Forest at Brisbane Road, playing in midfield in place of Terry Brisley and scoring the goal that enabled Orient to draw the game 1–1 – a goal he says he's unable to recall. George Petchey was suitably impressed, and Tony remained an ever present in the team for the rest of the season, playing in midfield, at right-back and left-back and clocking up 26 appearances. 'I still felt so young, though,' Tony says of that first season. 'But the older players helped me out. Tom Walley was a great guy. He said to me "Don't take any s\*\*t from these old boys. If there's any problems, talk to me. I'll sort them out." But I was frightened to tell him in case there was a punch-up.'

In January of that season Tony found himself up against Scotland legend Archie Gemmill in an FA Cup game against Derby County. 'He was a bit of a bastard,' Tony laughs. 'He was very aggressive and mouthy. All game he was going on at me, saying "I've got you in my pocket now, son," and so on. I didn't know what he was on about. I was only a young boy and I looked up to him as one of the midfield heroes of the time. Gerry Queen stepped in and told Archie to leave me alone as I was only a boy, and Archie said that I'd soon learn. Then you had these two Scotsmen yapping at each other.'

Such was Tony's enthusiasm about his first season as a footballer, it almost escaped his notice that Orient as a team were doing pretty poorly. The spoils of that season, such as they were, included 12th position in Division Two, 12 goalless draws and a sum total of just 28 League goals throughout the entire campaign – a record low. 'I was young and naïve, I was wrapped up in my own world,' he says. 'But the other lads were getting really wound up. They were very vocal at half-time and at the end of the game. They'd be in the tunnel eyeing everyone up. They'd say to me "If so and so is any trouble, kick him over to me and I'll sort him out." And if you made a mistake yourself someone would be over saying "pull your finger out or I'll give you a wallop in a minute." That frightened me at first. These were my own teammates!' Tony points to Tom Walley and Phil Hoadley as the big voices in the dressing room and on the pitch, but says that for him it was Peter Allen who proved inspirational. 'He was great in terms of encouragement and he taught me a lot as well. He always said keep yourself fit, do well for yourself, climb the ladder and don't s\*\*t on anybody when you get up there. He gave me great advice, Pete. Not that I ever took it!'

The following season of 1975–76 was one of grinding mediocrity for Orient – the club finished 13th in the League, were knocked out of the League and FA Cups at the first time of asking and amassed a grand total of just 37 goals in the entire campaign. Still, there were a few reasons for fans not to top themselves, in particular the form of youngsters Laurie Cunningham, Glenn Roeder and Tony himself. Once again playing in both midfield and full-back positions, the Irishman's performances began to attract attention – not least from the manager of the senior Republic of Ireland team, Johnny Giles. In 1976 Tony was selected for the squad and made his debut at right-back in a 3–0 friendly win against Norway on 24 March. He made one more appearance for the Irish team that season, in a 2–0 friendly win in Poland.

Tony took a fair amount of stick for his new-found international fame once back at Orient. 'A lot of them started taking the piss,' he laughs. 'They called me the plastic Paddy, or the Paddy from Cricklewood. "What part of Ireland is that in?" they'd ask. They'd say "well, if you can play for Ireland so can I." But there was no malice intended, no jealousy.'

During that 1975–76 season, rumours that bigger clubs were looking at Tony became an almost weekly occurrence. They prompted him to think a little about where his career was taking him. 'I did start to think that perhaps this time with Orient was like another apprenticeship, and that maybe it was about time I pulled my finger out and pushed on to get to a higher level,' he says. 'Especially once I'd got the taste for it after playing the two friendlies with the Irish team. But I thought to myself that the only way I could push on was to have another good season for Orient; that if I was good enough someone would come in for me.'

For the time being, Tony was perfectly happy at Orient. And not just on the pitch. He attests to a good social life, and singles out Bobby Fisher, Gary Hibbs and Nigel Gray as particular friends. 'We were young lads, and we just did the typical stuff young lads get up to,' says Tony. 'When we finished training we'd sneak a few beers here and there. Or we'd go and buy records and clothes or go to the cinema – or try to find a bird. On Friday nights I'd have two pints of Guinness with a spaghetti bolognese and a chocolate bar. I know it sounds terrible – but it was just to get my carbohydrates. And we'd always get home by 9.30.' He is possibly stretching the truth somewhat and when pushed adds 'More like 9.30 in the morning!'

After matches, the pub would inevitably be the destination of choice for Tony and friends. 'We'd have a few drinks in the bar and make our way home,' he says. 'Depending how the result went we might get s***-faced. But that wouldn't have taken long in them days – three or four pints. It was nothing outrageous.' And even if it was, Tony had a neat way of getting himself going of a morning. 'My dad always gave me a shot of sherry with a raw egg in it,' he laughs. 'He'd stand there watching me drink it to make sure I didn't run to the toilet. It's a typical Irish remedy – a typical myth. My dad would say "It'll put hairs on the back of your neck." Like I needed hairs on the back of my neck! It was horrible.'

In the summers Tony would often do a bit of work to top up his salary – in construction and labouring – and sometimes went on a lads' holiday with some of the other players. 'We went to Benidorm, Ibiza, places like that,' he says. 'Six or seven of the young pros, people like Dean Mooney and Tony Simpson, along with Bobby, Gary and Nigel. Glenn Roeder would never come with us. He was too strait-laced, bless him.'

The 1976–77 season was a bad one for Orient and, says Tony, for himself. The club struggled on the pitch, winning just nine League games all season and scoring only 37 goals, and suffered from severe financial problems. Attendances at Brisbane Road rarely topped 6,000. 'Personally, I don't think I played too well that year,' he says. 'I don't really know why, but I had a couple of injuries, and I couldn't get that rhythm going. There were other players too who felt that they let themselves down that season.'

It had potentially dire consequences. Orient had to avoid losing to Hull City on the final day of the season to avoid dropping into Division Three. Thankfully for the 8,400 fans who turned up, they managed it, with an Allan Glover goal helping them secure a 1–1 draw. It sparked the sort of jubilant celebrations in the stands that you would expect to see had the club achieved promotion. This didn't sit well with Tony. 'I couldn't believe the amount of satisfaction the lads were getting because we'd stayed up,' he explains. 'The fans were celebrating like we'd won something and we were told to go up to the directors' area and wave to thank them. But it wasn't the right thing to do in my eyes. One or two of us were reluctant to go up. I thought we should have been hanging our heads in shame because we'd let them down. I thought, Christ almighty we're better than this. None of us had done our duty in that sense as players.'

Slightly bizarrely, Orient's directors allowed George Petchey to stay in his job for the beginning of the 1977–78 season, only to sack him after losing the first two League games. Tony did not see it coming. 'I was shocked,' he says. 'For him to get the boot that early, well, no one could have read that. And obviously with George being my first manager it was a bit hard to take. I had a lot of respect for George and he taught me a lot. He treated me very well, but he wasn't averse to giving me a bollocking. He'd say things like "Pull yourself together, you're putting weight on." He could be quite ferocious when the 90 minutes were playing. But he was a great all-round manager.'

Petchey's exit allowed Jimmy Bloomfield to return to Orient in his second spell as manager. It was Tony's first experience of the former Leicester City boss. 'He breezed in like a bit of a wiz kid,' he laughs. 'He was always telling everyone how to dress, to tidy themselves up, to look smart, get your head up, don't slouch, look the part. To be honest it was a breath of fresh air. The older guys were a bit wary – they were thinking that they could be out of the door. But us younger lads enjoyed it, the different training methods and the fact everyone had to impress. Jimmy was very encouraging. There was a lot of enthusiasm.'

Orient at the beginning of the famous 1977–78 season. Back row, left to right: Bobby Fisher, Terry Long, Alan Stephenson, Peter Angell, Peter Kitchen. Middle row: Peter Bennett, Nigel Gray, John Jackson, John Smeulders, Bill Roffey, Tony Grealish. Front row: Allan Glover, John Chiedoze, Peter Allen, Phil Hoadley, Glenn Roeder, David Payne, Derek Clarke.

Certainly something inspired the players that season, if not in the League then in the FA Cup. The run began with wins over Norwich and Blackburn before a 0–0 draw with Chelsea at Brisbane Road in February. The Chelsea side still featured veterans such as Ron Harris and Peter Bonetti, along with rising stars like Ray Wilkins. Though not the finest side in the club's history, they nevertheless had beaten European champions Liverpool in the third round and were no pushovers. 'It was a tough old game,' Tony recalls. 'We were quite pleased with how everyone had performed but you think, Christ, you don't give a club like Chelsea a second bite at the cherry.'

Stamford Bridge, however, was to become the location for a famous Orient victory. Peter Angell was in temporary charge of the team as Jimmy Bloomfield was in one of his spells in hospital. 'Peter said to us "Go out there. You've got nothing to lose but this game,"' Tony recalls. 'Everyone started laughing. Peter was a bit nervous himself. But he just said that if we put in our work rate, everything else would fall into place. And he was bloody right.'

Orient won 2–1 thanks to two Peter Kitchen goals. Tony recalls, in particular, having to withstand the Chelsea onslaught for the last 15 minutes of the game. 'It seemed like an eternity,' he says. 'But our little crowd in the corner were great, and made more noise than the Chelsea fans. When the final whistle went it was just ballistic. I didn't sleep at all that night. My parents' pub was nearby so I celebrated there.'

A 2–1 replay win over Middlesbrough in the quarter-finals set Orient up for their first and so far only FA Cup semi-final. They would be playing an Arsenal side near the top of Division One and containing the likes of Frank Stapleton, Malcolm MacDonald, Pat Jennings and David O'Leary.

Did Tony think Orient had a chance of making it to the Final? 'To be honest, no,' he replies. 'On the one hand I was 21 years old and thought I could fight the world. I thought we had a chance if everyone played well and if this and if that. But there were too many ifs. When you looked at the players they had then you'd think there was no way on God's earth that we were going to get anything. I know it sounds terrible, but I thought if we got through it would have been a bloody miracle. You'd just hope it wasn't embarrassing. But in the end I just thought, who gives a s\*\*t, let's just go out there and see what happens.'

Tony was given the task of marking fellow Irish international Liam Brady. 'I found it embarrassing,' he says. 'I'd only just got to know the lads in the Irish team, and now I had to mark Liam and give him a bit of grief. Jimmy told me that if he went for a s\*\*t I had to go with him. So I niggled him a bit and tried to slow him down, and he got a bit huffy and puffy. But I did find it very awkward.'

Ultimately the game was an anti-climax, with Orient undone by two deflected goals from Malcolm MacDonald and another by Graham Rix. Describing the immediate aftermath Tony says

| THE LINE UP | | |
|---|---|---|
| **ORIENT** | | **CHELSEA** |
| John JACKSON | 1 | Peter BONETTI |
| Bobby FISHER | 2 | Gary LOCKE |
| Bill ROFFEY | 3 | Ron HARRIS |
| Tony GREALISH | 4 | Ian BRITTON |
| Phil HOADLEY | 5 | Micky DROY |
| Glenn ROEDER | 6 | Steve WICKS |
| Kevin GODFREY | 7 | Steve FINNIESTON |
| Nigel GRAY | 8 | Ray WILKINS |
| Joe MAYO | 9 | Tommy LANGLEY |
| Peter KITCHEN | 10 | Ken SWAIN |
| David PAYNE | 11 | Clive WALKER |
| | 12 | |
| Colours: White Shirts Red side stripes White Shorts Red stripes | | Colours: Royal Blue Shirts and Shorts with white trim |

Magazine Production: Editor: Mike Blake  Design: John Monks  Print: Ward & Woolverton Ltd.

The programme denoting the team line ups for Orient's fifth-round FA Cup tie against Chelsea on 18 February 1978.

Tony in the FA Cup sixth-round match against Middlesbrough on 14 March 1978, fighting for the ball with John Mahoney.

Tony is put under pressure by Bryan Robson in the Republic of Ireland's European Championship qualifier against England at Wembley on 6 February 1980.

'Everyone was sad and choked. It wasn't just that we'd lost, it was the way we'd lost it. Those two horrible goals. And once they'd got those goals they relaxed. They started to take the mickey. But Peter Angell came in and told us that we'd had a fantastic run, that we'd been fantastic for the club and that we shouldn't forget who we'd beaten to get that far. Then he opened a bottle of beer and said "Here's to you, lads." That broke the ice. Then we all got hammered.'

Unfortunately, once the hangovers subsided, it was back to the grim reality that Orient were involved in a relegation battle at the end of the 1977–78 season. Thanks to a final day win over Cardiff City at Ninian Park, Orient survived. But after the FA Cup run and his international appearances, Tony began to think more about his future. 'I had such a fantastic feeling playing against Chelsea and Arsenal, and I started thinking, wouldn't it be great if you played in that sort of atmosphere every week, in front of those crowds,' he says. 'And going away with the Irish team also opened my eyes. I'd be in Denmark or Germany or Holland playing in front of 50,000 people alongside the likes of Steve Heighway, Don Givens and Frank Stapleton and I'd think, bloody hell, these players do this every week – it means nothing to them. I realised I wanted to play in bigger grounds. I thought it would lift my game no end. But I suppose I was a bit naïve, because I didn't think that I needed to leave Orient to do it. I just thought it was part of my job to keep myself fit and do the right thing. I thought that if I did that and had a good year, I'd get a good move, make a few quid for myself and start climbing the ladder.'

These, of course, were pre-Bosman days, so Tony had little control over his career anyway. The press speculation about a move continued – Liverpool and Spurs were among the clubs supposedly having a look – but he heard nothing concrete. And so, while he says he felt confident he could play at a higher level – 'The bigger the stage the better' – Tony began the 1978–79 season still in Division Two.

He probably wished he had not bothered, for the season was one of numbing mediocrity on Orient's part – a mid-table finish, no Cup runs and not even a relegation battle to keep fans entertained. It proved to be Tony's last season in an Orient shirt. He was coming to the end of a four-year contract and was not happy with the new terms he was being offered. He was due to get married in June 1979 to Pippa, a Fulham girl he'd met a few years earlier at a friend's 21st birthday party, and wanted security. 'I wasn't asking for the earth,' he says. 'I wanted about £20 a week more. There were some lads coming in at the end of their careers getting extra money, and I thought that if the club considered me an asset then I should get the same. I'd been stuck on the same wages for four years, and I thought if I wasn't going to be treated fairly then that was it. So I stood my ground. But I must admit, I was shaking like a leaf. In those days if the manager barked you'd cower.'

The new freedom of contract rules that had come into football the previous year meant that other clubs were allowed to approach Tony once June arrived. On the first day of the month, just days before his wedding, he received a call from Luton manager David Pleat. He invited Tony to come and take a look at the club. He obliged, and within 48 hours had signed on as a Luton player, with Orient getting £150,000 in the deal. 'David was a very persuasive talker,' Tony says. 'He wined and dined me at a hotel and that was it. I signed and then told him I had to go and get my wedding suit.'

Luton had just finished four points below Orient in Division Two and were attracting similar attendances. After all his dreams of playing in front of big crowds at the highest level and the continuous speculation about interest from above, it seems a little strange that Tony signed for Luton so swiftly. 'It was quick,' agrees Tony. 'Everyone asked why I signed when I had another six or seven weeks before the season started. Jimmy told me it was a step down. I was entitled to speak to other clubs, but I'd have felt a bit of a wally ringing people up and offering my services. Looking back on it I could have held out and it would have been interesting to see who did come up. But I'd have looked a right Charlie if no one had come in after six or seven weeks. I suppose I just wanted a bit of security for marriage. Luton were going to pay for my removal fee and storage for moving up there.' There was also the attraction of playing for David Pleat, who was creating a name for himself as a bright young manager. 'I've got nothing but admiration for George Petchey and Jimmy Bloomfield, but David Pleat was another League up,' says Tony. 'He just told me to express myself on the pitch.'

Tony made 79 appearances for the Hatters over two seasons as they pushed for – though ultimately failed to achieve – promotion from Division Two. In July 1981 Tony finally achieved his ambition of playing in the top tier when he was transferred to Brighton for £100,000 in July 1981.

He played a part in the Seagulls' famous FA Cup run of 1983, when they reached the Final and drew 2–2 with Manchester United before getting thumped 4–0 in the replay. 'I loved every minute of it,' says Tony. 'As a kid I used to stay at home watching all the build-up on the television. At that time it was every player's dream to play in the FA Cup Final.'

In March 1984 Tony moved to First Division West Bromwich Albion for £75,000. It was while there – in November 1985 – that he made the last of his 45 appearances for the Republic of Ireland. In October 1986 Tony joined struggling First Division side Manchester City for £20,000 but stayed only until the following August, making just 11 appearances. From Manchester City he joined Third Division Rotherham at the start of the 1987–88 season and stayed until August 1990. He then moved on to Conference side Bromsgrove in May 1992 and also had spells with Moor Green, Halesowen Harriers, Sutton Coldfield Town and as player-coach with Evesham United before returning as coach to Bromsgrove at the beginning of the 1994–95 season. In September he became caretaker manager, taking over the position permanently in December. He was fired three months later. In May 2000 he became assistant manager at Warwickshire-based Southern League outfit Atherstone United, while also working at West Bromwich Albion's youth academy. He also worked in the insurance and scrap metal industries. In 2004, after separating from wife Pippa, he moved to the south coast of Spain, near Estepona, where he makes ends meet by painting, gardening and selling spa baths. He has a daughter, Jordana, who was born in August 1983, and a son Geraint, born in December 1985.

Tony and Brighton manager Jimmy Melia celebrate winning the FA Cup semi-final against Sheffield Wednesday on 16 April 1983.

Looking back at his time at Orient, Tony can become quite emotional. 'They were good people at Orient,' he says. 'I still remember that to this day – it was a friendly club where everyone looked out for each other. I felt at home there.' Orient fans of the 1970s were glad that he did, and every one would surely attest that, despite what his school report might have said, Anthony Patrick Grealish really did make something of himself.

# Chapter 8
# GREAT SCOT
## Tommy Johnston 1956–58 and 1959–61

Tommy during his first spell with Orient.

Few players attain such legendary status that they need only be referred to by their first name, but when the word 'Tommy' is uttered in reverential tones at Brisbane Road, it can mean only one thing. Thomas Bourhill Johnston, to give him his full title, blew apart the Orient record books during the late 1950s and early 1960s, scoring a phenomenal 123 goals in his 190 appearances for the club, including 36 in 32 games during his defining season of 1957–58. Stats aside, Tommy was a leader, an icon, a craggy Scot who came to east London via the mines of Loanhead and five League clubs north and south of the border. He did not look too much like a footballer – the bitter winds of Scotland had etched lines into his face prematurely – but he sure played like one. 'He had two good feet, he could head a ball, he was mobile – he was the perfect centre-forward, and he couldn't stop scoring goals,' says fan Alan Harvey, who saw Tommy in his prime.

The sight of Tommy's raised hand – he wore a distinctive white bandage on his left wrist, the legacy of a nasty mining accident – became a beacon at Brisbane Road. It meant he wanted the ball and, more often than not, with the precision passing of the likes of Phil White and Phil Woosnam, he got it. Pretty soon after that it would be in the back of the net. 'You'd go to a game expecting him to get a hat-trick,' says fan Mickey Kasler. 'He was just incredible. There is no comparison with any other strikers Orient have ever had.' And while Tommy could certainly score goals with his feet, it was his heading ability that set him apart from mere mortals. 'At times he was unplayable in the air,' says supporter Dick Richards. 'He used to hang there, and he had such a powerful header.' Mickey Kasler agrees: 'He could head a ball harder than he could kick it. That's not an exaggeration. He'd head it like a rocket from the edge of the penalty area.'

Remember, too, that in those days leather footballs had all the springiness of your average block of concrete and bore laces that would embed themselves into the skull of anyone foolish enough to attempt to head the damn things. This did not seem to trouble Tommy too much. 'He was a hard man,' says Mickey. 'If the ball came in low, it didn't matter if boots were flying about, he'd dive in and head the ball into the net.'

As hard as nails on the pitch, Tommy could be pretty uncompromising off it, too. The Scot was notorious for refusing to sign autographs, something he readily admits to all these years later. 'It's true that I wouldn't do it if people asked at the wrong time,' Tommy says. And that time was? 'Walking to the station to catch the train home,' he says. 'But I signed them outside the club and signed countless autographs when I was over in England in 1989. I wouldn't mind a pound for every one I've signed.' A family man, he married his wife Jean when he was 25 and has been with her ever since. He enjoyed socialising with his teammates and could regularly be found in the Monkham Arms near his home in Woodford Green, drinking Mackeson's milk stout. 'Tommy was quite a character,' says Stan Charlton, who played alongside the great man. 'He was quite a hard man, but he had a good sense of humour – you had to if you played for the Orient! He was a popular member of the team.' Though he now lives over 10,000 miles away in Australia, Tommy remains close to the hearts of Orient fans who, in 1999, voted him the club's greatest ever player in a Millennium poll.

It all began on 18 August 1927 in Loanhead, a small town just south of Edinburgh in Midlothian, when Tommy was born to parents Bob and Meg. He has five brothers, a sister and a half-sister. His father, a coal miner, was the family's only breadwinner. Tommy says that he was not interested in learning at school, believing – like all Loanhead boys – that his destiny was to end up down the mine. But he did find himself to be a pretty handy footballer and would spend hours kicking a small ball barefoot around the yard. At the age of 10 Tommy was selected for the school team as an outside-left and scored two goals in his first game. Predictably, both were headers. By the age of 13 Tommy was captain of the school team – he once scored 19 goals in one single game – and also played for a local under-17 side, Loanhead West End. He left school just short of his 14th birthday in June 1941 and a couple of months later, in common with all his older brothers, began working at the local coal mine.

Tommy continued to play for Loanhead West End before joining another local side, the delightfully named Gilmerton Drumbirds. It was there that he was converted to a centre-forward after the regular striker failed to turn up for a match. In February 1945, at the age of 17, Tommy suffered a serious accident in the mine when he caught his arm between two hutches – the box-like wheeled trucks used to transport coal. His left wrist was badly crushed and doctors initially believed that his arm would have to be amputated. Two years of surgery and skin grafts saved the limb, though it retained a distinct bend on the outer side of the wrist. Henceforth Tommy would wear a bandage on it whenever he played football.

By March 1947, Tommy, now 19 years of age, was cleared to return to the football pitch and he signed up to play for local semi-professional outfit Loanhead Mayflower. In August of that year, he joined Peeble Rovers, who played in the East of Scotland League, one level below the Scottish Football League, and he spent the next two seasons there, scoring over 50 goals. During this time he went on trial with Falkirk and Third Lanark – both in the top tier of Scottish football. He was also offered a trial at Bolton Wanderers, then in Division One, but he turned it down in favour of remaining in his native country. 'I was happy in Scotland,' says Tommy, simply. 'I was near my family and I didn't want to leave.' Eventually, in November 1949 he elected to sign for Kilmarnock, then residing in the second tier of Scottish football. He remained there until April 1951, scoring 20 goals in his 26 appearances. His next move took him south of the border, to Division Three North side Darlington. He stayed just under a year, scoring nine goals in his 27 appearances. Oldham Athletic – residing in the same division – took him on, though he was unhappy at the club's refusal to let him play as an attacking centre-forward and made only five appearances, scoring three goals.

Norwich City manager Norman Low was at Tommy's last game at Boundary Park and offered him a contract to play for the Division Three South club. The Scot was impressed with Carrow Road, but there was one thing holding him back. In April that year in Oldham he had met a local trainee fashion model, Jean Waite, and was rather smitten. Luckily the feeling was mutual, and on 19 July 1952, having known each other just four months, the couple wed and moved to Norwich together. These were happier times on the pitch for Tommy: he scored 15 goals in 27 appearances for Norwich during the 1952–53 season and 16 goals in 33 appearances during the 1953–54 season. Included in the latter were the two headed goals that knocked Arsenal out of the FA Cup on 30 January 1954 in front of over 55,000 fans at Highbury. That same month Jean gave birth to the couple's first child, a boy they named Neil.

Things began to turn sour for Tommy in the 1954–55 season when, he says, the directors of the club began to wield too much influence over the team's style of play. In particular they wanted Tommy to play as a deep-lying centre-forward in the style of Don Revie at Manchester City, a new fad in football since Hungary employed the system to great effect in beating England 6–3 at Wembley in 1953. Tommy was having none of it and asked to leave. An offer came in from fellow Division Three South club Newport County, and on 16 October 1954 Tommy signed for the Welsh club for a fee of £2,100. Tommy enjoyed life in Wales and scored 53 goals in 68 appearances. By January of 1956 his performances had alerted Leyton Orient who, at that time, were riding high in Division Three South and, following the departure of Vic Groves to Arsenal, were on the lookout for a centre-forward to help their push for promotion.

The story goes that on the way home from the away game against Coventry City on 14 January, chairman Harry Zussman asked the team if anyone had a suggestion as to a striker who could strengthen the side. Captain and centre-half Stan Aldous shouted out 'Yes, I reckon we ought to go for that fellow Johnston at Newport, he always plays a blinder against me. He's an absolute menace to play against and in the air he's unplayable.' Zussman took his captain at his word, and by the time Newport came to Brisbane Road on 18 February Orient were ready to make an offer. 'When Newport's manager Billy Lucas told me of Leyton Orient's interest, I said "If they pay me my present wages, I will go"', says Tommy, simply. They did, and a week later Tommy was turning out in the blue of Orient after Zussman had paid money from his own pocket to meet the £6,000 transfer fee, which also saw striker Mike Burgess move to the Welsh club as part of the deal.

Tommy's first meeting with his new teammates was approximately an hour before the kick-off of Orient's game against Swindon Town at the County Ground. 'My first impressions were that Leyton Orient were a good side and seemed more professional than some of my previous clubs,' he says. The craggy Scot introduced himself the only way he knew how: with a goal. The *Walthamstow Guardian* enthused 'Tom Johnston had to wait barely 24 hours to prove that he can play a large part in Orient's promotion bid. In the first 20 minutes at Swindon he got a goal and made one and generally looked like solving one of Orient's problems – making their goals-for column look as prosperous as their great defensive record.'

Orient won the game 2–1, one of nine victories in Tommy's first 10 games. This, clearly, was no coincidence. Tommy was happy, not least because Orient's manager at the time, Les Gore, was allowing him to play as an attacking centre-forward, rather than employing the Revie system the striker so despised. 'Les Gore was a good acting manager,' he says. 'He was a real gentleman who got the best out of his players. He should have got the job permanently.' Unfortunately for Tommy, it was not to last. In April of that season Alec Stock returned as manager of Orient after just 53 days at Arsenal, claiming he had missed Brisbane Road too much. Scribbled into his tactics book was the Revie plan. 'He started telling me to play deeper and deeper,' Tommy says. 'I felt the Revie plan wasn't played correctly at Orient; that Alec Stock didn't get the message over properly. And the players didn't enjoy this sudden change. I was not happy about that and told him so. He threatened me and told me he could get someone else in to take my place who would play his style. I replied "Well, you just get them in and you find me another club"'. Thankfully for Orient fans Stock did no such thing, and that was the end of the matter.

On 26 April it was Tommy who scored the winning goal – whipping in behind the defence to crash home a looping header from Stan Aldous – in the 2–1 victory over Millwall that confirmed Orient's promotion to Division Two for the first time since 1929. Tommy, who ended the season with eight goals in his 15 appearances, was elated. 'I was delighted to have achieved promotion for

Tommy (far right) celebrates winning promotion from Division Three South after Orient beat Millwall on 26 April 1956.

Orient's Division Three South-winning side of 1956. Back row, left to right: Ken Facey, Harry Gregory, Pat Welton, Sid Bishop, Tommy Johnston. Front row: Phil White, Les Blizzard, Stan Aldous, Phil McKnight, Phil Woosnam, Johnny Hartburn.

Tommy in an aerial clash against Fulham on 8 December 1956.

ourselves and the fans,' he says. 'It meant they would be seeing a better class of football the next season.'

But 1956–57 started badly for Orient, with three losses and a draw in their first four games and Tommy yet to register a goal. He made up for it in style in the fifth game of the season against Bury at Brisbane Road. Orient were 3–1 down with 15 minutes to go until goals from Johnny Hartburn and Stan Willemse brought the sides level. In the dying seconds Hartburn floated over a corner. The *Walthamstow Guardian* reported what happened next: 'Johnston came in like a ton of bricks to belt it into the net. It was a wonderful finish.' Orient won the game 4–3.

In September Tommy was involved in an incident that nearly sparked a riot at Brisbane Road, when he clashed with Doncaster Rovers centre-half Charlie Williams in the 60th minute as a free kick was struck into the Doncaster area. The *Walthamstow Guardian* reported: 'As the ball soared towards them Williams appeared to move forward and his elbow struck Johnston. I'll swear the Leyton leader did not move a muscle. Yet as the Orient forward's arms went up in appeal the referee came in running and pointing. I was aghast when Johnston got his marching orders. Orient men ran from all over the pitch to plead in vain against what seemed a fantastic decision. As Johnston walked off disconsolately towards the dressing room, the crowd rose to cheer his every step from the pitch.'

After the game, the crowd also ensured that the Doncaster team needed a 20-strong police escort to get them to their coach and that referee Mr J. Baradell was snuck out of a side door to prevent further trouble. Tommy was not one to forgive and forget, as teammate Sid Bishop explains. 'He was no mug. If anyone started handing it out to him he'd get some back a bit quickish. And when we went up to play Doncaster Rovers again that season, it was actually Williams that got sent off. I'd loved to have seen Tommy's face when he did, because Tommy had got his own back on him.'

While Orient struggled to make much of an impact on Division Two that season – they eventually finished in 15th position with 40 points – Tommy was still regularly finding the back of the net, and scored 27 goals in his 43 games. On 6 December 1956 Jean gave birth to the couple's second child, a girl they named Alison and, as if to show the new arrival exactly what daddy did for a living, Tommy scored four goals in his next three games.

Many of Tommy's goals that season – and throughout his entire time at Orient – were provided by Phil White. Fan Dick Richards remembers how important the diminutive right-winger was in creating chances for the big striker. 'You can't talk about Tommy Johnston without talking about Phil White,' he says. 'He made so many of his goals. Phil would get the ball on the wing – he wouldn't mess about with it – and he'd look up into the penalty area. Then you'd see Tommy's arm go up – with his big white bandage – and it was like a signal for Phil. And then the ball would come over, and it would always be within a foot of Tommy.'

Phil Woosnam, too, was also a great provider. 'Phil was a superb player,' says fan Mickey Kasler. 'He'd make time for himself, look up and pick a pass out. He was a schemer and he was skilful on the ball.' Tommy himself speaks highly of his two partners in crime. 'I had a great understanding with Phil White and Phil Woosnam,' he says. 'We could play blindfolded.'

The 1957–58 season began with the departure of Alec Stock, who left to take a job managing Roma in Italy. Possibly not coincidentally, it turned out to be Tommy's defining season at Leyton Orient, during which he scored an incredible 36 goals in 32 games before being transferred to Blackburn Rovers in March. He scored two in the first game of the season against Grimsby at Blundell Park before netting nine times in five matches during September. He scored a hat-trick against Swansea in

Orient in the 1956–57 season. Back row, left to right: Stan Willemse, Harry Gregory, Ken Facey, Dave Groombridge, Alex Forbes, Jimmy Smith. Front row: Phil White, Dave Sexton, Stan Aldous, Tommy Johnston, Ronnie Heckman.

Tommy is just beaten to the ball by Doncaster Rovers goalkeeper Harry Gregg in 1957.

October and then went on a quite phenomenal scoring run: in the nine League games between 23 November and 11 January, he netted 18 times. During that spell, he scored a hat-trick in a 5–1 victory over Grimsby at Brisbane Road on 21 December, after which the *Walthamstow Guardian* reported: 'You can't talk about Orient's win – or even talk about Orient at all – without somehow getting back to this man Johnston – the craggy Scot who finds it easier to score great goals than to talk about them; the soft-spoken leader who hits the ball as though he loathes leather and is always, in everything, the complete master of his trade. This time Johnston hit three superb goals, made another and from first whistle to last made Grimsby centre-half Roy Player wish he had caught a trawler headed north instead of a train south.'

Humbly, Tommy puts his incredible goalscoring feats that season down in large part to his fellow players. 'We played as a team,' he explains. 'There were no prima donnas. Everyone worked together, and it was most enjoyable.'

Even in those days of high-scoring games, Tommy's goal-getting exploits were creating a stir, and there were repeated calls in the press for his inclusion in the Scotland squad. Selectors had watched the centre-forward in two games that season: the one against Grimsby when he had scored a hat-trick and a match against Bristol City in January, in which he also netted three times. What more could he do? That year the Manchester United manager Matt Busby had been appointed temporary boss of the Scottish national team and Tommy says 'I knew for a fact that he liked the way I played and was looking for something different up front.'

Tragically, Busby was seriously injured in the Munich air crash just a month later in February 1958, and the Scottish committee decided not to replace him as manager, instead relying on trainer Dawson Walker to take them to the World Cup Finals in Sweden. Players from the Scottish League made up the majority of the squad, and the few that did come from English clubs certainly were not playing for anyone as deeply unfashionable as Leyton Orient, who were to football what the emerging

Cliff Richard was to rock and roll. Tommy's chance had gone. 'I still think that if Busby had been in charge for the World Cup tournament in Sweden he would have chosen me at centre-forward,' he says. 'But it never happened, and perhaps it was never meant to be.'

As well as dreaming of playing for his country, Tommy also wanted a shot at playing in Division One. He was, by now, 30 years old and he realised it could be his final opportunity. 'I was happy at Leyton Orient and had no thoughts of leaving,' he says. 'But it was my last chance to play in the higher grade, and I wasn't going to achieve this with Orient.' When, in February 1958, Tommy heard word that former manager Alec Stock was to return to the club from his stint in Italy, he realised it was time to leave and put in a transfer request. He believed that Stock was using the club, always leaving for better jobs then returning when things weren't working out, and he didn't enjoy playing under him. 'Day to day I got on perfectly well with Alec Stock,' he says. 'I went for a drink with him occasionally and attended a few games with him. But his idea of playing the game was different to mine and I wasn't going to change the way I played at 30 years of age. And besides, I didn't like the way he spoke to the players.'

Certainly Tommy's form had alerted the clubs in the top tier, and that month, when Orient played a friendly against Bradford City, there were representatives from Spurs, West Bromwich Albion and Sunderland in attendance. Most keen were Blackburn Rovers who, under the stewardship of soon-to-be Orient manager Johnny Carey, were riding high in Division Two. The club had bid £10,000 for Tommy in December 1957 but were turned down. But on 7 March 1958, with an improved offer of £15,000 and Tommy ready to leave, they were finally able to secure their target. 'I was excited,' says Tommy. 'It had been an ambition of mine for a long time to play in Division One, and I thought Blackburn had an excellent chance of promotion.' He was right. Tommy played in Blackburn's remaining 11 games of the season, scoring eight times, and helped the club to second spot in the League and promotion to Division One. Finally the burly Scot had his

Orient manager Alec Stock, with whom Tommy had a difficult relationship.

chance to play at the highest level. He was no slouch either, and he scored five goals in his first three games of the 1958–59 season.

At the end of January 1958, having scored a hardly unimpressive total of 15 goals in 27 appearances, Tommy was dropped by new manager Dally Duncan who, he says, was trying to fill the side with youngsters. Tommy realised it was time to move on again, and his first call was to his old friend Les Gore. 'On reflection, I made a very big mistake in moving away from Orient to Blackburn,' he says. 'The way I was going I could have easily got very close to or even broken the long-standing record held by Dixie Dean of 60 League goals in a season.'

Orient were happy to have their talismanic striker back. Or at least some people were. Tommy claims that Alec Stock was against re-signing him but was overruled by chairman Harry Zussman, who paid Blackburn £7,500 to secure his services. This, says Tommy, is what prompted Stock's resignation in February 1959. But with Les Gore taking the reins once again, Tommy was happy to be back to the club where he'd had so much success. 'I was pleased to be going "home" and playing with the old team,' he says. 'The whole atmosphere of the club was totally different than at Blackburn. The climate there didn't suit me at all. I always seemed to have coughs and colds. I missed Leyton Orient terribly.'

Tommy was rejoining a team deep in relegation trouble. Having accrued just 19 points from 28 matches, Orient were a hair's breadth away from the drop zone. Initially Tommy struggled to make an impact, failing to score in his first three games as Orient crashed to defeats against Fulham and Liverpool and failed to beat fellow relegation candidates Lincoln. But then the creaking limbs of veteran trio Tommy, Eddie Baily and Eddie Brown – with a combined age of 93 – began to work the old magic and, with seven wins in their last 11 games, Orient ensured they would be playing Second Division football again the following season.

Tommy scored 10 goals in his 14 games for Orient that season, including the header in the 1–0 victory against Bristol City at Ashton Gate that ensured safety. Teammate Stan Charlton recalls the high spirits as the players travelled back to London on the train: 'Harry Zussman had said we could have whatever we wanted to drink. Tommy was sitting next to Ken Facey, and I was sitting next to Eddie Baily. Ken suddenly said to Eddie "I reckon that Tom can drink more than Stan." And Eddie replied "No, I think Stan can drink more than Tommy." So Tommy and I tried to outdo each other, drinking more and more. At that time Tommy and Jean were still living up north so that night he was staying in a hotel in Whipps Cross and I dropped him off there in a cab. But by then it was so late that they'd let his room out to someone else. Next day he came in to training and said to me "What do you reckon, Stan – they kicked me out of my bed!"'

Such problems were solved when Tommy and Jean moved to a club house in Buckhurst Hill in the summer of 1959. Tommy turned 32 as the new season began and, with 33-year-old Eddie Brown and 34-year-old Eddie Baily alongside him, fans were concerned that Orient's forward line was more of a worry to the queue for bus passes than it was to opposition defences. Tommy answered in the only way he knew how, with goals: nine in his first eight games of the season. But there was no use denying that by now Tommy's powers were beginning to fade a little. 'The skill was still there,' he says. 'I wasn't waning, but I was slowing down a bit. A knee injury was causing me a good few problems.' Yet still the goals came, and there were some great moments for Tommy during the season. In November he bagged his 200th League goal in a pulsating 4–3 loss to Liverpool at Anfield. At the same ground in January, in an FA Cup tie, Tommy's sparkling performance even had Liverpool fans showing their approval. Tommy ended the season with 25 goals in his 40 games, and Orient finished in a respectable, if unexciting, 10th place in Division Two.

During the summers Tommy would often take a part-time job to boost his income. 'One of the local builders got close-season jobs for the players,' he explains. 'We swept the terracing steps, tidied around the grounds, concreted new steps…Any jobs that needed doing, we did them.' Teammate Sid Bishop remembers doing some work on a construction site with Tommy. 'We were doing some ground preparation, and the first job was to dig out a 4ft trench, about 2ft wide and 30ft long,' he says. 'My trench was all jagged, with bricks and lumps in it, but Tommy's was all lovely and smooth. I said to him "I know mine doesn't look right, Tom, but I think it'll blend in better than having straight sides." He said to me "If you say so." I said "Well, you did used to be a bleedin' miner." I still don't know how he got his sides so straight. He went along like a worm – his trench was spotless.'

The 1960–61 season was to be Tommy's last. He began it the way he had so many other campaigns, scoring four goals in the first three games. But Orient began to struggle and by the beginning of October sat just one spot above the relegation zone. Though Tommy was still knocking in goals it was not with the same ruthless regularity of previous campaigns, and he was getting little help from those around him. 'What Orient really want is a new pair of legs for the craggy Scot, rather than new players,' wrote the *Walthamstow Guardian* at the time. 'He still has so much to show his colleagues about the game his presence has enriched for nearly 20 years.'

In March 1961 the writing was on the wall for Tommy in 6ft-high letters, as Orient brought in the experienced centre-forward Dave Dunmore from West Ham. He and Tommy actually played alongside each other for the remainder of the season, and it was Tommy who scored the goal in the 1–0 victory over his old club Norwich City that prevented Orient from dropping into the Third Division. It was his 17th of the season and the last he would ever score for the east London club.

In the summer of 1961 Orient appointed the ex-Blackburn Rovers and Everton manager Johnny Carey. It was Carey who had taken Tommy from Orient to Blackburn, but given that the striker was now 34 he told him that Dunmore would be the first-choice centre-forward that season. Carey asked Tommy if he would play in the reserves to help bring the younger players on. 'I was quite

Tommy with his wife Jean in December 2007.

happy to do so as I enjoyed coaching the younger players,' says Tommy. 'But only providing my wage remained the same. Carey refused to consider this and wanted me to take a £2 cut in salary. You don't do that when you are the leading goalscorer of the club. Carey told me that another club was interested in me, which sounded like an invitation to leave, so I signed for Gillingham.' So, on 20 September 1961 Tommy became a Gillingham player in Division Four. 'Leyton Orient was a great chapter in my life and as a player and as a man I was very sad it was all coming to a close,' he says. 'I expected to play out my days at Leyton Orient. I should have listened to my wife Jean – she didn't want to leave Essex.'

Tommy scored 10 goals in his 36 appearances for the Kent club that season, helping them avoid relegation, before signing up as a player-coach for Southern League side Folkestone Town in 1962. In May 1964 Tommy was told by the chairman that the club could no longer afford his wages. Now coming up to his 37th birthday, the Scot took it as his cue to retire from the game. Tommy and Jean moved to Poulton-le-Fylde near Blackpool and in November 1964 opened a betting shop called Tom Johnston Bookmakers. But there was to be one last hurrah on the football field when Tommy signed as a player-coach for the Lancashire Combination League side Lytham St Annes FC in October 1965, making approximately 10 appearances.

In January 1972 Tommy and Jean moved to Australia, where they thought there would be more opportunity for their children Neil and Alison. They settled in the small town of Dapto, near Wollongong in New South Wales. Tommy took a job as an inspector for a firm of electricians and also coached a local works' football team. At the age of 44 he played for the reserves, alongside his son Neil, and scored 15 goals. After suffering a neck injury at work in 1988, Tommy retired at the age of 61, and the couple moved to nearby Sanctuary Point. A year later, he and Jean returned to the UK for a holiday, and took the chance to return to Brisbane Road for the first time in 28 years.

In September 1991 Tommy was diagnosed with bowel cancer and had to undergo surgery. He had 19 inches of his bowel removed. He recovered well enough to continue playing the odd game of golf or lawn bowls, but in 2000, after further surgery, he had to accept that, at 73, his sporting days were over. In September 2004 Tommy underwent surgery to have a double heart bypass. Five weeks later he had an operation on his carotid artery. But, tough as ever, Tommy recovered well. He remains in good health today and enjoys spending time with his five grandchildren. His wife Jean says 'Tommy's only problem at the moment is his legs. He uses a stick and can't walk too far. He has short-term memory loss, which happens a lot to people of advancing years. But he has a good memory for anything to do with football, particularly his time with Orient.'

Looking back, Tommy has a special place in his heart for Brisbane Road. 'It was a club where everyone from the chairman down treated you with respect,' he says. 'There was a good manager in Les Gore, good teammates and great supporters.' And those supporters continue to hold their goalscoring hero in the highest regard. Tommy says that to this day he continues to receive many letters from fans requesting an autograph.

These days he signs every single one of them.

# Chapter 9
# KING KITCH
## Peter Kitchen 1977–79 and 1982–84

Peter after winning the *Evening Standard* Player of the Month award for January 1978.

*'Kitchen sinker!'*

*'On the boil! Kitchen whistles in to score Orient Cup stunner!'*

*'Chelsea dished by Kitchen!'*

Rarely in their history have Leyton Orient had a natural goalscorer with as tabloid-friendly a name as Peter Kitchen. In fact, rarely in their history have Leyton Orient had a natural goalscorer full stop, which is why the moustachioed Yorkshireman is held in such high regard by fans of the club. They are not likely to forget him in a hurry, since a bar and one of the apartment blocks at Brisbane Road are both named in his honour.

In the 1977–78 season Kitchen cooked up 29 goals – only eight less than the entire team had managed in the previous year's Division Two campaign – and helped take Orient to the brink of an FA Cup Final. For a few heady weeks the east London club were the talk of football, being referred to in words other than 'Who are they again?' or 'Haven't they gone bankrupt yet?' – and Peter Kitchen was at the vanguard, flashing past defences in that striking white-and-red-braced kit.

In his two spells at Orient, Peter scored 62 goals in 134 starts and five substitute appearances, including the two that famously knocked Chelsea out of the FA Cup. In his entire career – which also took in Doncaster, Fulham, Cardiff, Chester, Dagenham and Margate – he found the net 211 times in 520 starts and 26 substitute appearances. Goals were an addiction. 'I've never snorted cocaine but I can imagine that the reason people do it is because they want to get the same sort of high I got from scoring,' he says – not that he's advocating the use of recreational drugs, of course. He continues 'Whatever level you play at, scoring a goal is a sublime moment. You get a big kick out of it. And when you score in front of a lot of people and they're chanting your name, it's an amazing feeling. Right through my career, up until I was playing vets football at over 50 years of age, I loved scoring goals. I enjoyed making goals and being involved in the build-up when someone else scored, but I'd only ever feel happy after a game if I'd scored two or three goals myself. I felt that if I hadn't, then I wasn't doing my job effectively.'

And yet for all the goals, all the glory, all the adulation, Peter's career is touched by the sadness of unfulfilled ambition. He left Orient in February 1979 under a cloud, frustrated at being played out of position and at odds with manager Jimmy Bloomfield over tactics. Five years later, after another two seasons back at Brisbane Road, he was released, despite his belief that he had more to give. It was a decision, he says, that 'defied logic'. But perhaps Peter's biggest disappointment was that he never got the chance to play in Division One. He came close. Not with Orient, obviously, but at various times in his career there were offers from clubs such as Leeds, Spurs, Ipswich and Norwich. Circumstance, timing and luck conspired against him, as did the almost total lack of player power in those pre-Bosman, pre-agent days. 'I still believe now that I should have played at a higher level,' he says, poignantly.

Peter now lives in Ightham, near Sevenoaks in Kent, with his partner of seven years, Katherine, a beauty therapist, nutritionist and fitness instructor. He's the operations director of a company that runs leisure centres and a golf course in Kent. Softly spoken, his Yorkshire accent has been dulled by over 30 years away from the county he grew up in – 'I see myself as a naturalised southerner,' he declares. He can be quite philosophical when talking about both his own career and the wider issues of football. At one point he says 'I'm not religious or anything, but I think about Buddhist principles.' Not the sort of thing you'd expect from your average ex-player. He became cynical about the game once he retired and did not kick a ball for 18 months after hanging up his professional boots, but he still holds Orient very dear. And fans will be thrilled to hear the following: 'I've always got affections for Doncaster and Orient, but out of the two it's probably more Orient, even though I spent longer at Doncaster, because I have continued to live in the south and have always maintained contact with people involved at the club. I also try to attend a couple of matches each season. I love the club; I have such an affinity with it and so want the Os to do well.'

Peter was actually born Michael Peter Kitchen on 16 February 1952, although he has always been known by his middle name. He grew up in the small South Yorkshire town of Mexborough. His father, Harry, was a coal miner, while his mother, Dorothy, had ranging jobs, from working in a peanut factory to dinner lady and nursing assistant. Peter has an older sister and brother, Rita and Gordon, and a younger sister, Janice.

He describes his childhood as 'idyllic', playing for hours on end in the countryside surrounding his home. He spent a lot of time with his brother Gordon, who was four years older, playing football with him and his friends in a pair of old brown leather football boots with a strap across the front.

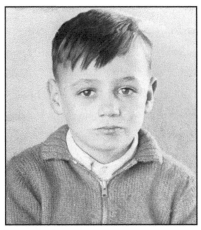

Peter aged six.

Peter says that mixing it with these older boys helped him develop his skills, and when he attended Roman Terrace Junior School having just turned seven, he found himself picked in the under-11 side. He held his own. 'I felt that I was a very good footballer even within that age group,' he says.

When Peter joined Mexborough Secondary Modern at the age of 11 he continued to bang in the goals, representing both the school and the district sides. As a teenager he had a brief flirtation with music when he formed a band with his friends and took lead vocal duties. And while in later life his haircut and moustache made him a dead ringer for a member of Eurovision Song Contest winners Brotherhood of Man, it quickly transpired that the world of rock was not for him. 'I couldn't sing to save my life,' he admits.

Peter achieved six O levels and five CSEs and went on to the sixth form college at Mexborough Grammar School. Playing for both the school's first XI – alongside Alan Sunderland, who later went on to play for Wolves, Arsenal and Ipswich – and the representative Yorkshire Grammar Schools side, Peter began to develop a reputation as a goalscorer.

At the age of 17 he represented the Northern Counties against the Southern Counties, played for the England Schools B team and began to turn out for the Doncaster Rovers youth team. It was with them, in June 1970, that he was taken to a week-long FA training course at Lilleshall in Shropshire. Many of the coaches and scouts present showed an interest in the young talent, prompting Doncaster manager Lawrie McMenemy to offer Peter a professional contract. 'I'd already been involved with Doncaster and, though I had other clubs asking about me, it was my only concrete offer,' he says. 'I'd just finished my A levels – I passed three – and I needed to start a career and earn money.'

In retrospect, Peter may have been a little rash in rushing to play for Doncaster, who were residing in Division Three at the time. The very same night that Peter put pen to paper on the contract, he received a visit from a Leeds United scout. This was during the Don Revie era, and the team – which included legends such as Billy Bremner, Norman Hunter and Johnny Giles – had won the First Division title in 1968–69 and finished second in 1969–70. Yet Peter says that at the time he was relatively unfazed by this just-missed opportunity – the first of many – to play for a top-tier club. 'It didn't really frustrate me because I was just happy that I was going to be a professional,' he says. 'I'd already signed for Doncaster when the scout arrived at my house, so it never got to the stage of finding out exactly what Leeds were going to offer me. I was young at the time and didn't have any long-term aims.'

So, Donny it was, and in the same summer he became a professional footballer, Peter married Susan, who he'd met a couple of years earlier at school. Peter spent seven seasons there, scoring 108 goals in 251 starts and seven substitute appearances for the club who, after relegation in 1971, were residing in Division Four. During that time he and Susan had two children, Michael and Darren. At the end of the 1976 season, Peter says he realised that he had to move on. 'I was 24 years old by then and no longer the up-and-coming youngster. I thought that if I was going to get anywhere and play a higher grade of football I needed to get a transfer.' He put in a transfer request but found that Doncaster were as determined to keep him as he was to leave, and he turned down offers from a number of clubs, including Southend, Huddersfield, Mansfield and, auspiciously, Orient. Peter ended up playing the entire 1976–77 season, and scored 27 goals in 49 appearances.

In May 1977 Peter went on a month's trial with Ipswich who, under Bobby Robson, had just finished third in Division One. Peter recalls 'At the end of it Bobby called me in and said that I'd impressed them and that they were interested in signing me. But in the end they couldn't agree a fee with Doncaster. Ipswich wanted to pay around £25,000 but it wasn't enough.' Another stab at Division One had passed Peter by. 'It was frustrating, but I didn't feel that I had any choice in the matter,' he says. 'In those days the power was with the clubs.' But all was not lost because waiting in the wings were Orient. Strangely, tales of this beautiful oasis of football in Leyton had not quite reached Doncaster. 'I didn't know anything about the club,' Peter admits. 'I'd only been to London two or three times on school trips. In fact, I had said to myself that I would be happy to move anywhere but London. I suppose I was very parochial. I had a perception of what London was like: a big city, very impersonal, smoggy and full of traffic.'

But Peter was so desperate to leave Doncaster that he was willing to give anything a go, and agreed to travel to the capital to meet Orient chairman Brian Winston and manager George Petchey. They made their way through the smog and traffic to Brisbane Road, where Winston and Petchey intended to woo their potential new striker with their swanky stadium. It backfired. 'I must admit I was disappointed with the ground,' Peter confesses. 'There was no grass on the pitch at the time, as it was being resurfaced, so it was just a muddy field. George Petchey said to me "What do you think, then?" and before I could answer Brian Winston said "By the look on his face, not very much."' But if the pitch did not impress Peter – and he points out that, once re-laid, it was a good surface – the people did. 'I couldn't have been made more welcome. It seemed like a fantastic, homely club.'

Although still yearning for a move to a Division One club, Peter came to the conclusion that Orient was the right move for him. 'I had to go for it and see what happened. It was an opportunity to play two divisions higher up, and I saw it as a stepping stone, a chance to prove myself. And I thought that if I couldn't settle in London I could always go back. It was very much a leap in the dark.'

Peter agreed to join the club on a two-year deal, but on returning to Doncaster to await the official written contract from Orient, he discovered that another club had made a firm offer for him: Keith Burkinshaw's Tottenham side, featuring the likes of Glenn Hoddle and Gerry Armstrong. Not yet having put pen to paper on his Orient deal, Peter could have gone to White Hart Lane. And while Spurs had actually been relegated the previous season and were hence plying their trade in Division Two alongside Orient, clearly the north London club would have afforded Peter a better opportunity to reach the very top. But Peter chose to honour his word to Brian Winston, which, in today's footballing climate, is frankly bonkers. 'I suppose I've got an old-fashioned view of integrity,' Peter laughs. 'Those were the values I got from my upbringing. My parents didn't stop me from doing much – they were very liberal in many ways – but there were basic guidelines of behaviour, such as being honest, not swearing in front of women, avoiding trouble with the police and keeping your word. If only these values were instilled today!'

Surely he must have been tempted? There's a long delay before Peter responds 'To be honest, I wasn't really. I just put it out of my mind. I just said to myself that I'd given my word, we'd shaken on it so that was it. It's really strange. I can't understand why I did it. When I think back, it's ludicrous. It wouldn't happen today and if it did I would probably just say "Sorry, I can't sign for you, I've had another offer." But at that time, although I was gutted about the timing, I wasn't tempted to do that.' Peter admits to occasionally wondering what might have been had he done the dirty on Orient and signed for Spurs. But this is where the Buddhist principles come in. 'There's no point in worrying about something if you can't do anything about it,' he says. 'You just have to get on with things and deal with what you've got.'

Anyway, Peter soon found that things were not so bad on the east side of London, and he speaks warmly and enthusiastically about the friendliness of the club he joined. 'It's an unpretentious club and it didn't have delusions of grandeur. I turned up at the stadium and the groundsman Charlie Hasler came up to me and welcomed me to the Orient. It struck me that all the people who were involved with the club were supporters as well. Brian Winston gave me a bottle of whisky and a silk scarf for my wife, and the director Harry Zussman gave me a big, fat Havana cigar. From then on, whenever I scored two goals he'd come into the dressing room and give me one of these cigars, which I'm sure he must have had flown in from Cuba. I didn't smoke, so I'd give them to my dad.' He was also quickly impressed with his new teammates. 'There were some really good players around me but there were no egos – nobody thought they were better than anyone else,' he says. 'It was probably the perfect team environment for me to come into.'

Clearly everything had fallen into place for Peter at the right time, and that season turned out to be his best ever as he scored 29 goals in 56 appearances. Attempting to explain where it all went right, Peter says 'For one thing I think that if I was ever determined to do something in my life, it was

Peter with sons Michael and Darren in 1978.

then. I was determined to score goals and show that I could play at that level. I had an instinct that it was going to be right. I felt confident in my ability. And I suppose that there were no big expectations. I'd arrived from Division Four so I don't think anyone expected me to have such an impact. If I'd scored 15 goals everyone would probably have thought I'd done pretty well. Also, I enjoyed living near London and settled quickly into the Epping area, which I really liked. There were no pressures or problems such as being homesick, and all the factors were right.'

He also points to his partnership with Joe Mayo as significant. 'We were a great combination. We clicked straight away, and complemented each other in our styles of play and our attitudes. He was an honest, hard-working player and the sort of genuine person I warm to.'

Peter made his debut against Fulham in the League Cup on 13 August 1977 and, unsurprisingly, marked his arrival with a goal. 'It wasn't a classic,' he laughs. A couple of weeks and two League defeats later, Peter found out that manager George Petchey had been given the boot. Replacing him was Jimmy Bloomfield, returning to Orient after six years in charge of First Division Leicester. And, according to Peter, he wasn't shy of letting the players know where he truly believed his managerial skills lay. 'He told us that he was a Division One manager and that's where he expected to be. He breezed in wearing a three-piece pin stripe suit and was so arrogant. I reckon he thought that coming to Orient was a good move for him because he was at the stage of his career where he wanted to move back near his family in north London. But I don't think he was the right personality for Orient at the time.'

Peter quickly found that he was at odds with the way Jimmy wanted the team to play football. 'With Jimmy it was all about stopping the other team,' he explains. 'He'd tell me and Joe that we had to spend our time trying to stop their full-backs bombing forward. I'd say "What if I'm trying to get on the end of a flick-on?" and he'd tell me that if I wasn't going to get there then hold back. It didn't seem right. Scoring goals is all about getting in the box, anticipation, gambling on a knock-down, taking the chance that you're going to get a flick-on or a loose ball. I tried to do what Jimmy said, but found that every time we got the ball I was in our own half, facing our goal. I'd have to chase back up and felt like I was running around like a headless chicken. I agree that we had to have some defensive duties for the team and close down the opposing defenders, but it shouldn't have been the most important part of our game.'

In the second match under Bloomfield, Orient lost 3–1 to Derby in the League Cup, a game at which a number of Peter's former Doncaster teammates were in attendance. 'They told me that I wasn't playing my own game at all,' Peter recalls. 'It made me stop and think. They were right. I was just chasing shadows. So I made the decision that from that point on I wouldn't chase back all the time. I literally ignored what Jimmy was saying to me.' His blatant disobedience would have landed him in hot water, save for the fact that in his next game – a 5–3 victory over Oldham Athletic – Peter scored two goals. 'I started to get my confidence back,' he says. 'And if I was scoring, Jimmy couldn't criticise me.'

By Christmas Peter had clocked up 13 goals, including a hat-trick in a 4–2 win over Mansfield Town. He was enjoying his time off the pitch, too. 'I got on very well with a lot of the players,' he says. 'After training we'd go to the Atlantis Fish Bar on Leyton High Road, and I'd have rock and chips with one of those great big gherkins. I'd never had rock eel before I'd come down to London – I was only

Peter scores the second of his two goals against Chelsea in the fifth-round FA Cup tie at Stamford Bridge on 27 February 1978.

used to the cod and chips we got up north. I'd also go to the Oliver Twist pub on Oliver Road with Derek Clarke, who I often shared lifts with as he lived nearby.'

It was after Christmas – and at the beginning of Orient's famous FA Cup run – that Peter really began to fly. He scored in both the 1–1 draw and the 1–0 replay victory over First Division Norwich in the third round, then bagged two goals in the 3–1 trouncing of Blackburn in the fourth. That brought Chelsea, and after a hard-fought 0–0 draw at Brisbane Road the Os faced an

Manager Jimmy Bloomfield presents Peter with the *Daily Mirror* Player of the Month award for March 1978.

intimidating trip to Stamford Bridge where, naturally, they were expected to be spanked. After going 1–0 down, two goals from Peter enabled the east London club to secure one of its most famous victories ever. It is a day Peter describes as 'one of the finest moments in my footballing career'.

In common with all Orient fans of that era, Peter remembers well his famous opening goal, in which he appeared to weave around the entire Chelsea defence. 'I picked the ball up on the right-hand side of the goal and went on a mazy dribble. It was a totally instinctive goal – I just dropped my shoulder as opponents came towards me. As I was straightening up to shoot with my right foot, I saw Ian Britton coming across and flicked it to the left-hand side. It was only then that I got my head up and hit it with my left foot, low to the left of Peter Bonetti.'

Peter, by now, was national news. His distinctive moustache and flowing mane no doubt helped, as did the fact that, on occasion, he did interviews dressed up as a pearly king. He won the *Evening Standard* and *Daily Mirror* Player of the Month awards in January and March respectively and enjoyed the attention – up to a point. 'I'd have to say that I liked it, but at times I found it a little embarrassing,' he says. 'I almost got too much attention, and it took some of the prestige away from the rest of the team, who were doing their jobs as well. Football is a team game.'

The sixth round brought a trip to First Division Middlesbrough and, after a 0–0 draw at Ayresome Park, the Os recorded a highly impressive 2–1 victory at Brisbane Road. Joe Mayo got one goal. No prizes for guessing who got the other. It's a goal Peter describes as his greatest moment in an Orient shirt. 'It wasn't typical of the goals I tended to score. Phil Hoadley played it to my feet, just outside the box on the right-hand side of the goal. As it came to me I sort of flicked it up and half-volleyed it. It was totally instinctive. I saw it sailing under the bar. After that, the last 15 minutes of the game were like the siege of the Alamo. But we held out and got through to the semi-final.'

Peter describes that semi-final against Arsenal – which Orient lost 3–0 – as a huge disappointment. 'I think we all became very nervous. We realised we were one game away from Wembley. From my own point of view I was very tightly marked, and I didn't have enough of the ball. John Chiedoze wasn't playing – we didn't have any width and we weren't creating many chances. When they scored, it deflated us and it was very difficult to come back, especially because of the nature of their first two goals in the opening 20 minutes – both own-goals but claimed by Malcolm Macdonald.'

Worse still, once the Cup run was over, Peter and his teammates had to face the reality of a relegation battle. Just three League wins since the start of the year had left the team needing to beat Cardiff City on the final day of the season to avoid the drop to Division Three. It was Peter who saved them, scoring in the 1–0 win that preserved their Division Two status. 'It was a toe-poke from a few yards out,' he says. Peter believes it should never have come to that and that Orient, given the

Peter scores one of his three goals against Sheffield United on 27 March 1978.

squad at their disposal that season, should have been pushing for promotion, not slumming it in the relegation zone. It is something that clearly rankles with Peter, and he lays the blame at the feet of Jimmy Bloomfield. 'With a different mindset we could have achieved much more,' he explains. 'His cautious approach of stopping other teams playing meant we drew a lot of games we should have won. I think he put negativity into our game and the approach was a reflection of his own attitude. He was approaching middle age, and he'd probably achieved everything he expected to achieve in football as he'd been at a top club in Leicester City. I believe that he didn't have the ambition or the drive.'

The publicity Peter had garnered during the FA Cup run meant that other clubs were soon enquiring after the moustachioed striker with long hair. During that 1977–78 season, Second Division Crystal Palace offered £100,000 plus Neil Smillie for Peter's services and First Division Norwich put £140,000 on the table. Both offers were refused. 'I could see the same thing happening as when I was at Doncaster,' says Peter. 'I was being priced out of the market. I knew that after having such a fantastic season that this was the time I had to move on to Division One. I was desperate to do so. But I knew that if I kept on scoring goals for Orient then Jimmy couldn't keep turning down offers.'

He kicked off the 1978–79 season with a goal against Sheffield United, but then both Peter and the team went through a terrible slump. Throughout September, Orient failed to score, let alone win a game. At the beginning of October, Bloomfield brought in striker Ian Moores from Tottenham Hotspur. Peter was not impressed. 'Jimmy tried to find a way to accommodate him, Joe and myself into the team. He played those two as the target men and me in behind them. I was playing more like an attacking midfielder and I never felt that I could be effective there.'

That was the final straw. 'I just felt that I was never going to achieve what I had the previous season,' says Peter. 'I felt that I wanted to get away even more so and I was very unhappy. In the summer the club had also sold Glen Roeder to QPR and Phil Hoadley to Norwich, which identified to me that there was no real ambition at the club, and I could see that we were only going to be fighting relegation yet again.' In November Peter told as much to the reporters he had become friendly with during the FA Cup run and, when the story ran, he was fined £50 by the club. 'It was a bit of naïvety,' he says. 'What I didn't realise was that the press will take your comments out of context and make them into a story.'

Still, he stood by the sentiments he aired and put in a transfer request. The whole thing culminated in a huge row with Bloomfield in January. 'I ended up losing my temper,' Peter admits. 'It was out of character for me – I'm not a particularly aggressive person. I'd gone in to tell him that I didn't think I was playing in the right position to be effective for myself or for the team. I said that I wanted to leave and asked why he wouldn't accept an offer for me. He said that there hadn't been any. But I knew that this was untrue – Terry Venables, the Crystal Palace manager at the time, had told me himself that they'd put in a bid. I lost my temper and said to Jimmy "You're a ****ing liar." And he told me that I couldn't speak to him like that. I replied "I'll speak to you any way I want to. I don't want to ****ing play for you."'

Peter is slightly embarrassed by the recollection and admits 'I wouldn't normally swear at people. Once I left the club I actually arranged to go back and see him to apologise for my behaviour because I thought it was inappropriate. But I'd got to the stage where I was so fed up that the situation had been allowed to carry on. It was a terrible situation to get in.'

Peter signs for Fulham in February 1979, with manager Bobby Campbell.

It was February 1979 – by which time Peter had scored nine goals in 29 starts and one substitute appearance – before a move finally came about. Fulham – also in Division Two – made an offer of £150,000 plus the 19-year-old striker Mark Gray. Orient were willing to accept the offer and Peter was happy to go. Looking back, he says the move was a big mistake. 'I went for the wrong reasons. I moved too quickly and I was tempted by the money offered. I received a signing-on fee of £20,000 plus a new Toyota Celica, and I was given a basic salary of £275 a week rising to £325 in the third year. But my relationship with Jimmy had become so bad and I was so desperate to get away that I didn't look at it objectively. I was inexperienced and did not have anyone to help or advise me, so I jumped from one situation into another.'

What then, with the benefit of hindsight, does Peter think he should have done? 'I should have played the season out with Orient,' he replies. 'If I'd have done that I would have been out of contract and, wherever I moved, the transfer fee would have been sorted out by a tribunal. I think I would have got a better move.' A move to Division One, perhaps? 'Probably,' Peter replies. 'Orient may have been a struggling Division One side, but I might have got the opportunity. It's hypothetical, but it was probably my last chance to get a move to the top tier.'

It is another moment of missed opportunity and frustrated ambition in Peter's career. Perhaps it was the defining one, for at 27 years old he was hitting what should have been his peak as a striker. Sadly, he was never given the chance to show it at Fulham. 'The manager Bobby Campbell was a great talker and he sold me the club,' Peter says. 'But after three weeks of being there I thought to myself, what have I done? He was the wrong type of manager for me – he was a coach, not a man-manager, and at times he verbally abused players because, in my opinion, he had no control of his behaviour or his emotions.'

Peter played 17 games and scored five goals in the remainder of the 1978–79 season, but at the start of the next season was injured in a pre-season friendly and lost his place to Gordon Davies. In the 1979–80 season he made just four starts and three substitute appearances, despite scoring over

30 goals in the reserves, and had become *persona non grata* at Craven Cottage. Understandably, Peter says that this was the lowest point in his football career. It coincided with problems in his marriage, and in 1980 he separated from his wife Susan – they eventually divorced in 1982 – and moved into a flat in Enfield. 'Separating from my children was the hardest decision I ever had to make in my life,' he says. 'It was a difficult time. I'd started to become disillusioned with football and begun to doubt my own ability. I felt that my dream of playing First Division football was slipping away.'

At the end of the 1979–80 season he was given the chance for a fresh start when, after rejecting overtures from Rotherham and Sheffield United – both Third Division sides – he accepted a £120,000 move to Cardiff City, then a Second Division team under the management of Richie Morgan. 'I thought that they might be a more ambitious club who had the potential of getting into Europe through the Welsh Cup,' says Peter. 'But within three or four months of arriving I realised that they were a team going nowhere. It was a backwater in terms of football.' And so, despite the fact that on a personal level Peter's first season was pretty successful – he scored 19 goals in 45 starts and one substitute appearance – he asked to be transfer-listed at the start of the 1981–82 season so he could move back to the London area. Although there were offers, nothing materialised, and Peter ended up staying for the whole of that campaign, in and out of the side, eventually making 29 starts and two substitute appearances and scoring 11 goals. One of the failed offers came from Orient, who put £60,000 on the table to bring their one-time star back to Brisbane Road. 'I would have gone back then, but the money they were offering was half of what Cardiff wanted,' says Peter.

Peter arriving at Hong Kong airport in the summer of 1982.

Peter still had an affinity for the Orient and the East, though going to Hong Kong was perhaps taking things a bit literally. But in what was a somewhat strange move for a 30-year-old footballer, that is where Peter ended up at the start of the 1982–83 season. He had offers from Third Division Doncaster and Fourth Division Scunthorpe, Hereford and Hull, plus a chance to go to Dutch club Sparta Rotterdam on trial. He rejected them all in favour of a move to a club called Happy Valley. 'I didn't know anything about Hong Kong football but the money was good,' Peter admits. 'I'd split up from my wife and had a girlfriend, Sharon, who was a totally different personality and was very much into travelling. I suppose that was an influence. I also had to support two families, so the money I was offered became more of a factor. I also thought it would be an interesting opportunity. I had no idea what it would be like living in Hong Kong, but I thought that maybe it would be somewhere I could make a new career, perhaps coaching or whatever. So I went with an open mind.'

Unfortunately it was less Happy Valley, more Depressing Canyon. Despite enjoying the lifestyle, Peter found himself homesick, missing his sons Michael and Darren. He says the standard of football was not good, and he found that the Happy Valley coach was – you've guessed it – obsessed with stopping the other team from playing. In November, after just a handful of games, Peter elected to call his boss '****ing useless' in a moment of frustration. Evidently the manager did not require the use of an interpreter on this occasion, and Peter quickly found his contract terminated. In December 1982 he returned to England.

Peter was now on the market again. He says 'I realised now that I was a journeyman footballer and had given up hope of playing at the top.' It seems a sad, poignant admission, but by that stage Peter was happy to get to play in England, especially since he ended up re-signing for Orient. He asked the club – now residing in Division Three – if he could train with them to get match fit while awaiting his international clearance and was then offered an 18-month contract by manager Ken Knighton. 'I loved the club, and it was an ideal opportunity,' says Peter. 'I had bought a house back in Epping with Sharon while I was at Cardiff and rented it out when I was in Hong Kong, so it was good to be able to move in. It was déjà vu, but I felt happier than I had been for a long time.'

Even though he had been away only three and a half years, Peter noticed that things at the club had changed. 'It had lost its drive and direction,' he says. 'Harry Zussman had died and Brian Winston was leaving the club that season. Neville Ovenden took over as chairman, and although he was a nice guy he didn't have the same ambition for the club as Brian. I'm sure that this became a factor in me eventually leaving the club the following season.'

There is no denying that these were catastrophic times for the club, both financially and on the pitch, and Frank Clark, at that point assistant to Ken Knighton, recognises that this made things difficult for the returning striker. 'It was an unusual situation because Peter had been a great hero at Orient,' Frank says. 'There's always a danger that fans look for something that isn't there any more

Peter scores against Bournemouth on 28 December 1982.

or think that a player is better than he really is. We were struggling as a team and the club was in dire straits financially. It was just a case of survival, not of winning football matches. So it was hard for Peter to come into a fairly ordinary team, but he was OK and he did alright for us. He was experienced, a good professional and a great example to the younger players.'

Peter says that despite the troubles, the friendly atmosphere and lack of egos that characterised his previous stint at the club still persisted among the squad. 'There were a few different faces but I think I got on with everyone well. And there were some good players there, such as Bill Roffey, Kevin Godfrey, Shaun Brooks, John Cornwell, Barry Silkman and Mark McNeill.' Up front was Keith Houchen, and although the Middlesbrough-born forward went on to make a name for himself with Coventry City, scoring in the 1987 FA Cup Final, he was not to Peter's liking as a strike partner. 'He wasn't a bad player, but I didn't rate him as highly as others I had played with. Physically he looked the part – he was tall and slim – and he held the ball up well, but he had little awareness of what was going on around him and could be greedy at times.'

On 17 December 1982 Peter ran out at Brisbane Road once again in a match against Preston North End. News of his potential appearance had obviously spread like wildfire through east London, for a whopping 1,668 spectators turned up to see him. 'Maybe no one had told the fans I had returned,' Peter says, wryly, and adds 'You'd have thought that there would be more interest in me coming back after having such a great time in my first spell. It was almost surreal. But it was an appalling winter's night, raining and windy. Despite all that, it was great to be back at Brisbane Road. It's always a lovely pitch to play on, and there's something about it that made me feel like I was back home.' And Peter picked up where he left off, scoring the winner in a 2–1 victory. 'Someone ran on the pitch and shook my hand,' he laughs. 'I thought it was really nice that he'd done that.'

The win lifted troubled Orient out of the relegation zone and was one of six in the next seven games. 'I'm not being arrogant but I think my return helped to keep Orient in the division that season,' Peter says. 'There were a lot of good players in the team but they had no confidence. Before signing, I'd watched them get thrashed 5–1 at home by Oxford United. Having someone come in who could score goals helped to bring the team together.'

Peter says that although he was obviously a few years older than during his first spell at Orient, his form was good. 'I wasn't as good as before because I was losing a bit of pace. I was unable to do as much off the ball and relied more on the service I was getting, but I still think I was playing well and I think I had a good return of goals per game.'

Peter scored nine in 20 appearances that season, including one against Sheffield United on the final day that helped Orient to the 4–1 victory that enabled them to avoid the drop to Division

Peter takes on Preston's Dave Jones at Deepdale on 14 April 1984.

Four. Manager Ken Knighton, however, paid the price for the generally poor performances. 'Ken didn't really make much of an impression on me in terms of his coaching or his personality,' says Peter, simply. Knighton's assistant, Frank Clark, took over as manager, and Orient began to enjoy slightly better results in the 1983–84 season. But Peter is ambivalent about the Clark effect. 'I wouldn't say I had a relationship with Frank, good or bad. He wasn't someone who was very outspoken. I got the feeling he didn't like any stars in his team, players who were overly popular with the fans. He didn't like anyone who got above their station.'

Peter made a handful of appearances at the start of the campaign, scoring a goal against Aldershot in the League Cup after coming on as a substitute, but was left out of the team by Clark for a long spell during October and November. In his absence Orient coped well, losing only two of 10 games and allowing fans to set themselves up for disappointment by entertaining the notion of promotion. Peter, as was his habit, reintroduced himself to the side with three goals in four games. He felt things were going well again. Then, in an away game against Brentford in March, Peter was brought off at half-time, despite scoring a goal. Peter thinks this was bizarre, and he has a theory – pure speculation, granted – as to why. 'There was no reason for me to be taken off. As a player you know when you're playing well and not playing well. I got the feeling it was because I was getting too close to the number of goals I had to score to get a bonus.'

In April Clark called the striker into his office. 'He told me that I'd done very well,' says Peter. 'He asked me if I wanted to stay, and I said yes, and he told me that he would offer me a new contract at the end of the season.' That same month Peter scored four goals in a 5–3 victory over Millwall. 'A couple of them were tap-ins,' he confesses, 'but I made the other goal in the game as well. It was one of those days when everything I did went right.'

Orient finished a respectable 11th in the League and Peter scored 15 goals in 29 starts and three substitute appearances. 'I felt like I'd had a very good season, especially considering that I had not played as much as I would have liked and missed quite a few matches,' he says. But as the campaign ended Peter found that, contrary to his earlier conversation with Clark, he was not going to be offered a new contract after all. 'I must admit I was very, very surprised and very disappointed because I'd had a good season,' Peter says. 'I felt that maybe there was something personal behind the decision; because Frank didn't like the fact I was very popular with the fans. Also, Brian Winston had said to me that he saw the potential for me to be a player-manager, so perhaps that got back to Frank.'

Clark claims that, in fact, the reason Peter was not offered another contract was more prosaic. 'Finance,' he says. 'At that time we were operating with 15 or 16 players and salaries were very low. There was nothing personal between Peter and me. I don't recall any particular problems, and if I left him out of the team on occasion it would have been for football reasons. I never allowed anything else to interfere with my judgement about putting the best team on the pitch.'

Peter is not entirely convinced, saying 'I was only earning about £300 a week, not a fortune at the time. I was probably one of the highest earners at Orient, but that was for someone who was guaranteed to get you goals. It's not like I wasn't scoring. I was the top scorer that season and fit enough to have played for at least two more. I believe that I was proved right as the following season Orient were relegated to Division Four. I have always felt there was something more to it than the finances.'

Where next, then, for Peter? He had heard that Bournemouth, then a Division Three side, were looking at him and there was apparently interest from semi-pro clubs such as Enfield. But Peter admits 'There was no clamour of clubs trying to sign me. And by then my ambition and drive had gone. I had become disillusioned with the English League game. It was becoming so tactical that I thought it had become boring. I think I would acknowledge that at that point I had become a journeyman footballer just trying to make money.' One offer did pique Peter's interest. It came from the United States, and after a trial that summer at the JVC Centre at Highbury, he was given the chance to join the indoor soccer team the Las Vegas Americans. 'I loved America at the time, and I thought that this might be an opportunity to create a career over there, in a different environment,' says Peter. Sadly it was not to be. Peter says he, Sharon and her two children enjoyed the lifestyle out there, but he could not adapt to the frantic nature of indoor soccer. He played only seven League games for the Las Vegas Americans and, unusually for Peter, failed to find the net on a single occasion. He was released just three months into his contract in December 1984.

After travelling around the States for a couple of months, Peter and family returned to England in February 1985. He had just turned 33, but accepted an offer from former Orient boss Ken Knighton to play for his Southern League outfit Dagenham when retirement might have been a more obvious option. 'I was buying time,' Peter admits. 'I was putting off the inevitable decision when I had to recognise that my career was coming to an end. But I had bills to pay and I thought, what am I going to do? So I went to Dagenham and played for four or five weeks, but I must admit that I hated it as the standard of football was very poor. My motivation had completely gone.' After seven goalless appearances for the Essex side Peter received a call from Micky Speight, the caretaker manager of Division Four club Chester City. 'He asked me if I'd be interested in going up there as a player-coach,' Peter recalls. 'I thought I'd give it a go and signed on non-contract terms.' He made three full and two substitute appearances for Chester and scored his last-ever League goal, against Aldershot, while doing so. But it was not a move he wanted to make permanent. 'I didn't want to move up North, and I thought that playing in Division Four was no longer for me,' he says.

Peter applied for a job as an assistant recreation officer in the leisure department at Harlow Council and, to his surprise, he got it. 'I knew then that was it for football,' he says. He confesses that by that point it wasn't hard for him to accept that his playing days were over, and he didn't kick a ball in an 11-a-side match for the next two years. 'I was very disillusioned with football, with the people in football,' he says. 'I'd lost any innocence I had and any belief in the honesty and integrity of people. I realised that we're all just pawns in people's games. I had become so cynical.'

Was he bitter about the way football had treated him? 'No, I wasn't bitter about that,' he replies, before passionately stating 'I think football is a great game. Played as it should be, it's an art form. But in reality football isn't always like that. It's more the "kick, bollock and bite" mentality. But what had disillusioned me was some of the people. Lawrie McMenemy and Stan Anderson had been great for me at Doncaster, as had the coach Peter Angell at Orient. But then there were managers who treated me and other players badly. I accept that managers have to make decisions and leave people out of the team, but they should just be honest with players. They should just say "Your form is crap at the moment." Players can accept that. But when they ostracise you, when they treat you like s**t, it's wrong.'

From the outside, given that Peter clashed seriously with the majority of managers he worked with, it would be easy to surmise that Peter himself was part of the problem. It's something he's intelligent enough to consider. 'I don't believe these things were only one person's fault,' he says. 'I've always been my own biggest critic as well as my own admirer, and always been aware of my own weaknesses as well as my strengths. I think at times I could have been more communicative. And maybe at times I came over as having a bit of an attitude problem. If I felt that someone wasn't a genuine person then I wouldn't go out of my way to talk to them. I'd tend to go quiet and introverted. And that could be perceived in a different way. In football, people tend to like those who are chirpy and cocky and loud, even though it's a façade. I'm too intelligent and not that sort of personality.'

Peter still feels that he was denied the chance to prove himself in the top division, and maintains that he would have acquitted himself well there. 'At the peak of my career I was supremely confident in my ability to play at the highest level. I think my style of play, my ball control and my intelligence as a footballer would have enabled me to make that transition. I was also very quick over short distances and when I got in front of goal I was quite composed. Another point is that when you play at a higher level it becomes easier in some ways. Players give you more respect and don't just come in and chop you down. And there are better players around you who put the ball where you want, when you want it. It certainly would have played to my strengths rather than my weaknesses. Imagine having Trevor Brooking, Tony Currie or Glen Hoddle passing to you from midfield in my era or David Beckham or Cristiano Ronaldo putting in the quality crosses that they do now.'

Though at times circumstances conspired against Peter proving himself, he is aware that there were those who had their doubts about whether he was good enough to cut it at the very top. 'You'd get feedback from people, you'd hear things,' he says. 'The main criticism was that, although I was quick over five or 10 yards, I didn't have the power and pace over a longer distance. Or that I couldn't play outside the penalty box.'

Can he recognise those weaknesses in himself? 'I think it was a fair criticism that I didn't have that sort of pace,' he says. 'But having said that, neither did Teddy Sheringham or Kenny Dalglish. It's more about the sort of player you are and how you fit into a team. The other thing was that I used to be able to instinctively ride tackles. If I felt that I wasn't going to get there for a 50–50 ball, I wouldn't go for it. It wasn't that I was a coward, I just knew I wouldn't get it so I wouldn't dive in. But then you get players like Bryan Robson who'd steam in, and while he might have won some of them he also got injured a lot. So maybe they're the reasons why I didn't get those moves to the top. It's also about market forces and how much clubs are able to spend. But I still believe that you can't score 20-odd goals season after season and be that bad a player or not be able to reproduce it at the highest level. I am absolutely certain of it and, in fact, I did score against almost every Division One team that I ever played against during my career – and there were quite a lot.'

In 1988, after two years of studying on day release at Harlow College, Peter was awarded a CNAA Diploma in Management Studies, and a year later began working as the manager of a leisure centre in Edenbridge, Kent. Surprisingly, there was to be one final act in his football career. In August 1991, at the age of 39, he agreed to a request from ex-Orient player Tommy Taylor to turn out for his Southern League side, Margate. Over four months he made 11 full and seven substitute appearances and scored four goals. It seems the old magic was still there, though perhaps a little more Paul Daniels than David Blaine. That same year, Peter – who'd obtained his FA Preliminary coaching badge when he was at Cardiff – began to coach the Wimbledon FC youth teams a few evenings a week. In the nine years he held the role, he brought the likes of West Ham and Aston Villa midfielder Nigel Reo-Coker and one-time Orient loanee Mikele Leigertwood through the ranks. Peter also began to turn out every week for the Corinthian Casual School Veterans football team.

In April 1994 Peter, by now holding a UEFA B coaching licence and managing the Wimbledon Under-15 team, declared his interest in managing Leyton Orient who, at the time, were embarking on the chaos that was the John Sitton-Chris Turner comedy double act. He never formerly applied for the job and heard on the grapevine that he was not on chairman Tony Wood's Christmas card list after he'd criticised the club's transfer policy in a newspaper article. He also applied to be manager of Doncaster Rovers that same year but was unsuccessful. It seems that his interest in management was but a passing one. 'It was more a dream than a burning ambition,' he says. 'I looked at the way Kevin Keegan went back to Newcastle and totally rejuvenated the club and thought maybe I could have the same effect. I thought my popularity at Orient and Doncaster may have helped me get the opportunity, but it wasn't to be.'

In 2003 Peter suffered tragedy when his son Darren died of a brain haemorrhage at the age of 28. His other son Michael lives and works in Osaka, Japan, with his wife Yoko, and they have given Peter two grandsons, Alfie and Tommy. Peter continued to play football for the Corinthian Casuals right up until 2005 when, at the age of 53, he figured that the game was probably up. Incredibly, he scored 280 goals in 228 appearances for the team. He still manages to get to Brisbane Road once or twice a season, and is always warmly welcomed. In 2006 he released his autobiography, *The Goal Gourmet*.

Looking back on his career, Peter says 'I'd have to say it was fairly successful. I played a lot of games and didn't get too many serious injuries. And I had a very good ratio of games to goals. I'm content with what I achieved. And I did enjoy it. I've got great memories. I learned an awful lot about people. I think it's made me a better and more well-rounded person.'

And despite the disappointment, he is reflective about the move to a Division One club that never was. 'I prefer to have been a hero at Doncaster and the Orient than to have gone to Ipswich or Spurs and been just another squad player,' he says. 'I would have hated it if I'd gone to a First Division side and just had a few games, then drifted back down the divisions – although I don't believe that would have been the case. I had a great couple of years at Brisbane Road and made such an impact. So at least I've now earned my place in Orient's history, which is fantastic.'

# Chapter 10
# THE 12-YARD BANDIT
## Matt Lockwood 1998–2007

Matt in 2007 during his last season at Orient.

'Anyone who has seen me play knows that I can't tackle. I'm not the quickest, I'm not the strongest and I'm not the best in the air.'

Few Orient fans could argue with Matt Lockwood's rather candid assessment of his own abilities. Then again, few could dispute that, despite this, the frizzy-haired defender was the club's most significant player of recent times – a penalty-taker who virtually never missed, a dead-ball specialist, a driving, inspirational, creative force and a lower League player who could actually control a ball without it spooning off his knee into touch. As Matt himself says 'I'm not your stereotypical left-back.'

When Matt joined Orient in August 1998 he was convinced that it was a club destined for promotion from the bottom division of the League. And he was right, it was just that it took another eight seasons to achieve it. During those wilderness years there were brief chinks of light in the dark despair, and more often than not it was Matt who was shining the torch. It was his cool penalty in the shoot-out of the 1999 Play-off semi-final against Rotherham that sent Orient through to Wembley. Two years later, his 35-yard thunderbolt won another Play-off semi-final, this time against Hull City. In 2005–06 Matt's eight goals were a significant factor in the club's promotion to League One, as were his 10 assists. Aside from that there was the consistency, creativity and forcefulness of his performances over the period and the fact he was voted into the PFA Divisional Team of the Year on four separate occasions, not to mention that his presence allowed the club to sell Billy Jones, something for which fans will always be grateful. Yet for all this, it was actually Matt's final season at the club in 2006–07 that secured his status as a Brisbane Road legend. It is no exaggeration to say that he single-handedly kept Orient in League One. He scored 11 goals from left-back, many of them crucial points-gaining ones, not least the incredible hat-trick he scored against Gillingham when Orient were 3–0 down at Brisbane Road with just 13 minutes to go.

There was, however, always a sense that Matt should not really have been at Orient. He was too good. Chairman Barry Hearn was fond of saying that his left-back was a Premier League player in League Two. ('That was Barry just trying to big up his property,' Matt laughs. 'He wanted a million for me. He's a businessman.') And yet no move ever materialised. There were always rumours – West Ham, Tottenham, Charlton and Ipswich, to name a few – but they came to nothing. In 2001 Reading, then an ambitious club one division above Orient, wanted him but, finding the price too high, opted to take Matt's understudy, Nicky Shorey. The fact that Shorey now plies his trade in the Premier League and has two England caps to his name is something that rankles with Matt. 'Every time I see him on the television I think, that could have been me,' he says. 'It's a bit of a sore subject. He was my understudy when he was at Orient and if he'd stayed he'd still be my understudy.'

He is not being arrogant, but rather philosophical. 'It's funny, it's just luck,' he says. 'You've got to be in the right place at the right time and Nicky couldn't have been in a better place at a better time. Don't get me wrong, he's a good player. He's gone to Reading and done well. I might not have done that. But he couldn't get in above me when he was at Orient so you never know. I'm not saying I'm good enough to play for England because I'm not, but if I'd gone to Reading then, when I was 24, I could have stepped up to the next level.'

In the end Matt did get a move, perhaps at the time fans least expected it. At the end of the 2006–07 season, aged 30, he signed a new three-year contract with Leyton Orient, intending to beat the all-time appearances record. Yet come August he was turning out for Nottingham Forest after he was snapped up as part of the club's innovative transfer policy of looking at the previous season's PFA Divisional Team of the Year (Matt had made it for the fourth time in 2006–07) and then buying all of it. And though Forest were at that time in the same division as Orient, only the most deluded of Orient fans would begrudge the loyal Lockwood his move to what is clearly a bigger club. But talking in March 2008, nine months after his transfer, Matt still rather affectionately refers to Orient as 'we' rather than 'they'. When Nottingham Forest played Orient in January 2008 he refused to take a spot-kick against his former club. 'On the Friday before the game the gaffer asked who would take a penalty,' Matt says. 'Everyone looked at me, but I said that I definitely wouldn't take one against Orient. I couldn't – I'd have felt out of order. I would have been scoring against my team.'

Matt says he still harbours a burning ambition to return to the club one day in some capacity. For now he lives in a tastefully flashy apartment in the centre of Nottingham with his wife Sally, a Leigh-on-Sea girl who he is due to marry in the summer of 2008 after meeting through friends three years earlier. 'Matt can talk!' she says, and she is not wrong. He is an Essex boy, after all, born and raised in Rochford, where he stayed throughout his time at Orient. He is not brash or cocky, but friendly and easy to warm to, and he is thoughtful and insightful about football and his part in it. He is also unafraid to voice his opinions, particularly about the way he was treated in the earlier part of his career, and it is easy to marry the resolve he shows on the football pitch with the personality of the man himself.

Born on 17 October 1976, Matthew Dominic Lockwood grew up with dad Stuart, a market trader, mum Patricia, a housewife, and older sister Francesca. Football was his main interest, and he would force his father to play in the park for hours on end. At the age of six, Matt's dad took him along to train with local boys' side Thorpe Invaders, where he was selected for the under-9s team. By the time he was actually nine he was running rings around everyone else. 'I used to play up front and score all the goals,' he says. 'I could get the ball anywhere on the pitch, take everyone on and score. If I didn't want to get tackled, I wouldn't.'

Thorpe Invaders were a pretty handy youth team, and when Matt was 10 they reached the Final of the local Cup and played at Roots Hall. There he was spotted by West Ham scouts, who asked him to come to training with them at Chadwell Heath every week. He did so for the next six years, while also representing his school teams – he attended Hamstel Junior School and Shoeburyness Comprehensive – and the South East Essex district side. But, when he was 16 and at the point where West Ham could offer him YTS terms, he was released by the club. 'They told my dad that I needn't come back again,' he says. 'I'd spent six years there and they didn't even have the courtesy to tell me to my face. I was obviously gutted because I thought that my chance had gone, but more than that I was disappointed with the way I'd been treated, like nothing. It was because I was a little lad, and they always knew that eventually they'd get rid of me. I knew that I was better than the other lads technically, but they were bigger and stronger than me.'

Matt, it should be pointed out, is not exactly pint-sized. These days he stands at 5ft 9in, and while he accepts he was one of the smaller kids, he is hardly Ronnie Corbett. Anyway, Matt's not bitter. He describes his release by West Ham as 'the best thing that's ever happened to me'. Finding himself club-less, he took the direct approach of knocking on the door of Southend manager – and former Orient full-back – David Webb, who lived around the corner from the Lockwoods. Matt went for a trial and was offered apprentice terms on the spot. 'I went from being a tiny fish in a big pond at West Ham to being the big fish in a little pond at Southend,' he says. 'I was the main man there.' And while Orient fans might consider Southend United less of a pond, more of a stagnant puddle, Matt enjoyed his two years there. By then he was playing as a central midfielder and doing well, but unfortunately his time coincided with one of managerial upheaval at the club. As he came to the end of his two years in April 1995, he found the club were more concerned with internal politics than giving professional contracts to their apprentices.

Matt was released, but was offered a week's trial at QPR by their youth team boss, Billy Bonds. Training alongside the likes of Les Ferdinand and Trevor Sinclair, Matt acquitted himself well enough to be offered a year's contract. 'I couldn't believe it,' he says. 'I went from being released by Southend to getting a pro contract at a Premier League club.' Still playing as a central midfielder, Matt established himself in the reserve team and felt that he was progressing well. Unfortunately, at the end of that season QPR were relegated from the Premier League and manager Ray Wilkins had to trim the squad. Matt once again found himself club-less. He admits to feeling a little bit disillusioned, but adds 'It made me even more determined to make it.'

Matt's regular appearances for the reserves ensured that there was interest in signing him, and he recalls that around eight teams came in for him that summer of 1996, including Colchester, Blackpool, Crewe, Stoke and Bristol Rovers. Stoke City tried to lure Matt by inviting him to play in a special game behind closed doors. When Matt found out that the opposition were to be the Italian national side, warming up for their first match of Euro 1996, he was up there like a shot. 'They were all there: Paolo Maldini, Alessandro Del Piero, Gianfranco Zola, Fabrizio Ravanelli…' Matt recalls. 'I tried to nutmeg Paolo Maldini. I just thought it was the only chance I was ever going to get. It didn't work – he tackled me and ran off with the ball. After the game I was in such a daze I forgot to swap shirts with anyone, so without thinking I ran into their dressing room and asked for one. The kit man ushered me out and told me to wait a minute. He came back and gave me a key ring. I was absolutely devastated. But it was a fantastic day, and I've still got the key ring.'

Despite Stoke City's courtship, in July 1996 Matt elected to sign for Bristol Rovers, then in the third tier of English football under the management of his former QPR teammate Ian Holloway. It was at Bristol that Matt became the left-back that Orient fans know and love. He explains 'When I was at QPR the reserves played against the first team and I got shunted out to left-back. I was up against Trevor Sinclair, who at the time was playing for the England Under-21 team, and for some reason whatever he did that day, he couldn't get past me. After the match Ian Holloway came up to me and said "Decent". That's all he said. But as soon as I joined Bristol Rovers, Ian told me that he honestly believed that I'd make it as a left-back. He put me there for the first game of the season, and I've not looked back since. It's the right position for me. I wouldn't want to play anywhere else now. I think if I'd remained a central midfielder I wouldn't have made it. There's too much competition.'

Orient fans would probably agree that Matt would not have been under too much threat for a central position from the likes of Billy Beall, Scott Canham or Carl Hutchings once he moved to Brisbane Road, but then again he could probably have commanded a place in any position – including goalkeeper – during some of the club's less illustrious seasons. Nonetheless, it was left-back from then on for Matt, and he established himself as Bristol Rovers' first-choice number-three, making 66 starts and six substitute appearances and scoring one goal. In the second season he helped the team reach

Matt during his first season at Orient, against Cardiff on 10 April 1999.

the Play-off semi-finals, where they lost to Northampton. He was offered a new contract by the club but was not happy with what was on the table. 'I wasn't being greedy, I just wanted to be paid the same as everyone else,' he says. 'They let me go for the sake of an extra £100 a week.'

This was 10 days before the start of the 1998–99 season. He got on to the PFA straight away to notify them of his availability and the next day was invited to a trial at Leyton Orient, where he was struck by the club's legendary warmth and friendliness. 'No one whatsoever spoke to me!' Matt says. 'All the squad had their blue training kit on, and there was myself and a couple of other trialists in a red kit. Everyone blanked me and I was just stood there like a lemon. I thought they were a bunch of a***holes.' Matt says he later realised why he had been treated like a pariah, and it wasn't his choice of aftershave. 'Tommy Taylor used to like to bring in trialists; he had hundreds through the door. I guess the lads just thought I was going to be another one of them.' He was not, and he turned out in a pre-season friendly for Orient against Kingstonian. He was immediately offered a contract. Despite an offer from Bury – then residing in the second tier of football – Matt had little hesitation in signing. 'I spoke to a few people who told me that Orient were an ambitious club going in the right direction,' he says. 'They told me that it was likely that they'd be promoted and Bury would be relegated, so the next season I thought they'd both be in the same division anyway.'

Who were these people with such confidence in Orient? Not fans, that is for sure. But anyway, they were right on one count – Bury were indeed relegated. Orient proved a little more problematic, although in that first season it did seem that Matt's faith in the club's potential was well-placed, and they ended up sixth in the League, qualifying for the Play-offs. The semi-final was a two-legged affair against Rotherham United: 210 minutes of goalless football that Matt tactfully describes as 'the worst ever'. He says 'In the away leg I spent the whole game just running up and down with their right-sided player, hardly touching the ball. At one stage he said to me "Blimey, how boring is this game?" I said "Yeah, you're not wrong." It was a non-event. With the big crowds and the prize waiting at the end, no one wanted to make a mistake.'

Matt says that Orient had not practised spot-kicks in the run-up to the game – 'Tommy used to say that there was no point in practising because you couldn't recreate the pressure' – and that the penalty takers weren't assigned beforehand. But he knew that he would nominate himself for one. After successful strikes by Dean Smith, Martin Ling and Dave Morrison, coupled with two saves by goalkeeper Scott Barrett, it turned out that Matt's penalty was the one that could send Orient to Wembley. 'The pressure was off me,' he says. 'Even if I'd missed we had one more we could have scored to go through. I knew what corner I was going to put it in even before the penalty shoot-out started. And I knew I was going to score.'

He did. 'Even now I can remember being in the dressing room at the end of the game, jumping up and down with the chairman and singing and going mental – it was unbelievable,' says Matt, fondly.

The Final was on 29 May 1999 against Scunthorpe United. Matt went into the game brimming with confidence. 'We felt we were the better team,' he says. On the day, however, it was the northerners who prevailed, scoring a goal early in the first half that Orient could not find a response to. Matt has his theories on what went wrong. 'I think the manager tried to make everyone happy,' he says. 'He played a back four of Roger Joseph, Stuart Hicks, Dean Smith and Simon Clark, something we hadn't done all season. We'd always played with three centre-halves. It seemed like Tommy was trying to let the older lads play at Wembley because they were never going to get the chance to do so again. But

Matt, fourth from the left, takes to the Wembley pitch before the Play-off Final of 1999 against Scunthorpe.

Matt during the Play-off Final of 1999 against Scunthorpe.

I think playing a system we were unfamiliar with didn't help us, and in the first half we were awful. In the second half we reverted back to our usual system when Alex Inglethorpe and Graham Maskell came on and we started playing really well but just couldn't score. I believe that if we'd started the game with the correct system we would have won. The manager maybe got it wrong on the day and we ended up losing 1–0 to a header that should have been defended, especially as we had four centre-halves on the pitch.'

Naturally, Matt was devastated. 'All the hard work over the course of the season had been wasted in 90 minutes. It was a horrible feeling, especially as we should have won the game and were the better team. People tell me that I should have enjoyed the occasion of playing at Wembley, but I couldn't enjoy it because we lost.'

The following season of 1999–2000 started abysmally for Orient – not so much a hangover from the Play-off Final, more like blood poisoning and acute liver failure. By Boxing Day they were bottom of the table, with just 14 points from 22 games and a goal difference of minus 18. Bury suddenly may have seemed like an attractive option to Matt after all. He struggles to explain what the hell was going on. 'It's weird because you're not conscious of a change in your mentality. I don't think the team was any worse or any better than the year before. We just ended up letting in a few too many silly goals.'

A post-Christmas run of seven wins in eight games ensured that Orient pulled away from the relegation zone, but a final League position of 19th was hardly a demonstration of the supposed ambition and potential of the club Matt had joined two seasons earlier. Still, his own form had been good that season – he made 47 appearances and scored eight goals – and he was already regularly attracting rumours about supposed moves to bigger clubs. 'One time that season, after we played Hartlepool away in October, Tommy pulled me aside and told me that Charlton had come in for me and that we were going to go and talk to Alan Curbishley the next week and get something sorted,' Matt says. 'But nothing came of it. I don't know if Orient wanted too much money. I got injured a couple of weeks later and that was the last I heard about it.' Did all this unsettle him? 'No, not really,' he replies. 'I just thought, if it happens, it happens. I didn't have an agent – agents are crap. I'm not the kind of the person to go banging on the door saying that I want to leave. Maybe I should have. But I was happy at Orient and I loved the club.'

During that ill-fated 1999–2000 season Matt signed a new three-year contract. He also became the team's official penalty taker and it soon

Matt scores a penalty – one of many – against Lincoln on 16 October 1999.

transpired that he liked nothing better than staring down the barrel of a 12-yard spot-kick. He says 'After I scored the penalty in the Play-off semi-final the season before, Tommy had said to me "I like the way you took that, you were very cool. Do you want to be on them?" I said "Yes, definitely." So I was on them for the Final and I've been on them ever since. It's a massive part of my game.'

Matt takes the matter very seriously. If you casually point out that he probably only missed a handful in his time at Orient, he's quick to fill you in on the detail. 'I missed four,' he says. 'I scored 36 out of 40.' And those four clearly still hurt, because he has a scarily precise knowledge of each. For the record: 'The first one was in the first game of the 2001–02 season, against Cheltenham away. As I placed the ball I didn't know which way to go and I knew I was going to miss. I hit a lame effort down the middle, quite slow, and the keeper got a foot to it. But it came straight back to me and I scored the rebound. The second was away at Carlisle on a Tuesday night in the 2002–03 season. We were 3–0 down, it was the last minute and the keeper saved it.

'Then the next season I missed one against Cambridge at home on the final day. I took the penalty and scored but the referee made me take it again because their players were in the box! I knew the keeper was going to dive the way I went the first time, but I wanted to prove he couldn't get it even if he did dive the right way. But I miskicked it slightly and gave him the chance to save it. I should have dinked it down the middle. The last one was in the promotion season of 2005–06 against Darlington at home, when I slipped – the ground gave way under my foot and I scuffed it into the floor.'

Still, 36 out of 40 isn't a bad record, especially since Matt claims never to practise. 'When Tommy first put me on them I went out to start practising but he told me not to,' he explains. 'He said to me

"You don't miss, so don't practise." So I never do. I know it's weird, but I just go and take them; pick my spot and stick it in.'

Matt says that he always expects to score, but adds, surprisingly, 'I don't like taking penalties.' Really? 'Well perhaps that's not the right wording,' he reflects. 'But it's not a nice feeling because the pressure is on you to score, not for the goalkeeper to save it. You're playing cat and mouse with the keepers, especially once everyone knew who I was. I had to mix it up and change it. In the promotion season I had to take some big, high pressure penalties – Mansfield away and Peterborough at home. But I was never going to let anyone else take them at Orient because I wouldn't have trusted them.'

Matt says that he took a bit of stick over the years off various strikers who were keen to up their goal tallies by putting away a few spot-kicks. 'Carl Griffiths actually nicked two penalties off me when he came back to the club in 1999. It was the home game against Chester City and we got awarded one in the first half. He sprinted up to get the ball, so I said to him, "What do you think you're doing?" And he said "Oh go on, let me take it, I haven't scored since I've been back." And I thought, oh God, you've got to handle forwards with care to get their confidence up so I told him he could have that one. He scored it and got another goal, then we were awarded another penalty in the second half when he was on a hat-trick. So I had to let him have that one too. But after the game I said to him "That's it, you're not having any more." And he agreed. He said he'd take his hat-trick and run.'

Similarly, in a revelation that will fill Orient fans with horror, even in retrospect, Matt says that Gary Alexander was also keen to take them. 'Gaz always used to say to me that if I missed one then

he was on them. He'd say "Imagine if I took all the penalties, I'd be right at the top of the scoring charts." But I just said to him "Gaz, you wouldn't score them." And he wouldn't have done.' The fact that Alexander often had difficulty hitting the net from six, let alone 12 yards, backs Matt up on this one, and Orient fans were always safe in the knowledge that nine times out of 10 – and that's a statistical fact, remember – Matt would score from the spot.

Matt about to score another penalty, this time in a 1–0 win over Carlisle on 19 August 2000.

The 2000–01 season began well for Orient, and by Christmas the club sat third in the table. Then, on 24 March, with Orient still pushing for promotion, Matt sustained a serious injury at Brisbane Road when his face collided with the elbow of York City player Chris Brass. Matt recalls 'It didn't really hurt when he did it, but I went down on my hands and knees and I could see blood pouring on to the ground. I went into the dressing room and the doctor said "It's the worst one I've ever seen." Apparently you could see my skull. I went that night to see a surgeon and he had to sew the muscle together inside the wound so that my eye didn't droop. I've got a massive scar, but it makes me look tougher!'

Matt was out for six weeks, but returned for the final game of the season at Macclesfield, where Orient secured the win needed to seal their place in the Play-offs. First up was the away leg against Hull City, a game Orient lost 1–0. The home leg saw the east Londoners go in at half-time with a 1–0 lead, thanks to a Steve Watts header. Then, in the second half, Matt scored what remains one of the truly great goals at Brisbane Road – an Exocet into the top right-hand corner of the goal launched from fully 35 yards. Matt recalls it vividly. 'About five minutes before I actually scored, Steve Castle had said to me "Next time you get it have a shot. If you don't shoot, you don't score." Then the ball came to me on the half-way line. I had a touch and there was no one for me to pass to. But there was no one in front of me, so I had another touch, and another touch and I thought, it's now or never. And I just hit it. And as soon as I did, I knew it was in. I'd caught it absolutely perfectly. Even now when I see it on video it makes the hairs on the back of my neck stand up.'

The 2–0 victory booked Orient a place in the Final at the Millennium Stadium against Blackpool. But it was to be a day out in which Orient fans would go home with nothing but the taste of Welsh beer in their mouths – Blackpool won the game 4–2. 'Two years earlier I felt we were unlucky against Scunthorpe, but this time the best team won; they outplayed us,' Matt admits. 'Of course I was disappointed we didn't go up, but it didn't hurt as much as the Scunthorpe game.'

So, after three seasons with Orient, Matt's promotion dreams were once again in tatters. Did he, at that point, not feel that it was time to move on? 'It's funny,' he says. 'I remember watching the video of the Final, and at the end the camera panned in on me and the commentator said "Could this be Matt Lockwood's last game in an Orient shirt?" And I thought, well, maybe it could be. Maybe another club will come in for me now.'

In the 2001–02 pre-season it did genuinely look as if Matt would be off. After a friendly with Millwall, Tommy Taylor touted his left-back to their manager, Mark McGhee, who agreed to take Matt on tour to Germany with his side. 'I thought it was a bit weird really,' says Matt. 'I felt that I had enough of a reputation not to have to go on trial at clubs – either they wanted to sign me or they didn't. I was in two minds as to whether to tell them to stick it, but I thought I didn't want to cut my nose off as Millwall had just been promoted to what's now the Championship. So I went away to

Germany for a week, and at the end of it Mark McGhee said "Yes, you've lived up to your reputation, I really like what I've seen, I want to sign you. I'll get our chairman to talk to your chairman and hopefully you'll be here by the end of the week." Then they made an offer which wasn't in the price range of what Barry Hearn wanted so it hit a bit of a stumbling block. But I didn't think that'd be the end of it, I thought they'd come back in. But that was close to the start of the season and three weeks later I ruptured my spleen, which put paid to any move that I was going to get. Obviously they weren't going to sign someone who'd nearly died.'

Matt is not being overly dramatic – he really could have gone at any minute. The incident occurred on 25 August in the away fixture at York City. Initially, it seemed an innocuous injury. 'I'd bumped into the centre-half while attempting to shoot,' Matt says. 'I felt like I'd been winded, but I stayed on the pitch. Then someone passed me the ball about two yards in front of me and I just watched it roll past. I thought, I have to come off. I was in excruciating pain. The doctor said that maybe I had a broken rib, and I sat on the bench for the rest of the game curled up in a ball with my head between my knees.

'On the coach, Scott Houghton turned to me and said that he didn't want to worry me, but that when he was at Spurs someone had ruptured their spleen and the symptoms were really similar to mine. At that I ran to the toilet and was sick. Tommy told the coach driver to take me to a hospital – the lads were loving that, stuck outside A&E for two hours, still four hours away from home. They X-rayed my ribs and said there was nothing broken. They told me it was probably just some internal bruising, gave me some painkillers and sent me home.

'But throughout Sunday I was still in a huge amount of pain, so on Monday I went back to the doctor, and was booked in for an ultrasound scan the next morning. That night we were due to go on a team bonding night and I didn't want to pull out. So I was walking around London on a pub crawl with what I later found out was a ruptured spleen, and although I wasn't drinking, I could have keeled over and died at any time.

'At the time, Roger Joseph had this habit of walking around the back of people and jabbing them in the side of the ribs. A few weeks later he said to me that he was going to do it to me that night, but for some reason he didn't. If he had done I'd probably have dropped down dead.

'Next morning I woke up and drove myself into London for the ultrasound scan. And then I knew that something was wrong because all the doctors were buzzing around and whispering behind my back. Then they told me that they had to rush me in for an emergency operation because if they didn't I could literally go at any time.'

Matt had his spleen removed, spent the night in intensive care and the next week in hospital and now bears a six-inch scar down his stomach. 'It done me a treat,' he says, somewhat understatedly. But he wasn't about to let the mere fact that he'd had a major organ removed stop him getting back on the football pitch, and less than three months after his operation he returned as a substitute in a 0–0 draw with Exeter City. 'It was the worst thing I ever did,' Matt admits. 'With hindsight, I should have stayed out for six months, but at the time I was desperate to get back playing. The lads were on a good FA Cup run and my target was to play in the fourth round against Everton at Goodison Park. Also, in the back of my mind was the fact that Millwall might still want to sign me.' Matt did make it into the starting line up for the FA Cup tie against Everton – Orient lost 4–1 – but says it was a total disaster. 'Literally, after five minutes I couldn't breathe. I thought to myself, what am I doing? I'm a nutcase. I think it was the worst I've ever played.'

The season itself was one of upheaval at Orient, and in October, while Matt was out injured, Tommy Taylor had been replaced by first-team coach Paul Brush. 'It wasn't a surprise that Tommy went,' says Matt. 'It had got to the stage where the fans wanted him out, and it was getting nasty. It wasn't that he'd lost the dressing room, but we weren't doing very well and something had to give.' Matt says that he always got on well with Taylor. 'I liked Tommy. A lot of players didn't because he was very abrupt. You either liked him or hated him. He didn't mince his words, but you knew where you stood with him and I liked that. I'd rather someone was honest with me. I was gutted to see him go, but I realised it was time.'

Sitting at home 'twiddling his thumbs', as he puts it, while recuperating from his operation, Matt naturally expected a telephone call from the new boss. Bizarrely, he did not get one. 'It was a funny time,' he says. 'I literally heard nothing from him. Then I turned up to training one day when I thought I felt OK and he said "Oh, hello, where have you been?" I thought, what are you on about? Surely he should have rung me to find out how I was?'

Matt says that he did get on 'fine' with Brush and that he was a 'nice guy' but he doesn't believe the former West Ham player was cut out for management. 'He was the complete opposite to Tommy. He was too nice. He didn't really ever go mad or scream and shout. He didn't have that ruthless streak to drop people. You need someone to come in and hammer people if they're not doing their jobs, but he wouldn't do it. He's a great coach and a perfect number two, but I just don't think he was a manager.' Results under Brush would certainly bear Matt out on this one and the 2001–02 season ended with a whimper, Orient finishing in 18th place. The 2002–03 season, meanwhile, started with a whimper, had a bit of a whimper in the middle and ended with another whimper. Once again Orient finished in 18th place. Fans at the time were contemplating rupturing their own spleens. 'We weren't going anywhere and we were struggling constantly,' says Matt.

Still, Matt was still enjoying his time at the club and maintains that in all his time at Brisbane Road there was an excellent team spirit. 'As a group we always got on. We always had a nucleus of lads who'd been there a long time, but new players slotted in really easily.' Over the years a number of teammates lived near Matt in Essex – Scott Barrett, Andy Harris, Lee Harrison, Wayne Purser – and while there was not too much socialising, they all got on well and would drive in to training together. Matt was not a big drinker – these days he is teetotal – and he would spend his spare time on the golf course, where he plays off a handicap of four.

By October of season 2003–04, Paul Brush paid the price for taking Orient into the relegation zone with a paltry seven points from 10 games and was given the boot. 'It was definitely the right decision,' says Matt. 'I was actually out injured when he was sacked. When the lads told me, I thought, bloody hell, I miss all the entertainment!' The club went through a rather public process of recruiting a new manager and let it be known that all manner of big names could think of nothing better than managing a struggling League Two side. And while no doubt Sir Alex Ferguson, Arsene Wenger, Fabio Capello and so on were sorely tempted, in the end the job actually went to Paul Brush's assistant, former Orient player and youth-team boss Martin Ling. It was a decision Matt says the squad was fully behind. 'He was the logical next step. He'd done well with the reserves and the youth team, and we all knew what he'd done as a player. I was as pleased as anyone because, coming from within the club, he knew all about me and what I could do. It was a bit weird because we had to go from calling him "Lingy" to "gaffer" overnight, but I was experienced enough to realise that it was just as hard for him as it was for us.'

Things began to pick up under Martin Ling, and Matt is quick to highlight his former teammate's managerial qualities. 'He's a nice bloke, but he's got that side to him where if it's not going right he'll tell you. He knows when to have fun on the training field and when to be serious. He's worked with some good managers in his career and he's picked up good points from all of them. His record speaks for itself.'

With a smattering of eye-catching new signings – such as Lee Steele, Wayne Carlisle, Andy Scott and Michael Simpson – there was a fair degree of optimism at the beginning of the 2004–05 season. And it seemed well-placed: by October, Orient were top of the League. Unfortunately, concurrent injuries to strikers Gary Alexander, Lee Steele and Jabo Ibehre during December and January meant that Orient were reliant on loan signings for the goals that would maintain a challenge. It was not to be, and the team finished the season in 11th place. 'The injuries hurt us,' Matt confirms. 'We needed Gary and Steelo up there banging in the goals for us. There was too much pressure on the back four to keep clean sheets because as soon as we let one in we thought we'd lose. I think it has been our problem over the years at Orient: that apart from Carl Griffiths we haven't had anyone who would score 20 goals a season.'

The next season of 2005–06 was the one where Matt finally achieved the promotion he had been expecting when he joined Leyton Orient in 1998. He says that the team were confident from the outset. 'Every season you start off thinking, this is going to be our year, but that season I don't think there were too many decent teams in the League, so we knew we had a good chance. And we didn't have many injuries that year, which made such a big difference. We learned how to play with each other and we got into the winning habit.'

The season also saw another impressive FA Cup run, when Orient beat Fulham at Craven Cottage in the third round and then took Charlton to the 90th minute at the Valley before a deflected goal won it for Alan Curbishley's side. Matt says that the games gave the team a huge confidence boost for their promotion challenge. 'It made us think that if we could beat Fulham and take Charlton to 90 minutes then we could beat anyone.'

Also key to Orient's season was the fact that for seven games between February and April the team did not concede a single goal at Brisbane Road. 'The back four we had was solid every week,' Matt says. 'We got used to playing together and we were proud of that record.' Matt points to the centre-back pairing of John Mackie and Gaby Zakuani as critical. 'That was a really good partnership. John was mental, chucking himself in front of everything, and Gaby was a great defender.'

Zakuani himself, meanwhile, is quick to highlight the importance of Matt in the quartet. 'He was a quality player on the ball, and he was a massive help to me,' he says. 'He'd pull me to one side and give me little bits of advice. And if I made a mistake he'd tell me that it wasn't the end of the world, so I played with a lot more confidence knowing that there was someone looking out for me. He was the player I respected most at the club, and he was a great role model and professional.'

Ultimately, it all came down to the final game of the season. To achieve promotion, Orient had to travel to Oxford United's Kassam Stadium and equal or better Grimsby's result against Northampton. Fuelling the fire of one of the most incredible games in Orient's history was the fact that Oxford needed to win to avoid relegation to the Conference. 'The atmosphere was amazing and the number of Orient fans that turned up was fantastic,' says Matt. 'But it wasn't an enjoyable game because of the pressure. There was so much at stake, and I bet most fans expected us to slip up at the final hurdle as we had done before.'

With the game going into five minutes of injury-time at 2–2, and Grimsby winning 1–0 against Northampton, it looked as if any doomsayers would have been right. 'I felt it slipping away,' Matt admits. 'We knew that Grimsby were winning because Martin had shouted on to the pitch that we needed to get one. I was gutted, I was thinking, oh God, not the Play-offs again. I didn't want to go through that. But you have to keep believing, you don't want to give up. You're just running around in a daze thinking, I just want to score, let's just win. We were so close, just five minutes away from promotion or five minutes away from another three weeks of pressure.'

Suddenly, there was an almighty roar from the Orient fans. 'We knew straight away that Northampton must have equalised,' says Matt. 'But then the ball broke and there were about five of us lined up in the box waiting to score because we were all so desperate to get through. But it was fitting that Lee Steele got the winner – the fans loved him. The relief was unbelievable. We all just piled on each other. I got caught underneath. I thought I was going to die! I literally had to push everyone off and crawl out on my hands and knees. When the final whistle went it was my best moment at Orient. It took long enough to get promotion, but it was definitely worth the wait. Everyone involved with the club can look back on that season and say that it couldn't have finished on a better day.'

As a postscript, Matt adds that he is convinced that Orient would not have been able to negotiate the Play-offs had it come to that. 'We definitely wouldn't have gone up if we hadn't done so that day,' he says. 'We wouldn't have been able to lift ourselves for those three games. The teams who just made it into the Play-offs would have beaten us.'

Orient began the 2006–07 season in the third tier of English football for the first time since

After eight seasons with Orient, Matt finally gets to celebrate promotion at Oxford United on 6 May 2006.

1994. There was not a major strengthening of the squad, with Martin Ling trusting the promotion-winning players to acquit themselves at the new level. 'I agreed with that,' says Matt. 'I didn't think the difference in standard between Leagues One and Two was so great. We looked at Southend who'd

Matt after the 3–2 victory over Oxford United that ensured promotion to League One on 6 May 2006.

gone up the year before us, then gone straight up again. But maybe the difference was more than we thought.' Results would certainly suggest so, and by mid-October Orient were bottom of the table. 'We realised that you got punished for your mistakes more,' says Matt. 'It was a learning curve, but I think we learned quickly and we managed to fight our way out of it.'

Despite – or maybe because of – the generally poor performances of the players around him, the season was actually Matt's defining one for Orient. With 11 goals and five assists, he was second-top scorer to Gary Alexander with 12, and it is safe to say that without him Brisbane Road would have been welcoming Dagenham & Redbridge and Accrington Stanley the next season rather than Leeds and Nottingham Forest. Matt is too modest to claim sole responsibility for keeping Orient in League One but does say 'I feel that was probably my best season since I'd been at the club. I don't know what would have happened if I hadn't been playing but most of the goals I scored were important ones, goals that got us three points or one point. And given we only stayed up by four points it was obviously a massive help to the club.'

Matt celebrates scoring his ninth goal of the season with Luke Gutteridge in a 2–1 victory over Port Vale on 3 February 2007.

Of his hat-trick against Gillingham in September, which rescued a point after Orient had been 3–0 down with 13 minutes to go, he says 'That night was unbelievable for me on a personal level. Even now I can't believe that I did it. When I was running through on goal for the third one I could have crossed it for Gary Alexander, but I thought, no chance, I'm on a hat-trick. It was a pretty tight angle, but I gave the 'keeper the eyes and went near post. That was a crazy, crazy night.'

At the end of that season, Matt signed a new three-year deal with Orient, one that included a testimonial. Given that he was 30 at the time, it seemed to fans that despite all the rumours and near-moves, Matt Lockwood would end his playing career in east London. Did Matt himself see it that way? 'I signed a new contract because I was happy at the club,' he replies. 'I still hoped that I could play at a higher level, but I hoped that I could do it with Orient. I felt that Orient was my club, and I just wanted to stay there forever. I loved everything about the club. My idea was to do my coaching badges and end up becoming manager, and I wanted to beat the all-time appearances record.' Was beating Peter Allen's record that important to him? 'Massively,' he replies. 'It's hard to say why, but seeing my name in the record books for being a top Orient person would have been a great thing to achieve.'

Throughout June, then, Matt was looking forward to the new season with Orient. There had been a big overhaul in the squad, and he felt that the new players coming in meant there was plenty of potential for a good year. Then, on June 30, while Matt was at a wedding with Sally, he got a call from Martin Ling telling him that Nottingham Forest had come in with an offer for him. 'They'd actually been sniffing around me in the January transfer window,' Matt reveals. 'I knew that they were looking for a left-back and that their manager, Colin Calderwood, liked me as a player. I spoke to Martin about it at the time, but he told me that Barry Hearn wanted a certain amount of money for me otherwise Orient could get relegated. So when I signed my new contract there was a minimum release fee clause in it, and in the summer Forest came in with that fee. So I spoke to the chairman about it and he said that no one at the club wanted me to leave, but that they couldn't stand in my way as it was a massive opportunity for me. I thought I had to go for talks in Nottingham at least.'

The offer gave Matt a huge dilemma. 'I didn't eat or sleep for four days,' he says. 'I just didn't know what to do. I just didn't want to leave Orient. In a way I wish a smaller club had come in for me, because I would have said no instantly. But I remembered playing Forest the season before and the ground was massive, and I knew that playing there meant playing in front of 20,000 people every week. Everyone I spoke to said that at my age I'd be mad to turn it down because I'd never get the chance to play for a club like that again. I said, yes, but will I ever get the chance to break the appearance record at Orient? Will I ever get the chance to become manager there?' In the end it was a conversation with Orient assistant manager Dean Smith that helped Matt to make up his mind. Smith had made a surprising move to First Division Sheffield Wednesday in 2003, just before his 32nd birthday, after many years' service at Brisbane Road. 'Dean told me that he wouldn't have swapped it for the world,' says Matt. 'And he said "Look at me, I've come back to the club, there's no reason why you couldn't." So in the end I decided to go. I thought that I would regret not going to Forest more than I would regret leaving Orient. It was something that I couldn't say no to.'

Matt's first season at Forest didn't go quite as planned. An ankle injury in the first game of the season kept him out of the side until December, by which time Julian Bennett had established himself as the first-choice left-back. But Bennett sustained an injury, giving Matt the chance to play against his old club when Orient visited the City Ground in January 2008. 'It was weird to say the least,' he says of the game that Forest won 4–0. 'But I was blown away by the fans' reaction towards me. During the game they were singing my name and afterwards I went over to thank them. I was always going to do that.'

Unfortunately, when Forest came to Brisbane Road in March, Matt was not even named as a substitute, something that he remains furious about. 'I knew I wasn't going to be playing, but I thought the manager would have put me on the bench because I'd played in the previous game and set up the goal, and of course because we were playing Orient. I didn't find out until I was in the dressing room before the game. The gaffer came up to me and said "You're not on the bench today." I didn't say a word. I just walked out. I was gutted. I thought it was bang out of order and I was well upset. But football's not about sentiment so I had to grin and bear it and watch from the stands.'

In March 2008, at the time of writing, Matt says that not being first-choice left-back is a 'culture shock' and adds 'It's not a feeling I want to get used to – I'm wasting my time. When you see what team the manager picks, it's all very young, very big, very strong and very athletic players. And young, big, strong and athletic aren't qualities that I have, so I can't compete with that. The manager is very defence-orientated, and he's picking the other lad for his defensive qualities over mine.' Does he regret leaving Orient? 'Not at all,' he replies. 'I had to give it a go. If anything I regret going in for that tackle in the first game of the season because if I hadn't got injured I would have played every game.'

Rumours abounded throughout the season that Matt would return to Orient and, according to Matt, it is a realistic scenario. 'I want to play as many years as I can, and if the opportunity ever arose to go back to Orient I'd bite their hand off. Maybe one day I can still break that appearances record. I'd love to go back.' He is serious about going into management too, saying 'I think being a manager is all about getting the best out of your team and knowing a good player when you see one. And I've learnt from the managers I've worked for, good and bad. It just depends whether I ever get the opportunity; whether I'm in the right place at the right time.'

Looking back on his career, Matt says that he is 'obviously gutted' that the reported moves to Premier League clubs never came about, and he remains convinced that he could have acquitted himself at that level. 'I've got weaknesses in my game, but you learn how to use your own strengths. Again, I look at Nicky Shorey and think that, like me, he's not the quickest or the strongest. But he doesn't get caught out in the Premier League. I think I've got good technique, good touch, good distribution and I'm not too bad at set plays. I think to myself, yes, I could have done well at the top level. But I'll never know.' But he's not one for wallowing or regret, and says 'What have I got to be upset about, though? I was doing a thing I'd loved all my life and playing for a great little club. Granted, I wasn't earning £20,000 a week, but I was still happy. Orient is my club and I loved my time there.'

# Chapter 11
# DON'T MESS WITH DENNIS
## Dennis Rofe 1968–72

Dennis in his Orient days.

You would not mess with Dennis Rofe. Not back in 1968 when, though only 17 years of age, he would go toe-to-toe with any winger who dared to take him on. And certainly not now because, despite the fact that he is pushing 60, he is still fit, compact and appears 10 years younger. And that fire in his eyes that made him one of the toughest defenders ever to pull on an Orient shirt still burns brightly.

Graeme Souness, no shrinking violet himself, tried his luck once. In 2003, when manager of Blackburn Rovers, he falsely accused Dennis, then first-team coach at Southampton, of trying to get one of his players sent off. Four security guards had to hold Dennis back. 'He was very lucky,' says Dennis, simply. He is not joking either, adding 'If someone pushes me I don't go backwards.' But don't get the wrong impression. Outside the confines of a football stadium Dennis is amiable, warm and imbued with a fair degree of Essex boy charm. He is into dogs. He and his wife, Sue, have two cocker spaniels and enter them in shows. They met each other in 1968 at a dog obedience class and fell in love through a shared interest in Labradors.

Football, naturally, is Dennis's other love, and he brims with pride and enthusiasm when he talks about his career. He has a large scrapbook of press cuttings and photographs, and the cap that signifies his solitary appearance for the England Under-23 team sits in pride of place on the mantelpiece. On the pitch, he was undoubtedly a hard and uncompromising left-back ('aggressive,' he says when asked to describe his skills as a footballer). But he was not simply a chop-'em-down merchant. Dennis had pace – a lot of it – and skill. He could score goals, perhaps a legacy of that fact that until turning pro he was an inside-forward, and he could create them.

During his four full seasons at Leyton Orient – from 1968 to 1972 – he made a name for himself as a classy, uncompromising defender. He was an integral part of the promotion-winning side of 1969–70 and the team that went on the great FA Cup run of 1972. And when he transferred to First Division Leicester City for £112,000, it made him the most expensive full-back in British football history. Dennis's playing career also took him to Chelsea and Southampton, and since hanging up his boots he has made a success of coaching at the top level. These days he works for the Football League as a regional youth development officer and lives in Chandler's Ford, Hampshire. He and Sue have three children – Daniel, a prison officer, Marcus, an assistant manager at a decorating centre, and Louisa, a hairdresser – and they remain close as a family. While Dennis was having a tear-up with Graeme Souness at Southampton, the Rofes were sitting nearby in the stands, urging him on. Go Dad!

Dennis was born on 1 June 1950 in Epping, Essex, and grew up in nearby Loughton. His father Ron was a bus driver and his mother Elaine worked at the Bank of England in Debden. He has one older brother, Alan. 'I had a really happy childhood,' says Dennis. 'I was a pretty cheeky young boy, but I remember that right from an early age all I wanted to be was a footballer. I supported Burnley – they were a top team at the time – and when they got to the FA Cup Final in 1962 I dreamt that one day I'd score a goal at that great occasion.'

The East London Boys team collect their trophy at Brisbane Road after beating South London Boys in a youth tournament. Dennis is behind the boy holding the Cup. Also in the side were Paul Went and Terry Brisley.

Dennis went to Hereward Junior School in Loughton and was immediately selected for the school and then the district team. 'I used to play centre-forward in those days,' he says. 'It was probably because I was quick. I can't think of any other reason. But I scored a lot of goals.' Dennis, clearly a bright lad, passed his 11-plus examination and attained a place at the Davenant Foundation Grammar School in Whitechapel, a school that, he says, turned out dentists, doctors and lawyers by the dozen. Luckily for Dennis, would-be dentists, doctors and lawyers rarely make good footballers, and once again he made the school team. His performances soon earned him a place in the East London Boys side. At the age of 13 he played in the Final of a competition against South London Boys at Brisbane Road. After the match Orient scouts Len Cheesewright and Eddie Heath invited Dennis along to train at the club every Tuesday and Thursday evening. Accompanying him would be Terry Brisley and Paul Went, who also went on to become Orient first-teamers.

At 15 Dennis was offered apprenticeship terms by the club, and he had to plead with his father to let him leave school a year early. 'He had reservations, but he listened to what I said and agreed to let me leave before I took O levels,' says Dennis. 'I was doing OK at school, but I was never going to be a genius. Dad had to pay £10 to the school so that I could leave early, which in 1965 was a lot of money. I still have the letter from the school giving me permission to leave early. At the bottom it says that they strongly advise that I continue with my education because you can't make a living out of football. Dad said to me "Promise me one thing: that you'll give it all you've got."'

As an apprentice, Dennis was paid £7 a week. 'I used to give my mum £2 and the rest used to last me all week,' he recalls. 'We'd train in the mornings and do jobs in the afternoon: cleaning boots, helping the groundsman roll the pitch, painting the crash barriers, cleaning the dressing rooms. You'd suffer a lot of mickey-taking from the older pros, people like Harry Gregory and Dennis Sorrell, but providing you did your jobs right they treated you well. There used to be a strict code of conduct about not entering the first-team dressing room unless you were invited in. But when new apprentices arrived we'd say, go straight in, it's OK. Then they'd get a right earful.'

In his years as an apprentice Dennis saw Benny Fenton, Les Gore and Dave Sexton all take charge of the club – 'I learnt a lot from these people,' he says – but it was the arrival of Dick Graham at the beginning of the 1966–67 season that was to have a significant influence on Dennis's career. Dick himself said at the time 'I moved Dennis Rofe to full-back. He was playing inside-forward, not that I thought he would make it. But he was a great helper to me in my general duties and I was determined to make something of him.' Dennis had no problem with being converted to a defender. 'I was just glad to play,' he says. 'I didn't mind playing at full-back and I think I did reasonably well there, so that's where I stayed.' Did he miss the glory of being a forward? 'No,' he says, 'but I do now because I would have made more money!'

Dennis playing for the Orient youth team in 1966.

New manager Jimmy Bloomfield addresses the Orient apprentices in March 1968. Dennis is on the far right.

Dick Graham had a reputation as something of a sergeant-major type manager, which, says Dennis, was a fair assessment. 'He had an element of the fear factor about him. If he felt you'd done something wrong, he'd ask you to explain yourself and then there'd be silence. And it was that period of silence that would be the most frightening because you never knew what was going to happen. He used to explode at me sometimes. But by and large he was OK. And he taught me a lot.' Dennis says that Graham was a very forward-thinking manager. 'He came in with a lot of new ideas. He introduced baskets of fruit into the changing rooms, and there were a couple of armchairs in there too. At that time the tradition was that the full-backs wore numbers two and three, but he'd make us wear numbers eight and 10 to try to confuse the opposition. I think it confused us as well!'

Dennis would spend many hours practising his skills.

It was Graham who offered Dennis a pro contract in the summer of 1967 – 'I was paid £14 a week,' Dennis recalls – but by February of 1968 the manager had resigned, frustrated at the lack of funds at the club. 'I was sad, but it came as no surprise because Dick was a man of principle,' says Dennis. 'And in truth he had pulled out all the stops to keep the club afloat. They were difficult times. I remember holding a bucket and going around the stands asking people to donate money to help save the club.'

Graham's departure opened the door to the arrival of ex-Arsenal player Jimmy Bloomfield as player-manager. 'Jimmy was fantastic,' says Dennis. 'The first thing I thought was what a smart man he was. He always wore a collar and tie and immaculate suits. And of course he was a very talented footballer: a marvellous passer of the ball with lovely control. He gained the respect of the players immediately, and he managed to combine the role of player and manager very well.'

Very well indeed, though it should be noted that in that 1967–68 season Orient were actually rubbish. When Bloomfield took over in February the team were languishing near the bottom of

Division Three, and they pretty much stayed there for the rest of the season. At this point Dennis was still only 17 years old, but on 30 April Bloomfield asked him to accompany the team on their trip up the M4 to play Bristol Rovers. 'I thought I was going just to get a bit of experience, to help with the kit, carry the skips, and generally get a feel of the atmosphere,' says Dennis. 'I didn't expect to be anywhere near the first team.' In fact, Bloomfield named Dennis as substitute. 'I was nervous, obviously, but I was elated,' he says.

At half-time Dennis was given his chance at left-back. He did not squander it, scoring one of the goals that helped Orient record a vital 2–0 victory. 'I went down the wing and played a one-two with Dave Harper on the edge of a box,' he recalls. 'The goalkeeper came out and I bent it by him. I took off at about 150 miles per hour as far as I could run. I would have beaten those greyhounds around Eastfield without a shadow of a doubt. It was fantastic.'

Dennis knew how proud his father would be. 'In those days there wasn't Teletext or mobile phones, and though my mum and dad knew I was travelling with the team they didn't know that I was going to be substitute. I got home from Bristol about 3am and went into their bedroom. My dad said to me "You won 2–0 then – who scored?" And I replied "Well I got one." He jumped out of bed

Orient in 1969–70. Back row, left to right: Terry Brisley, Peter Allen, Dickie Plume, Mike Jones, Brian Scrimshaw. Middle row: Terry Mancini, Steve Bowtell, Ray Goddard, Dave Harper, Peter Brabrook. Front row: Mark Lazarus, Mickey Bullock, Terry Parmenter, Barry Dyson, Dennis Rofe, Barrie Fairbrother.

and the lights went on. It was quite a moment. And then the next morning we got every paper to see my name in it. It was terrific.'

Dennis's performance was enough to earn him a place in the starting line up for the final three games of that season and, though Orient drew one and lost two of them, they managed to escape relegation. Dennis was on cloud nine. 'A whole new world opened up for me,' he says. 'It was stuff you could only dream of. Fortunately for me, things went quite well on the pitch and I began to feel very confident. I was young, fit and quick and in all truth felt I could take on the world.'

Firstly, Dennis had to take on the veteran left-back Bert Howe, who had joined Orient in January 1967 after nine years at Crystal Palace. At the start of the 1968–69 season, despite Dennis's potential, it was Bert who lined up in the number-three shirt. 'I was frustrated, but it makes you plug along,' says Dennis. 'Bert was a decent left-back in his day, but it's the nature of the game that I wanted his shirt. And although I wasn't in the team at the start of the season I was around it, and Jimmy told me that my time would come.'

It came in an away game against Barrow on 28 September and, after that, Dennis played in every single fixture for the remainder of the season. Unfortunately, Dennis's consistently good performances were not enough to drag the entire team out of the torpor of mediocrity and, once again, Orient found themselves swimming in the dregs of Division Three. 'It's hard to put your finger on why we were struggling so much,' says Dennis. 'But Jimmy instilled a belief in us that if we kept playing football we'd be alright. It wouldn't cross his mind that we could be relegated. He thought that we were too good for that. That belief transferred to the players, and we managed to stay up.'

Just. It came down to the last day of the season, when a 4–0 victory over the mighty Shrewsbury ensured another season of Division Three football would be played at Brisbane Road. 'I've always performed when my back's against the wall,' says Dennis. 'We won convincingly and, although I've seen the Orient ground rejoice on a number of occasions, none was quite like that day.'

The following season of 1969–70 also saw Brisbane Road rapturous on the final day, though unusually this time it was not because the team had narrowly escaped relegation. This was the famous promotion year and Dennis was a key component of the team, playing every minute of every single match. Dennis enthuses about the quality of the players around him that season. 'We had Tommy Taylor and Terry Mancini at the back, Peter Allen in midfield and Mickey Bullock getting goals up front. But most of all it was the two deadly wingers, Mark Lazarus and Peter Brabrook, tormenting defences. Peter helped me enormously. He used to get the ball, go inside and wave his arm for me to go by. He taught me when to overlap and when not to. It was terrific to play with those experienced players.'

Dennis also says that the team spirit in that season was a crucial part of the success. 'If you have a good team you usually find that you have a good dressing room. And it was never a dull place.

People like Mark Lazarus, Terry Mancini and Dave Harper played the game with a smile on their faces. There was a lot of East End humour. Everyone got on well together. We had a good spirit on the pitch but it was twice as good off it.' Dennis's main partner in crime was Tommy Taylor. 'We were just two young lads, full of the joys of life,' he says. 'We used to train hard, but we enjoyed it. And then afterwards we'd play snooker on the Leyton High Road or go tenpin bowling on Leytonstone High Street. On Thursday afternoons we'd go to Hackney dogs. You saw a lot of Orient fans over there. People used to give us tips but the dogs never seemed to win. On Saturday night we'd go to the Moby Dick on Southend Road or the Green Gate in Bethnal Green.'

Dennis, unlike some of his teammates, was not a big drinker. 'I was pretty religious about not drinking on Thursday or Friday nights,' he says. 'My dad kept me in check with that. It was drilled into me from a younger age. I liked a drink, but it'd come up after about two and a half pints. The Coach and Horses on the Leyton High Road was a regular venue for the boys, particularly when we used to get back from away games at about two in the morning. We'd bang on the back door and Jimmy Seal the proprietor would say "Come in lads, you know the prices, I'm going to bed." We used to have a beer and put the money on the counter.'

Clearly then, the team spirit – whether it be whisky, brandy or gin – was good. And it seemed to translate to results on the pitch. The first game of the promotion season saw Orient thump Rochdale 3–0, with Dennis himself claiming Orient's first goal. By April Orient were in a position to take the Division Three title. 'We were confident and we were rattling in goals,' Dennis says. 'We went out on to the pitch feeling like King Kong and just had the feeling we were going to win.'

A 1–0 victory over Shrewsbury in the penultimate game of the season sealed the title for Orient. 'We had a tremendous celebration that night,' says Dennis. 'There were several parties, certainly one

Dennis looks on as goalkeeper Ray Goddard saves from Charlton Athletic's Alan Campbell in a Division Two clash on 29 August 1970.

*Evening Standard London Football* No.3 1s

**ORIENT**

The big action series...
The story in pictures of
London's football clubs
NEXT: FULHAM

Dennis makes the front of the Evening Standard in 1970.

at the Coach and Horses. And as a reward we went to Benidorm for a couple of weeks. At the end of each night, no matter what part of town the boys had ended up in, we'd always congregate in the Melodia Bar and finish the evening by singing Frank Sinatra's *My Way*, led by Dave Harper and Mark Lazarus. They were phenomenal times.'

As Dennis began the next season in Division Two, his performances remained consistently good and rarely did a week go by without some club reportedly being interested in taking him away from Brisbane Road. 'There was a lot of speculation,' he admits. 'Huddersfield – who were a big club then – Chelsea, Tottenham, Everton. I've still got the paper cuttings. Things like "Orient defender to go north". North to Loughton, that's about as far as I went!' Joking aside, Dennis says that all the attention did not unsettle him or make him agitated to leave Brisbane Road. 'It was too regular to be unsettling. I'd pick up the paper and think, who is it this week? It was nice to be regarded as a bright prospect. I didn't let it prey on my mind too much. At that age I was just enjoying playing football. I thought that if I kept playing well, something would happen.'

The 1970–71 season was, in truth, pretty unmemorable, both for Dennis and Orient fans. With no new signings Orient bore-drew their way to a 17th-place finish, scoring just 29 league goals, the second-lowest total in the club's history. 'I did think it was a bit strange that Jimmy didn't add to the squad,' Dennis admits. 'I don't know whether there wasn't money available or whether he just had faith in us as a team. But we won the first game of the season 3–1 against Sheffield United and we thought, this division is alright, isn't it? But we didn't continue like that.' At the end of that season Jimmy Bloomfield left Orient for First Division Leicester, but the departing boss had a message for his left-back. 'He told me that he'd like to take me to Leicester,' Dennis says. 'But at that point that was as far as it got. I didn't know for certain if he'd come in for me.'

In the meantime Dennis had to ingratiate himself with new gaffer George Petchey, who arrived from Crystal Palace. 'He had an incredibly difficult job,' Dennis admits. 'He was taking over from a man that everyone liked and respected and who had got us promotion. But George handled it very well. He took time to speak to all the players individually. He told me that if I carried on playing the way I had been he wouldn't be able to keep me at Orient. He was very honest, a good coach, a very thorough man and a very trustworthy man. I liked George a lot.' Dennis was also impressed with Petchey's new style of coaching. 'He introduced a one-touch philosophy. I usually needed a few touches to control the ball! But whereas Jimmy would buy players and say, you know what to do, George really got the players to play the way he wanted.'

A couple of months into that season Dennis found that Jimmy Bloomfield had been true to his word. The Leicester manager made an offer to Orient for him. By now the left-back says that he was ready

**OFFICIAL PROGRAMME** PRICE 10p.

# ORIENT

v

# ARSENAL

F.A. CUP SIXTH ROUND — KICK-OFF 3 P.M.
Leyton Stadium, Saturday, March 18th, 1972

The programme from Orient's FA Cup quarter-final against Arsenal on 18 March 1972.

for the move. Orient, however, were not quite so keen to let him go. 'As far as I was concerned the deal was done,' Dennis says. 'At the end of September we went to play Burnley and we lost 6–1. I considered that my last game. But then afterwards I got called in to see the chairman, Arthur Page. He told me that Orient were in a bit of trouble in the League and that they didn't want to let me go. I said that I understood, but I'm not sure that I did. I wanted to move for no reason other than that Leicester were a First Division club under a manager I knew. I was a little bit worried that the chance wouldn't materialise again so it was frustrating.' So, for the moment, Dennis remained at Orient where, as fans will testify, he never gave less than 100 per cent. One game in particular stands out – a 1–0 loss to QPR at Loftus Road, in which Dennis was engaged in an almighty battle with winger Mike Ferguson. 'He elbowed me, and I set off after him,' Dennis recalls. 'But I didn't catch him as he disappeared over the other side of the pitch – he knew I was after him.'

While Orient's League form left something to be desired that season – they ended the season in 17th place – there was the brief glory of an FA Cup run to placate the fans. A 3–0 win over Third Division Wrexham in the third round gave Orient an away tie against – ironically, for Dennis –

Leicester. 'It put an extra edge on the game,' he says. 'Even though Jimmy knew me, I wanted to put on a good performance. It gave me a bit of extra impetus.' Was he frustrated that he was turning out in the red of Orient rather than the blue of Leicester? 'In a little way,' he says. 'It was the first time I'd been to Filbert Street, and it was a nice stadium, bigger and plusher than Brisbane Road. I knew that I wanted to be playing in the First Division.' Orient won the game 2–0, bringing a fifth-round home tie against Chelsea – then a Division One side and the European Cup-Winners' Cup holders. In other words, they were pretty tasty and proved as much when they went 2–0 up after 36 minutes. 'I thought, Christ, we're going to get walloped here,' Dennis admits. 'But at 2–0 the next goal is always important. If you get it, they start rocking; if they get it then it's game over. So we just stuck in there, which is all you can do. We had nothing to lose because everyone expected Chelsea to beat us.'

A goal from Phil Hoadley just before half-time gave Orient hope, and Mickey Bullock equalised. Then, with minutes left on the clock, Barrie Fairbrother scored the winner. 'I think I was down his throat about two seconds after he scored,' Dennis laughs. 'It was nice to score in the last few seconds as we didn't have too long to have to hold on to the lead. But then they hit the crossbar. It was heart-in-mouth stuff.'

The sixth round brought another glamour tie and another London derby. This time it was Arsenal, a side that featured the likes of Alan Ball, Charlie George and Frank McLintock. 'The FA Cup

Orient players in a question-and-answer session at Leyton Town Hall in 1971. From left to right: Mark Lazarus, Dennis Rofe, Dickie Plume, Barrie Fairbrother, Gordon Riddick, Les Bennett.

run started off as a bit of fun, but after we beat Chelsea I did start to dream a little bit,' says Dennis. 'Arsenal were a massive club and had a team littered with top names. But the game was at Brisbane Road so I thought, yes, we can beat them.' It was not to be – Arsenal won 1–0. But Dennis did take some positives from the game. 'I played OK, and it reinforced my belief that I could play in the top division,' he explains. 'I marked George Armstrong, and I'm not saying I was a world-beater, but I think I held my own. I knew I was ready and hoped a move would come about.'

There was interest from Queen's Park Rangers, then a Second Division side, but after talking to them Dennis declined the move. 'In other circumstances the move would have been ideal but they weren't First Division,' he explains.

There were no firm offers during that summer either and Dennis played the first three League games of the 1972–73 season. 'I just got on with life really,' he says. 'I'd spoken with George Petchey, and he told me not to worry; that a move would happen, he just didn't know when. So it was just a question of me accepting it.' In August Leicester made another bid for Dennis, this time £112,00, which, in those days, would probably have bought you half of Essex. It was the highest transfer fee for a full-back in British football history and one that the money men at Orient were more than happy to accept. Dennis was finally on his way.

Dennis instantly felt at home at Leicester – 'I walked into a community,' he says – and noticed that there were one or two cosmetic differences to the Orient. 'When I walked in the old boardroom at Filbert Street it was oak-panelled all the way round,' he recalls. 'Jim told me that he'd put Sue and me up in the Holiday Inn. I didn't know what the Holiday Inn was, but when I got there it was fantastic. It was palatial.' On the pitch there was a certain amount of pressure on Dennis to perform, despite the fact that he remained the most expensive full-back in British football for just 24 hours – Leicester sold his predecessor David Nish to Derby for £225,000. 'That was a weight off my shoulders,' Dennis laughs. 'But there was a lot riding on it. I was replacing a very good left-back, and I was very conscious that I was making my First Division debut. But I was confident in my own ability.'

Still, Dennis's first away trip with the club, to Manchester City, was something of a baptism of fire. 'I hurt my knee and came off after about 17 minutes,' he recalls. 'As I was going off Franny Lee said to me "You can open your eyes now," because it was a tough game up there, and I hadn't played that well. But I knew that I could sort myself out.' He did, and acquitted himself well for the remainder of that season, playing alongside the likes of Frank Worthington, Keith Weller and a young Peter Shilton. His performances alerted him to the national team hierarchy and that season he received a call-up to the England Under-23 squad that was due to tour Europe. 'Jimmy called me into his office to tell me,' says Dennis. 'Obviously I was delighted, but it was a double-edged sword because Leicester were going to Barbados for 17 days, which would have been the trip of a lifetime.'

So instead of the Caribbean, Dennis got Czechoslovakia, which, if Budvar beer and liver dumplings are your thing, is a reasonable exchange. After remaining on the bench for games against Holland and Denmark, Dennis finally got the chance to run out with the three lions on his chest against the home side. England lost 3–0, but it remains an intensely proud achievement for Dennis. 'When the cap came through I showed my father and said to him "Dad, do you remember when you asked me to promise you that I'd give football all that I'd got? Well, I gave it all that I'd got." It was an emotional moment.'

Disappointingly for Dennis, it was to be his only appearance for England. 'I felt like I must have been close to the full squad at the time, but it never materialised,' he says. 'My rivals at the time would have been people like Alan Kennedy at Liverpool, Micky Pejic at Stoke and David Nish at Derby. But I felt that the way I was playing, I deserved a chance. I feel that I could have held my own there. But I don't know what Alf Ramsey was looking for. I was quick, I put my foot in for a tackle. Maybe Alf was looking for people more comfortable on the ball? I wasn't the best dribbler in the world. But it was disappointing because at 22 or 23 years of age I felt I could stop a steam train if it was coming towards me.'

That season, in November 1972, Dennis married his dog-loving girlfriend, Sue. They'd been courting for most of his time at Orient. 'She didn't know much about football at first,' Dennis laughs. 'She told her mum that I played for Ulster or some Irish team. We got married in Chigwell and on that night we drove up to Leicester. The next morning I left with the team to play Norwich in the Texaco Cup, so the honeymoon was very brief. But that Sunday was the only day we could fit it in. Unfortunately *OK* magazine wasn't in existence in those days so the *Walthamstow Guardian* got the exclusive!'

Dennis played six seasons in Division One with Leicester before the club were relegated. He played a season and a half in Division Two, which enabled him to make his first competitive return to Brisbane Road on 30 September 1978 in a game Leicester won 1–0. He says 'I'd been back a few times to watch games – especially early on when Sue was still living down there – but this was the first time I'd gone there hot-blooded, so to speak. Getting changed in the away dressing room was a strange feeling, it put a bit extra on the game.' The crowd gave the returning left-back a decent reception – until, that is, he clobbered John Chiedoze. 'You could do that in those days,' he laughs.

In February 1980, after 323 appearances for Leicester, Dennis took what he calls a 'calculated gamble' and joined Chelsea for £80,000, believing they, not Leicester, would be promoted that season. He got it the wrong way round. And while Dennis thoroughly loved his time at Orient and Leicester, he speaks rather less enthusiastically of his Chelsea days. 'It was OK but not brilliant,' he says diplomatically. 'I just got the feeling that everyone was pulling in different directions and had their own agendas. There was a lot of in-fighting in the boardroom, and at that time Chelsea had an unruly element in their crowd that caused trouble wherever they went, which wasn't pretty.'

In July 1982, after 58 starts and one substitute appearance for Chelsea in the Second Division, Dennis moved to Southampton on a free transfer. Under manager Lawrie McMenemy, the south-coast club were going well at the time, having finished seventh in Division One the previous season thanks to the likes of Kevin Keegan, Alan Ball and Mick Channon. But Dennis found his first-team opportunities limited, eventually making only 18 starts and two substitute appearances in the League for the club. 'Of course I would like to have played more, but I knew the score when I joined the club,' says Dennis. 'Lawrie told me that I could go out on loan, but I didn't want to do that. I didn't want to go down the Leagues and end up scratching around.'

Besides, Dennis's career was taking a new direction. At Chelsea he had taken his preliminary coaching badge after a week's course at Bisham Abbey, and in his first year at Southampton he completed his full licence. So when the reserve-team coach of Southampton left, Dennis asked for,

and was given, the opportunity to take over as player-coach of the reserves. Soon Dennis found it difficult to combine both roles, and after an injury to his knee – he trapped a nerve, paralysing his foot – he decided, at 34 years of age, to bring his playing days to an end. 'It was the best thing I ever did,' he says. 'It enabled me to concentrate everything on the coaching. I wanted to finish playing and leave myself and other people with the impression of a good player.'

In 1987 Dennis was made first-team coach, under manager Chris Nicholl. The pair of them were sacked in 1991 after a 14th-place finish in Division One – 'It seemed a bit strange to me at the time, but that was their prerogative,' says Dennis. In July 1991 Dennis joined Second Division Bristol Rovers as

Dennis exchanges words with his Sunderland counterpart Steve Robbin during his spell as assistant manager of Southampton on 28 December 2002.

assistant manager to Martin Dobson. When Martin left just a few months later in October – with the club bottom of the table – Dennis was made caretaker manager, taking the job on permanently after Christmas. He pushed the club up to 13th in the table. In November 1992 Dennis resigned, unhappy that the club had made former Crystal Palace and Middlesbrough manager Malcolm Allison his assistant against his wishes.

Dennis then had a spell as the reserve-team coach at Stoke City under Joe Jordan, before being cleared out in October 1994 when Lou Macari returned to the club. He then returned to Southampton as youth-team coach under Dave Merrington but was part of the backroom staff clear-out when Graeme Souness took over in 1996. Short spells at Fulham and Kingstonian followed before Dennis rejoined Southampton in April 1998, firstly to work in the academy and then as reserve-team coach under Dave Jones and Glenn Hoddle. He was promoted to assistant manager when Stuart Gray took over in 2001 and remained in the position throughout the tenures of Gordon Strachan, Paul Sturrock, Steve Wigley and Harry Redknapp, adding an FA Cup Final to his CV in 2003.

It was during this period that he cultivated a reputation as something of a firebrand and, aside from the aforementioned spat with Graeme Souness, he also went toe-to-toe with Liverpool assistant manager Phil Thompson in 2002. And Orient fans will no doubt be amused that Brentford manager Martin Allen also incurred Dennis's wrath in an FA Cup tie in 2005. Dennis recalls 'Martin appealed for a penalty and I said to him "Martin, that was never a penalty." He replied "Sit down you little tramp," so I suggested that if he wanted to call me that again we could go outside right then. He didn't repeat it. That game was drawn, but we beat them in the replay at Griffin Park. It was a particularly rainy night and Martin was standing there in his suit, so when we scored the winner I jumped in the air and landed in a puddle right next to him. It wasn't deliberate, of course...'

In December 2005 Dennis once again found himself the victim of managerial changes when George Burley took over the top job and he was given the boot. Since then he has enjoyed his job as a regional youth development officer for the Football League. 'I get a real insight into clubs,' he says. 'It's a fantastic life and I'm happy doing what I'm doing. In my whole career, not a day has gone by where I haven't enjoyed going in to work, whether it be playing, or training or coaching.' But when asked if he still harbours dreams of managing a club himself, he answers 'Yes', quick as a flash. 'Saturday's a big day in football, and it's not a big day for me now,' he continues. 'I miss the buzz, the highs and lows. I'm realistic enough to know I'll never be offered a Premier League manager's job. But the Football League might be different.'

Maybe Orient then? 'Who knows?' Dennis replies mischievously. Certainly he still holds a great deal of affection for the club, saying 'When I was there it was a family club – everyone knew each other and everyone was willing to lend a hand. If it had been raining during the week and we had a game on the Saturday then Jimmy Bloomfield would go out on to the pitch with a fork and his wife would come out with a pair of wellies. That was the sort of club it was. I vividly remember a referee coming out to inspect the pitch and there being a particularly soft spot that was camouflaged. I can still hear Jimmy's wife saying "Jim, he's heading for that spot, Jim. JIM! He's gone down it, Jim!"'

So, as Dennis says, who knows? One day Orient fans might see the solid frame of their gritty defender back in charge of a team at Brisbane Road. And, were it ever to happen, one thing is for certain. No one would mess with him.

# Chapter 12

# TEENAGE KICKS

## Tommy Taylor 1967–70 and 1979–82

Tommy in his playing days at Orient.

Tommy Taylor must be something of a glutton for punishment. The last time he was at Brisbane Road in a professional capacity – as manager of the club – over 4,000 people were calling for his head. And yet he says 'To this day I'd still go back and work at Orient in any capacity if they wanted me to. As a scout, chief scout...anything. I would love to.'

Orient is his club you see. A precocious talent, he joined as a 10-year-old, was training with the first team at 13 and made his debut at 15. He was a cultured, artistic defender – certainly one of the best to ever pull on an Orient shirt – and he formed the centre-back partnership with Terry Mancini that helped the club win the Division Three title in 1969–70. After being sold to West Ham for £100,000 and spending nine years at Upton Park, he returned to Brisbane Road for a second spell and was made captain. Yet for all his footballing talent, it is his stint as manager – he was at the helm between 1996 and 2001 and guided the club to two Play-off Finals – that now defines him at Brisbane Road. At many points during that time the chorus of 'Taylor out!' was the soundtrack to every game. Tommy is sanguine about the fact that he would routinely go to work with thousands of supporters screaming abuse at him. 'People pay their money, they can say what they like,' he says. 'You get your good times and you get your bad times, but that is my work and I have to deal with it. I get paid for it. It's probably the only job in the world where someone can come and have a go at you. Football supporters, especially the men, only come to let off their steam. Their wife has a go at them every night of the week so they think, I'll go and have a go at the manager.' In person it is actually hard to dislike Tommy – despite the fact he once spent £50,000 on Billy Beall – for he is engaging, friendly and witty. He is cheeky, a joker and has a great line in swearing, too. Yet for all the insouciant charm, he is still a man who admits to having his ambitions as a manager frustrated. He is now in charge of Conference North side Boston United, but he yearns to take on the challenge of a Football League side again. 'Everyone wants to manage at the highest level,' he says. 'I'm still hoping to do that.'

Thomas Frederick Taylor was born in Hornchurch, Essex, on 26 September 1951. Dad Reg worked in the building trade and spent much time abroad, while Mum Daisy brought up Tommy and his sister Linda. Tommy claims that as a boy he was just like all other boys in that all he wanted to do was play football and cricket, though he dreamed not of playing at Wembley one day but of becoming a carpenter. From a very young age Tommy was taken to Brisbane Road by his next-door neighbour. 'He'd prop me up on the wall to watch the game,' Tommy recalls. 'I used to love it.'

Thankfully the young lad did not pick up too many bad habits from watching the Os because by the time he began to attend Dunningford Primary School in Elm Park he was turning out for the school team four years above his own age. Tommy says he was never anything but a defender: 'I was always at the back – because it was easy. You could see people running at you and where the ball was going to come. Even at a young age I could read the game quite well.' He was quickly selected for the Hornchurch district side and was part of a team that, he says, won nearly every competition going. It attracted the attention of Orient scouts Len Cheesewright and Eddie Heath, and when Tommy was 10 years old they invited him to come and train at Brisbane Road every Tuesday and Thursday night. 'I think I signed schoolboy terms with them for a Mars bar,' Tommy laughs. 'And we'd get one and six for expenses.'

By the time Tommy was 13 the coaches at Orient clearly realised that they had something rather special on their hands, so manager Dave Sexton took the highly unusual step of allowing the schoolboy to train with the first team as they prepared for the 1965–66 season. 'I remember treading on a centre-half's toes with my boots on while he was getting in the shower,' Tommy says. 'He asked me what the **** I was doing. His head was huge!' But the youngster was not intimidated by playing alongside seasoned pros, whatever the sizes of their heads. 'It was great,' he says, adding cheekily 'I was probably better than them anyway.'

Meanwhile, through the performances he was putting in for his school – Highlands in Hornchurch – and district teams, 14-year-old Tommy was invited to a series of trials that culminated in a North versus South England Schoolboys game. He was then selected for the full England Schoolboys side, captaining them on six occasions. Tommy left school at 15 and became an Orient apprentice the next day. And while it was an easy step for him to sign up for the club at which he had been playing since he was 10 years old, there were plenty of other teams circling the England Schoolboys captain, such as Tottenham and West Ham. 'Spurs in particular always wanted to sign me,' says Tommy. 'I went for a trial game there, but it just didn't feel right to me. I just told them that I was happy where I was.'

It is surprising it was quite so simple. Orient, after all, had finished the previous 1966–67 season turgidly, mid-table in Division Three. Spurs, meanwhile, had come third in Division One and boasted the likes of Jimmy Greaves, Alan Mullery and Terry Venables in their side. Surely he must been tempted to join the north London club? 'But would I have got in the first team at the age of 15?' Tommy counters. 'I wouldn't have got any more money either. It was just about being happy and playing the way I wanted to play. But I did say to Spurs – and to West Ham, who also wanted to sign me – that if I turned out to be any good then they'd have to come and buy me.'

So, in the summer of 1967 Tommy Taylor became an employee of Leyton Orient Football Club for the princely wage of £6.50 a week, working alongside fellow apprentices such as Dennis Rofe, Barrie Fairbrother and Terry Brisley. But just as he was getting into the swing of sweeping the terraces and cleaning the dressing rooms, Tommy found himself thrust into the first team for the second League game of the new season, against Torquay United at Brisbane Road. He was still a month short of his 16th birthday. Recalling the moment he was told he would be playing by manager Dick Graham, he says 'It was Friday night and I was doing my duties in the boot room with my overalls on. Dick came in and roared "You're in." I just said "OK, boss," and carried on cleaning the boots.'

Tommy was pretty unfazed by the prospect of playing with the big boys. 'I loved it,' he says. 'I loved playing in front of people. Even if 100,000 people had been there I would have loved it. I was 15, but I felt ready – it just felt natural. I didn't feel overwhelmed at all. I played very well. And after the game I went straight into the boot room and started cleaning the boots. I was still an apprentice, and I didn't get any special treatment.' After Tommy's debut Dick Graham chose to rely on more seasoned players such as Brian Wood, Vic Halom and John Sneddon in the centre-half spots. In February of 1968, however, the manager left the club, frustrated at the lack of funds. 'That was one hell of a man,' says Tommy of Dick. "He is the only man I've ever been frightened of in my life.' The new gaffer was former Arsenal player Jimmy Bloomfield, and Tommy cannot speak highly enough of him. 'He looked after me; he was like my guardian. He was closer to the players than any other manager I've known since.'

Bloomfield saw enough potential in the young Tommy to trust him as centre-half. Playing alongside Terry Mancini, who'd joined the club in October 1967, Tommy made a total of 16 starts and one substitute appearance that season. His assured, precocious performances and his habit of taking people on in the box piqued the interest of the press, and it wasn't long before he was being dubbed 'the new Bobby Moore'. 'There were loads of things in the papers but you don't take any notice,' says Tommy. 'I used to say "There's only one Bobby Moore, there's never going to be two of them."'

Given the attention, though, did Tommy view Orient simply as a stepping stone to greater things? 'Never,' he replies firmly. 'Orient were my club. And I was still just a kid really. There weren't many kids of my age playing in the Third Division. Or any division.'

During the 1968–69 season Tommy was awarded a professional contract of £12 a week. He and Terry Mancini formed the first-choice centre-back pairing, and Tommy made a total of 45 starts and one substitute appearance, also chipping in with his first two goals for the club. The season itself was another heart-in-the-mouth one for fans – it took a final-day victory over Shrewsbury to avoid relegation to Division Four. The following season of 1969–70, Tommy says that everything just clicked. 'We were a skilful team, and Jimmy wanted us to get it down and pass the ball.' Orient won the title and promotion with a victory over Shrewsbury in the penultimate game of the season. Tommy, though, took it all in his stride. 'It was great,' he says, 'but those sort of things never fazed me.'

Tommy had been living on his own in his parents' house in Elm Park since he was 15 while his mum and dad were living in Zambia as his Dad's job in the building trade often included long spells abroad. He had begun dating neighbour Pat a year earlier – they are still together today and have two sons, Scott and Lee – and she would come around and cook meals for him. Most of his spare time was taken up polishing his football skills. 'Dennis Rofe was my best mate, and we used to be on the training ground until six o'clock every night,' he says. 'We'd put dustbins on the ground and try to chip balls into them from 40 yards.'

Clearly his dedication to the cause was paying off, and it seemed only a matter of time before a bigger club would come in for the talented young centre-half. When they did, Tommy was taken completely by surprise. He had played the first 11 games of the 1970–71 season when, on Monday 12

Orient in 1968. Back row, from left to right: Bert Howe, Dennis Rofe, Terry Brisley, Malcolm Slater, Graham Archell, John Key. Middle row: Owen Simpson, Mike Jones, Ray Goddard, Steve Bowtell, Peter Allen, Peter Angell. Front row: Terry Mancini, Tommy Taylor, Vic Halom, Jimmy Bloomfield, Roy Massey, Brian Wood, Dave Harper.

Tommy in the early 1970s.

October, he was called into Jimmy Bloomfield's office. Tommy recalls 'We'd lost 1–0 to Hull City on Saturday and the goal had been my fault. I'd passed the ball back to the goalkeeper but it got stuck in a puddle and the centre-forward scored. Going into Jim's office I was thinking, here we go. I said "Sorry Jim, I know it was my fault." But he replied "Nothing to do with that." Then he told me that he'd sold me.' The club had accepted an offer of £78,000 plus utility player Peter Bennett from West Ham United, then in Division One. 'I asked Jim if he wanted me to go,' says Tommy. 'He replied "Of course I don't, but we've got to sell you because we need the money badly. If we don't sell you we won't have a football club."'

Bloomfield told Tommy that he was not to train that morning and that he would see him at Upton Park at midday. 'Jim drove there, but I had to get the train!' Tommy recalls. 'When I arrived the commissionaire stopped me and asked me who I was. I said "Nobody really, mate, but I think I've just signed here." Then he took me upstairs and Jim was there with the West Ham manager, Ron Greenwood. Jim said "Don't worry, I've done your contract for the next three years." I thought, oh, thanks Jim!'

So, just a few hours after innocently turning up to train at Brisbane Road, Tommy had become a West Ham player. 'I was devastated to leave Orient,' he says. 'No way in the world did I ever think I would leave. But I ended up having a great time at West Ham too.' Tommy's debut for the Hammers came against Tottenham, where he found himself marking Spurs legend and soon-to-be England striker Martin Chivers. 'I kept going round him, coming back then passing the ball,' Tommy laughs. 'When I came in at half-time I got the biggest roasting of my life. Ron said to me "You can't take the piss out of their centre-forward." I replied "Well, he isn't very good, is he?"' That was not the only thing that surprised the young Tommy that day at Upton Park. It seems the West Ham players' idea of pre-match refreshment was somewhat at odds with current thinking. 'Harry Redknapp and Ronnie Boyce were sitting in the corner sharing a cigarette,' Tommy laughs. 'They'd smoke one at half-time too. It's the funniest thing I've ever seen in football.'

Tommy went on to enjoy nine good seasons as a first-team regular at West Ham. He was part of the team that won the FA Cup in 1975 and reached the European Cup-Winners' Cup Final a year later, losing 4–2 to Anderlecht.

During his time at Upton Park, Tommy played for the England Under-23 side on 16 occasions. And while he was often said to be on the verge of making the full squad, he never did receive a call-up. He seems fairly ambivalent about it. 'It doesn't upset me,' he says. 'What should be, should be. What is not, is not. I had some great times, and playing for West Ham was just like playing for England because everyone was so good. It's always great to put the white shirt on, but your bread and butter is with your club.'

Tommy is perhaps being a little disingenuous. When asked if he has any regrets as a player he replies 'I should have been more serious. I knew I was good at my job, and I could get away with things. I would muck about during games, poke people in the eye, that sort of thing. I'd play one-twos when I knew I wasn't supposed to and take the piss out of people. I was a maverick. Once, after

an England Under-23 game, Alf Ramsey said to me that if I didn't muck about so much I'd be one of the best players in the world. So I think that if I had been more serious I might have achieved more.' Did that not occur to him at the time? 'No, because I just loved what I was doing. I would have played three games in a day. It's just the way I was. Even playing for West Ham in the top division, I found football easy. I could run, I could head a ball, I could definitely pass a ball, controlling a ball was easy, reading the game was twice as easy. But I think I could have done more.'

West Ham were relegated to Division Two at the conclusion of the 1977–78 season, and while Tommy remained with the club throughout the next season he began to hanker

Tommy after West Ham's FA Cup Final victory over Fulham on 3 May 1975. Behind him is former teammate Bobby Moore.

for a change of scenery. 'I wasn't disillusioned at West Ham, but I felt like I'd been going down the same road, looking at the same people, waiting at the same set of lights for nine years,' he says. 'It was like *Groundhog Day*. I wanted a new challenge.' Tommy had made a call to Orient scout Len Cheesewright to tell him he was thinking of leaving West Ham. Jimmy Bloomfield, back at Orient in his second spell as manager, was soon on the phone. 'I was more than happy to come back and play for Orient under Jim,' says Tommy. 'It was a new challenge because I didn't know what I'd be going back to, but you always knew that Jim would have good players, so it didn't worry me.' The move was completed in May 1979, with Orient paying West Ham £100,000 to bring back their former player. 'Everything was the same,' he says. 'The only thing that had changed was that Jim had put a telly and some chairs in the dressing room.' These fantastic luxuries were not the only thing that impressed Tommy. 'It was a brilliant team Jim had assembled,' he says. 'They were a good footballing side, with players like Bill Roffey and John Chiedoze.'

Bloomfield made Tommy his captain, a role which laid the foundations for his later foray into management. 'I loved it,' he says. 'I got on well with everyone, and I was honest with people. If they were s**t I'd tell them, if they'd hit a good ball I'd say, magnificent, well done.'

The 1979–80 season was a pretty forgettable one for Orient, finishing 14th in Division Two without even a relegation battle to keep fans interested. But Tommy did have reason to look forward to the following season of 1980–81, as Bloomfield had brought in former England internationals Stan Bowles and Peter Taylor from Nottingham Forest and Tottenham Hotspur respectively. Bowles in particular made a big impression on Tommy. 'Stan was magnificent,' he says. 'He was the funniest person I've ever met. There'd always be people knocking at the door, asking if he was there, saying he owed them money. And he'd be over the back wall. On one occasion all the players and their wives went to the dogs at Wembley. He told us all to put our money on one particular dog. He said that it could not fail. So we all put on a fiver each. He put on £2,000! It lost, but Bowlesy just said "Oh well, you win some, you lose some. Let's get a beer."' But while the players were clearly having a right old laugh off the pitch, things were not quite so amusing on it – Orient amassed just 38 points and finished 17th in Division Two. Joint-top scorers were Ian Moores and John Chiedoze, and when the latter was sold to Notts County for £600,000 at the end of the season, manager Jimmy Bloomfield was so incensed that he resigned.

Reserve-team coach and former player Paul Went was made caretaker manager. Under his leadership the team won their first League game of the season against Derby County, but then proceeded upon a losing streak that even by Orient's standards was staggering. They lost seven of their next eight League matches, drawing the other and scoring just one solitary goal throughout the spell. Tommy is at a loss to explain what happened. 'Paul knew the players ever so well and the players knew him ever so well, but sometimes the chemistry just doesn't work. Everyone wanted to play for Paul – he was good as gold – but these things just happen sometimes in football.'

Went was sacked on 12 October 1981, and the next day a new manager rode into Leyton: former Sunderland boss Ken Knighton. Tommy instantly refers to Knighton as 'the nob', suggesting that perhaps he did not have the greatest respect for the new gaffer. 'There wasn't much of a feelgood factor when that man came in,' he says. 'He was very, very strict, and the players weren't used to that.' Tommy did not agree with the way that Knighton wanted the team to play either. 'He just wanted us to get close to people and kick them. That wasn't our game at all.' But Knighton's biggest problem, according to Tommy, was a chip on his shoulder. 'He couldn't get to grips with some of the players being bigger than him,' he explains. 'I'm not being big-headed, but there were players like Bowlesy and myself that had done better in their careers than he had, and he didn't like that.'

To illustrate his point he recalls a game against Sheffield Wednesday in November when the team came in 3–0 up at half-time. He says 'We all came into the dressing room laughing and Ken asked "What's going on?" I replied "Excuse us, boss, but we're just enjoying ourselves." Then he said "You make me laugh, you southerners – you think you can go out there and take the mickey out of people?" I said "Well if we are beating them 3–0 now we can beat them 6–0 by the end of the game, so don't worry about it." But Bowlesy just told him to **** off. Ken said "Right, you're fined a week's wages." Bowlsey said "**** off" again. Ken said "That's two weeks' wages." Then Bowlesy said "You can go and **** yourself." Ken said "Why's that?" And Bowlesy replied "Because I've already got a month's wages in advance."' Unsurprisingly, this heralded the end of Stan Bowles's short but entertaining Orient career. And, as it turned out, Tommy wouldn't be far behind.

The Orient team Christmas party might have been an opportunity for Tommy and Ken to bond over a few drinks but, says Tommy, the manager was highly unimpressed with his choice of gift for assistant boss Frank Clark. 'We all thought that Frank looked like Blakey from *On the Buses*. So I went to the bus depot up the road and borrowed an inspector's suit and wrapped it up for him. He had to put it on. Ken didn't find it amusing, but we were only trying to have a bit of fun.'

Things came to a head on 16 February 1982 during an FA Cup tie against Crystal Palace at Brisbane Road. Orient had been awarded a penalty and Tommy was the designated taker. He takes up the story: 'I went to take it, but Ian Moores came up to me and asked me if he could take it as he was getting a bit of stick from the crowd and he wanted them back on side. I said, fine, just keep your head down and blast it. But he smashed it over the crossbar.' Knighton wasn't impressed. 'When I went in at half-time he absolutely blasted me for not taking the penalty,' says Tommy. 'I said to him "The forward asked me if he could take it, he had a lot confidence and so I let him take it. But it's my responsibility, it's my fault."'

In that same game, Tommy had an altercation with one of the linesmen over the awarding of a throw-in. The official reported him for abuse. 'Ken didn't say anything to me after the game, but it was clear he thought that it was my fault we'd lost 1–0,' says Tommy. 'Then the next day he told me that he was sacking me – for not taking the penalty and for abusing the linesman.' Surely there must have been more to it than that? 'Well, again, it comes down to the fact that I don't think he liked me being a bigger player than he was,' Tommy replies. 'And the fact that I said what I thought. He didn't like that.'

Tommy says that they had never had a big argument before that match, but admits that he would, on occasion, openly question the manager's decisions at half-time. 'Only when I thought he was wrong,' he adds. But surely the manager would perceive that it wasn't a player's place to do that? 'As captain I could,' counters Tommy. 'I was doing it for the team. Sometimes he would have a go at a player that didn't need having a go at. You could never have a go at Bowlesy, for example, because he just wouldn't play anymore. Ken didn't know how to treat people.'

Ken also did not know that there are employment laws in the UK that prevent bosses from sacking staff without just cause. Tommy got the PFA involved and they successfully argued that the maximum penalty the club could impose in this instance was a fine of two weeks' wages. So, unable to get rid of Tommy, Knighton sent him to train with the youth team. 'I was upset because I wanted to play for the first team and I wanted the club to do well, but I didn't mind training with the juniors,' Tommy says. 'I worked my nuts off with them and tried to make them play better football. And I kept myself super fit.'

With Tommy out of the side, Orient lost four and drew two of their next six games, and were mired deep in relegation trouble. Knighton came to Tommy and told him that he wanted him to play again. 'I thought to myself, why should I play for you?' says Tommy. 'But then I thought, it's my team as well. So I put the shirt on and started playing again.' His presence wasn't enough to prevent Orient finishing bottom of the League and dropping back into Division Three for the first time in over 10 years. Tommy now believed there was clearly no future for him at Orient. 'I still had a year left on my contract, but I couldn't stay at the club with that man still there,' he says. (Incredibly, Tommy says that Knighton actually tried to sign him for the club he was then managing, Dagenham Town, a few years later. 'I told him to go **** himself,' says Tommy, unsurprisingly.)

Tommy's first offer of new employment came from an unlikely place: Belgium. 'An agent rang me up and told me a top-division team were looking for a sweeper,' he explains. 'The next day I was gone. I was happy to play abroad.' He played two seasons for Koninklijke Beerschot Voetbal en Atletiek Club – though possibly without ever mastering the pronunciation of its name – before deciding that he wanted to return to play in England. Unfortunately he had signed a four-year contract and so, with the club unwilling to let him go or release his registration, Tommy simply retired. 'I didn't want to,' he says. 'I was fitter than I'd ever been in my life, and I was only 32. It was frustrating, but I wanted to go back to England and it was the only way I could do it. They've still got my registration today.'

Tommy took a position at Charlton Athletic as youth-team coach, and stayed at the club for two years. 'I'd wanted to go into the coaching side of the game from quite early on,' he says. 'When I was playing alongside younger players out on the field, I talked to them and they responded. I knew I could get things through to them.' He was then invited to manage Hamilton Wanderers in New Zealand, and stayed in the country for three years, managing Auckland City in his second year and Palmerston North End in his third. At the start of the 1989–90 season Tommy took a position as assistant manager to Keith Peacock at Maidstone United, who were playing their first season in Division Four. The club reached the Play-offs but lost in the semi-final to Cambridge. In January 1991 Keith Peacock and Tommy were sacked.

Tommy served as manager of Southern League side Margate between 1991 and 1993 before taking some time out to run a pub he had bought, the White Horse in East Ham. He was invited to become the youth coach at Cambridge United – then in the third tier – by manager Gary Johnson in 1993. When Johnson was sacked in April 1995 Tommy took over as manager, but winning his first three games was not enough to prevent the club's relegation to the bottom division. (Though, incidentally, they had 22 more points than Orient, who also went down that year.)

The next season started well for Tommy, and by the end of October Cambridge were lying second in Division Three. Tommy's contract, however, only took him up to December of that year, and the chairman of the club refused to offer him any more security than a rolling three-month contract. 'They just wanted to know that they could get rid of you without spending any money,' says Tommy. 'The chairman said to me, well, if you can find a job somewhere else, go ahead. And I knew that Pat Holland had been given the sack at Orient, so I made a phone call to Barry Hearn and asked if the manager's job was still going. He told me the job was mine if I wanted it.' Fans will no doubt be reassured that potential Orient managers undergo such a rigorous interview process. Presumably, though, Tommy and Barry were already acquainted? 'No,' says Tommy. 'I'd never met him before in my life. But he knew the job I'd done at Cambridge with a tiny budget.' Cambridge, with their bluff well and truly called, then decided to offer him the same money as he would get at Orient and twice as long a contract, but Tommy chose to go to east London and signed up as manager on 7 November 1996. 'Cambridge had their chance,' he says. 'I said to them "Up yours, I'm off."'

Tommy – who brought his assistant Paul Clark with him from Cambridge – was joining a team that proved in the previous season that they were the fourth-worst in professional football. They were currently sitting in 18th spot in Division Three – the fourth tier – and Tommy, understandably, was worried. 'I'm not being rude about the team, but I looked at it and thought we could get relegated out of football. There were some good players there, but it was an old team and they thought that they were better than they were, and they put themselves in trouble more times than they got out of it.' Tommy sought to address the situation by, well, bringing in some even older players, such as 47-year-old Peter Shilton and 40-year-old Ray Wilkins. To be fair, these were temporary measures and Tommy did manage to see out that season without too much of a relegation battle, Orient ultimately finishing in 16th position.

Chairman Barry Hearn called the 1997–98 season 'a season of no excuses,' and Tommy was under pressure to deliver promotion. He began to shape the team into his own. 'I brought in Dean Smith, Simon Clark and Stuart Hicks,' he says. 'We called them 'the three amigos'. We should have played 4-4-2, but with three good centre-halves like them, we had to play them.'

Things certainly improved, and by mid-March Orient were just two points off the Play-off positions. In April, however, the club were fined and docked three points after an administrative blunder by the general secretary meant three players were fielded in a game when they should have been suspended. Orient finished four points off the Play-offs, but Tommy says that the points deduction had a psychological effect on the players. In a season of no excuses, it seems Orient did actually have a genuine one.

Tommy gives a team talk during the 1998–99 season.

Still, onwards and upwards, as the 1998–99 season began pretty well, and Tommy made some key signings. He says 'I got Matt Joseph in, which gave us pace, and I signed Matt Lockwood, who was a hell of a player. Another big one was Wim Walschaerts. He used to win loads of balls in the middle of the pitch.' But it was another player who Tommy believes was his best-ever signing at Orient: former French international Amara Simba. 'I still talk to people now about what a great player he was. When I saw him on the training ground he was magnificent, and I got straight on the phone to Barry Hearn. I said "I think I've found a diamond here, mate." And Barry said "You tell me that every week." And then he asked me if he was a youngster. I said "Well, you could say that. He's 36." Barry yelled "Do what?" But I said "Barry, just watch him play."'

Simba's goals helped propel Orient up the table and by the beginning of March they lay third. That same month Tommy incensed some fans by allowing striker Carl Griffiths to leave the club at such a crucial time, releasing him to Port Vale for £100,000. 'I just told him that a club had come in for him, that I didn't want him to go but that I'd understand if he did,' Tommy explains. 'The money was going to be good for him, and he would have been playing a higher grade of football. I told him that the supporters wouldn't want him to go, that Barry and I would take a bit of stick for it but that I was leaving it up to him. But then he turned it around in the press and said that it was my fault.'

Could he not have done more to try to keep the striker? 'In my opinion, Griff was a money man, he loved a pound note,' Tommy replies. 'I just told him it was up to him.' Tommy seems to have mixed feelings about the striker. On the one hand he says 'Griff was always a luxury. And in that division you can't have luxury players, everyone's got to do a bit of graft for each other. Griff's feeling was, well, I score my goals and that's it; either we win the game or we lose the game. He'd do **** all, but he'd score a goal.' But then, when asked if he has any regrets in his career as a manager, the first thing Tommy says is 'I would have kept Griff. I wouldn't have let him go at all. He was a really good, clever centre-forward. One of the better ones.'

Without Griffiths, Orient still managed a sixth-place finish, which brought them a Play-off semi-final against Rotherham. With both the home leg and the away leg finishing goalless, the tie went to penalties. Tommy recalls 'Before the game everyone in the dressing room said, yeah, I'll take a penalty. But at the end of the game I said "Right, who's got the bollocks to take one now, boys?" And they all stood up. Scott Barrett said "I'll save two, don't worry about it." And he did.' Orient won the penalty shoot-out, enabling them to make the trip to Wembley for the Play-off Final against Scunthorpe. But it wasn't to be Orient's day. 'We had so many chances to score, but it just wouldn't go in,' says Tommy. 'Then they had one good chance and they scored. I'd said to the boys that they had to watch out for Alex Calvo-Garcia as he always comes on the blind side. And that's what happened. Losing that Final killed me.'

It also, so it seems, killed off the next season, which, even by Orient's reduced standards in the 1990s, was an abysmal one. By 28 December, the club were bottom of the Football League, the lowest spot they had ever held. Cries of 'Taylor out!' rang around Brisbane Road like a stuck record. 'Losing the Play-off Final was a massive blow,' says Tommy. 'Everyone was on a downer. But I knew that the players were good enough, and I didn't want to change the squad at all.' He did, however, re-sign Carl Griffiths from Port Vale, who inspired a mini-revival. The club eventually finished 19th in the division.

Tommy's faith in his squad proved to be justified, and 2000–01 was a much happier time at Brisbane Road, with Orient lodged in the upper reaches of the division for the entire season, eventually finishing in fifth position. A Play-off semi-final victory over Hull City meant the Os would face Blackpool at the Millennium Stadium for the chance to play in Division Two the next season.

Despite going 1–0 up after 27 seconds, thanks to Chris Tate, and taking a 2–1 lead later on in the first half, Orient eventually lost the game 4–2. 'Their boy Paul Simpson was too clever for us,' says Tommy. 'He changed the game every time he came inside from the right-hand side behind the midfield two. They were a good team and we missed a couple of good chances. It was hard losing in the Final again, and I felt for the players and the supporters. We should have been in the next division up – we had a good enough team to get there, but you have to do it for 40-odd games and we didn't.'

The next season started with a whimper rather than a bang, as Orient failed to register a victory until their fourth game. They won their next three matches but then went on a bad losing streak,

Tommy talks to his team before the Division Three Play-off Final at Wembley on 29 May 1999.

garnering just one point from six matches. The abuse began again, this time worse than ever, and got to the point where a group of fans would routinely wait outside the changing rooms singing their refrain of 'Taylor Out'. 'You're bound to get that,' says Tommy. 'The only thing that I didn't like was when my wife and kids were there and they took the abuse. They didn't deserve it. And Barry and his family too – the fans were having a go at him, but it was nothing to do with him.' On Sunday 14 October, after the previous day's 4–2 defeat at the hands of Shrewsbury, Tommy decided enough was enough and went to see Barry Hearn at his home. 'Barry went through enough abuse when Pat Holland was manager, and I didn't think he needed it chucked at him again,' he says. 'He said to me "Do you think it's time to go?" And I said "It's upsetting to say so, but it is." We shook hands, and it was the hardest thing for both of us to have to say goodbye.' Tommy has nothing but the highest praise for Hearn. 'You'll never find a better chairman than him in the Football League,' he says. 'He knows sport, and he knows people who go out there and give it all. He's a lovely man, and he's passionate for Orient.' Did they ever argue? 'Never,' Tommy replies. 'He used to tell me if he didn't think something was right, but I'd tell him that was the way I wanted to do it, and he'd say fair enough.'

Tommy accepts that the situation may have been affecting the morale of the team but denies that he had lost the players in any way. 'We were like a big family,' he says. 'If you ask any of the players how I treated them, not one of them would say I didn't give them what they wanted at any time. And I could say they gave me 100 per cent nearly every time as well. I couldn't moan at them. I thought the team we had at that point would still do well, it just needed one or two bits or pieces moved about.' The club announced Tommy's resignation the next morning, and he says that he was devastated at having to leave. He did not have the chance to say goodbye to his players either. 'I would have been so emotional with them. I couldn't have gone back, but all of them rang me up – everybody – and said they were sorry. I told them that that is football and to get on with it – and to make sure they didn't lose any more games.'

Since then Tommy has been on something of a managerial merry-go-round. He has taken the reins at Division Three Darlington, Conference side Farnborough Town and, for five months, Seba United in Jamaica. In October 2004 he was appointed manager of Southern League Premier Division side King's Lynn, before taking up a post as assistant manager of Peterborough in November 2006. In the summer of 2007 he became manager of Boston United, who had just been double-relegated from the Football League to the Conference North because of financial difficulties. Is he frustrated that, given that he's managed in the third tier and reached two Play-off Finals in the fourth, his managerial career has not taken him higher up the ladder? 'I think people are typecast,' he replies. 'I'm typecast as a manager who gets people out of the s**t – at clubs who haven't got any money. They get me in to run it on a shoestring, get them out of trouble, get them higher up the League.

Then they think, oh, we're a good club now, we can go for a bigger manager. Many clubs just want big names, even if they haven't managed before. It's very frustrating.'

Despite this, Tommy retains his good humour. One imagines you would need to if you were managing Boston United. And despite everything, he retains a lot of affection for the part of east London he calls 'his club'. 'Orient felt right to me,' he says. 'Everyone got on well with each other and they were lovely people. It was such a special place; it was unreal.'

ND - #0206 - 270225 - C0 - 234/156/9 - PB - 9781780913704 - Gloss Lamination